# Hindu Worldviews

## ALSO AVAILABLE FROM BLOOMSBURY

*The Bloomsbury Companion to Hindu Studies,* edited by Jessica Frazier

*Divine Self, Human Self,* Chakravarthi Ram-Prasad

*Hinduism and the 1960s,* Paul Oliver

# Hindu Worldviews

## Theories of Self, Ritual and Reality

**JESSICA FRAZIER**



Bloomsbury Academic
An imprint of Bloomsbury Publishing Plc

BLOOMSBURY
LONDON • OXFORD • NEW YORK • NEW DELHI • SYDNEY

**Bloomsbury Academic**
An imprint of Bloomsbury Publishing Plc

50 Bedford Square
London
WC1B 3DP
UK

1385 Broadway
New York
NY 10018
USA

**www.bloomsbury.com**

**BLOOMSBURY and the Diana logo are trademarks of Bloomsbury Publishing Plc**

First published 2017



**British Library Cataloguing-in-Publication Data**
A catalogue record for this book is available from the British Library.

ISBN: HB: 978-1-4742-5156-3
PB: 978-1-4742-5155-6
ePDF: 978-1-4742-5157-0
ePub: 978-1-4742-5158-7

**Library of Congress Cataloging-in-Publication Data**
A catalog record for this book is available from the Library of Congress.

Cover design and illustration © Alice Marwick

Typeset by Newgen Knowledge Works (P) Ltd., Chennai, India.
Printed and bound in India

*For Ann Ross Frazier*

# Contents

# Preface

Like the sage Śuka in the *Mahābhārata*, who began his liberation by taking a tour through the whole world (before departing to the higher realm of *brahmaloka*), this book takes a tour through the cosmos as envisioned in key classical Hindu sources and in some of their modern heirs. In the chapters that follow, it will try to reconstruct views of different realms and levels of reality as depicted in texts such as the Vedas and Upaniṣads, Sūtras and Śāstras, the *Mahābhārata* and later contexts of text and practice. It will examine central pillars of that worldview, including the self and its embodiment, the nature of reason and its attempts to comprehend the universe, and the way in which humans engage in the cosmos through ritual and religious practice. In doing so it also aims to show ways in which the world can be otherwise experienced than through the eyes of Western culture – that is, it aims to make the Hindu worldview available as a tool for what is here termed 'global theory'.

This project stands in contrast to approaches that take Hindu soteriology – largely consisting of traditions of *escape* from the embodied world – as their point of departure. For Western thinkers such as Schopenhauer, Hegel and Emerson, and also for modern Indian thinkers such as Swami Vivekananda, it was otherworldly doctrines concerning the eternal self or *ātman* and the belief in liberation of the self from the world that were of greatest interest – these, or the distinctive social philosophy of caste that placed such constraints on worldly life. It is certain that these aspects of Hindu culture form some of its most extraordinary and powerful themes. But they are neither the whole of Hindu thought, nor do they represent the main concerns of Hindu life which must, necessarily, proceed within the limitations of mind and matter.

In what follows the goal is to look at the world from the perspective of a person – a thinking, embodied, agent – who is located within the world that is described in these sources. This does not mean that all Hindus throughout the two millennia or more spanned by these texts necessarily thought this way; indeed, these are worldviews tied to quite specific texts and will not apply to the whole of India's diverse and complex cultures. Nor are these the only theories that could be (and have been) derived from these sources, since the sources themselves are not univocal compositions – most are oral texts redacted over long periods reflecting the speculations of different brahmins and nobles, families and 'schools'. However, the readings that follow aim to show what it means to exist, to think and to act according to concepts of materiality, reason, agency and the cosmos found in classical Hindu cultures. More than this, they aim to make these ways of thinking available to those in different periods and cultures who seek frameworks for comprehending human existence and the world in which it is embedded.

# Acknowledgements

This curious book of theories inspired by Hindu sources owes much to the patience of Bloomsbury and of Lalle Pursglove, who gave encouragement to the project. It also benefited greatly from the support of a Fellowship at the Oxford Centre for Hindu Studies that allowed me to pursue the project. Others have been helpful, including Ramprasad Chakravarthi, who invited me to a conference at Amherst in which I first began to think seriously about embodiment in Hindu sources; and Gavin Flood, whose combination of philosophical and historical approaches to Hinduism is always an inspiration. Particular thanks go to Lucian Wong for his thoughtful intellectual support along the way and to Rembert Lutjeharms for sharing his extensive knowledge; naturally these people are responsible for none of the book's shortcomings.

# Note on texts and translations

Mindful of the range of possible readers who may be unfamiliar with Hindu textual genres, abbreviations are not used for primary sources in the text and titles are cited in full. Again, existing translations have been used for primary texts with the intention that readers unfamiliar with these sources or their Sanskrit originals may be able to obtain translations and explore them in greater depth. These primary source translations are listed in the References section.

# 1

# Introduction: Hindu worldviews and global theory

This book is an experiment in doing with India's Sanskritic cultures what Western scholars have long done with classical Greek and Roman ones – that is, creating genealogies of key ideas and developing them into theories that are illuminating in themselves, potentially across different eras and regions of the world. This is a project with an old pedigree; in 1879 the German Indologist Max Müller translated the Upaniṣads, classical texts that stand at the root of much subsequent Hindu philosophy. He recommended them to a European audience with the hope that

> to the patient reader these [Hindu texts will] ... open a new view of the history of the human race, of that one race to which we all belong, with all the fibres of our flesh, with all the fears and hopes of our soul. (xxxvii)

Müller was writing at the point of a transition from the one-sided relation of colonialism towards the greater plurality and mutual exchange of globalism. Müller's interest in India was inspired by the hope of learning new ideas, but time forced him to acknowledge the difficulties attendant on that hope. His curiosity had been sparked as a product of his philosophical studies, having completed a dissertation on Spinoza and moved on to work with Franz Bopp, one of the first great European Sanskritists and an associate of both Charles Wilkins, the first translator of the *Bhagavad Gītā* into English, and Friedrich Schelling, a friend who suggested that Müller translate the Upaniṣads. Ultimately he sought a synthesis of European and Asian philosophies into a single grand-historical narrative of the evolution of ideas. It was a narrative that incorporated his own prejudices as well as enthusiasms (Immanuel Kant's German Enlightenment philosophy was, for instance, seen as the 'mature' fulfilment of Vedic thought). However, Müller's (1879: xxi) introduction to the *Sacred Books of the East* (1897) series struggles with the problem of incomprehension and clashing cultural tastes that readers 'who might expect to find in these volumes nothing but gems' would face in interpreting Asian sources. He wrote that

> Plato is strange till we know him ... so it is with these ancient sages, who have become the founders of the great religions of antiquity. They can never be judged from without, they can only be judged from within. We need not become Brahmans, or Buddhists or Taosze altogether, but we must for a time, if we wish to understand, and still more, if we are bold enough to undertake to translate their doctrines. (xxxvii)

Written more than a century after Müller's observations, the chapters in this volume seek to take Indian texts as valuable sources for global thinking – developing theories suited to a multi-culture with a shared history and common concerns and hopes. They aim to have an immediate use in that they help explain Hindu culture by bringing to light background beliefs that may be unfamiliar to readers, whether from other cultures and periods, or simply readers who are not aware of the ideas that have shaped their own tradition. Taking a broadly hermeneutic approach, it is assumed that *understanding* ideas (as well as simply knowing about them) requires a knowledge of the network of background beliefs that inform them. Thus, for instance, yogic meditation makes more sense against the background of Indian ideas about the way thought is constituted. The images of deities in Hindu temples make most sense when seen in terms of underlying beliefs about the nature of divine incarnation and embodiment; the typical materials used in Hindu rituals must be understood in terms of the liminal nature of sounds and substances. This approach to understanding is not new; in Classical Studies, for instance, the same interpretive process was at work in Friedrich Nietzsche's (1993) use of the chthonic symbolism of Dionysus to illuminate aspects of Greek drama, or in Michel Foucault's (1998) history of beliefs regarding the body as a way to explain classical attitudes towards gender and sexuality, or in Pierre Hadot's (1995) explanation of the way in which spiritual exercises informed the methods of Socratic and Stoic philosophy. Like such approaches, this books seeks to suggest interpretive 'keys' that can help to illuminate Hindu views on reason, self, body, agency, ritual and reality in the Sanskritic cultures of classical and medieval India.

But theories grounded in Hindu culture can also potentially have a broader value: the theories that are implicitly embedded in these texts, beliefs and practices have much to say to people *across* cultures, for they offer ways of approaching human experience. While in the past China has tended to draw on Chinese theories, India on Indian ones, Europe and the Americas on their own, it is nevertheless important to recognize that global media, trade, translation and migration have been creating a more permeable cultural resource for some time. It is due to this broadening of culture-specific theories across the widening structure of the global knowledge-economy that Nietzsche's contrast between the ancient Greek Dionysian and Apollonian perspectives is able to speak to modern Western distinctions between order- and excess-valuing cultures (see Benedict 1961), or Emile Durkheim's concept of the totemic sacred can be used to reveal the hidden religiosity of 'secular' societies (see Alexander 2006). The possibility of cross-fertilization between traditions of thought is being recovered in contemporary scholarship.

Yet while insights derived from diverse cultures are often applied to India by Western scholars, India's own rich intellectual heritage of theories is rarely put to use on a broader scale. This is in part due to ignorance about India's intellectual history, and it also reflects postcolonial trepidation about misinterpretation and misuse. The result is that understandings of India are too often overwritten by ideas of reason taken from Ancient Greece, the biblical heritage, the European Enlightenment and the social and natural sciences in their modern Western form. Against this, the present book assumes that all theory, made accessible, adds to the shared resource of ways of thinking – and that Europe has too long dominated that resource. One hope of this book is that fields such as religious studies, cultural anthropology, critical theory and other disciplines will find here ways of thinking that unmask Western assumptions and offer new paradigms for interpretation.

Thus, this book has two goals; first, to illuminate some of the worldviews that exist within Hindu contexts by highlighting underlying conceptions of reason, selfhood, ritual, action and reality. Second, it aims to extend those conceptions into broader insights that speak to contemporary theory in the social and human sciences; as such, it aims to reveal distinctive frameworks for thinking about the world.

## Thinking with India: the idea of a global theory

Müller's encouragement to his readers to explore the world's cultural resources was underpinned by his famous assertion that to know one is to know none – that no one can properly understand a single culture in isolation unless it is seen in relation to alternative pictures, paths and patterns of thought. Thus different cultures often appear as through-the-looking-glass worlds for each other, providing an alternative view of the cosmos as it would look if it were different at its very foundations. Müller's idea foreshadows Gayatri Spivak's (1997: 372) contrast – more than a century later – between those who see 'Indian' philosophy as a 'cultural artefact' and those who engage with it as 'an instrument for philosophising'. Spivak puts the word 'Indian' in quotation marks, as if to question the assumption that ideas are ever really possessed exclusively by a given culture.

In actuality, the West has often been more multi-cultural than it realized. It has incorporated influences from ancient Hebrew and Greek culture, Jewish and Muslim thought in the medieval period and afterwards, India via thinkers from Schopenhauer and Nietzsche to Jung and William James, China through the Sinophilia of nineteenth-century painters and composers, indigenous cultures of Africa, the Americas and Asia through the work of anthropologists such as E.B. Tylor and Levi-Strauss. Even Europe's own largely forgotten indigenous cultures which were transmitted through a range of sources from Norse Myth, Beowulf, Grimm's fairytales or even the reconstructed histories that arose in the twentieth century (including both National Socialists' imagined heritage of an imaginary lost Western island of Thule, and contemporary Eco-paganism and Feminist nostalgia for matriarchal cultures). The West has hinted at the 'global' in its thinking for some time; the problem was that its ideas usually stayed at the level of an approximate characterization rather than a more detailed development of the sources.

Some thinkers have attempted a more direct appropriation of Asian sources, either from original texts or from summaries and hearsay. In 1818 Arthur Schopenhauer (1818: 4) championed the potential value of Indian philosophical systems, declaring that the insights of the Vedāntic school of thought were useful for 'correcting the popular notion' of material reality. He asserted that access to the Indian classical texts was 'in my view the greatest advantage which this still young century has to show over previous centuries, since I surmise that the influence of Sanskrit literature will penetrate no less deeply than the revival of Greek literature in the fifteenth century' (xiv). But Schopenhauer's prediction did not come true; in comparison to the study of Greek texts that took place in the medieval and Renaissance periods, and the assimilation of those texts into the general educational system, nothing like the same energy was devoted to Europe's intermittent curiosity about India.

India did find its way into literature however, appearing as a symbol of mystifying otherness in E.M. Forster's *A Passage to India* (first published in 1924),[1] or untapped inner realities in Hermann Hesse's *Siddhartha* (1922). But rarely were ideas that had been rigorously derived from India's own intellectual life brought to bear on Western thinking, so that India often remained a straw man or imaginary interlocutor rather than a genuine generator of fresh concepts. Thoreau (1962: 135) captured this cavalier approach, writing that 'while the commentators are disputing about the meaning of this word and that, I hear only the resounding of the ancient sea, and put it all into the meaning that I am possessed of . . . for I do not in the least care where I get my ideas or what suggests them'. His words are indicative both of the nineteenth century's interest in India as a resource for thinking, and of the looseness of interpretation that would eventually dampen that initial enthusiasm.

The twentieth century saw a change within European universities, however, with Sanskrit coming to take its place alongside classical languages such as Greek, Latin and Persian. In Japan it was recognized as an important foundation for Buddhist scholarship. The twentieth-century Indologist and cultural historian Wilhelm Halbfass (1991) drew on his Indological training to articulate the observation that Indian perspectives were as valid – and likely to be more fruitful – a framework for interpreting Indian religions as Western ones. Trained as a philosopher, Sanskritist and historian of Southeast Asia, he based his own study on

> the premise that for understanding these realities the reflections and constructions of traditional Indian theorists are no less significant than the observations and paradigms of modern Western historians and social scientists. Indian thought has its own ways of dealing with the reality of the Indian tradition through the medium of Indian theoretical and soteriological reflection. (vii)

On this basis, Halbfass advocated using 'indigenous Indian reflections on the sources, the internal structure, and the inherent meaning of the Hindu tradition' to achieve an Indian-influenced methodology for studying Indian materials. He brought a long and wide familiarity with Indian sources to his more theoretical interests, but most scholars lacked the linguistic education needed to draw on primary texts, the sense of a shared cultural entitlement to those resources or the conviction that they were comprehensible and relevant in the first place. Subsequent thinkers tried to imbue greater precision into the enterprise by drawing on the methods of linguistic analysis or analytic philosophy. Bimal Krishna Matilal revolutionized the method of studying Indian thought by using analytic philosophy's more concise style of analysis as a medium for philosophizing with Indian concepts. Echoing the sentiments of Schopenhauer and Müller, Matilal (1986: xii) wrote hopefully that

> it is not easy to make a safe transposition of thought from the technical philosophical Sanskrit to modern intelligible English . . . Certain Sanskrit technical terms will eventually find their way into the modern writings about ancient philosophy when terms like dharma, pākṣa and sādhya will be as much tolerated as certain Greek words, endoxa, elenchus, and eudaimonia.

His project took on life in the work of a select tradition of subsequent philosophers who agreed with his suggestion that 'the field called the history of philosophy need not be a graveyard of dead philosophical ideas, for critical and creative research by modern philosophers can turn it into a blossoming beautiful flower garden' (2). Scholars such as Jonardon Ganeri (2001: 1) represent a generation of philosopher–Sanskritists who took up this theme in many ways, not least by correcting the model of 'Eastern Philosophy' with the acknowledgement that Indian cultures contain not one 'Eastern' philosophy but many different traditions pursuing a 'richness of projects and a diversity of methods'. Halbfass's indigenous hermeneutics and Matilal's analytic method have both contributed to the increasing sense that an archive of resources awaits use by modern heirs.

In recent years there has been considerable application of Western theories to South Asian materials, covering a wide range of objects and disciplines. The anthropologist Victor Turner's theories of ritual have been shown to be helpful in analysing the extended pleasures of certain kinds of religious pilgrimage (see Haberman 1994: 69–71); performance theory, drawn from thinkers such as Dennis Tedlock and Charles Briggs, has been put to use to show the role of imaginative association in ritual activity (see Patton 2005: Chapter two); Mikhail Bakhtin's notion of dialogical identity can shed light on approaches to the self in certain tantric traditions (Flood 2006); Max Weber's understanding of religious legitimation illuminates portrayals of Sanskrit as a 'language of the gods' (Pollock 2006), while Michel Foucault and Gilles Deleuze can help to explain the importance and uses of power in tantra (Urban 2010), and the post-Heideggerian notion of the divine as something that goes 'beyond Being' has been proposed as a useful framework for interpreting the Vedāntic philosophies of Śaṃkara and Rāmānuja (see Ram-Prasad 2013). In these and many other cases, theory has helped to add nuance to the interpretation of Indian sources. As the study of Hinduism has advanced towards more thorough understanding of those sources, so have advanced fields of theoretical reflection appeared increasingly relevant to the understanding of Hindu contexts and perspectives.

While these cases are fairly unilateral in their application of Western ideas to Indian contexts, they have provided a first step towards what Gavin Flood (2013: 5) calls theoretical and philosophical 'mapping ... across cultures'. They demonstrate that an indigenous concept can often be illuminated by insights gained from the analysis of similar concepts derived from other contexts; if one wants to understand Indian theories of meaning, for instance, it does not hurt to know the range of approaches that are taken elsewhere – the better to spot and plot out the Indian view in its unique character. This is less a 'comparative' practice in the old sense of seeking similarities than a hermeneutic practice using comparison as a tool to parse particular concepts. One of the most effective means of cross-cultural mapping has been the exposition of indigenous concepts that are able to help the reader's understanding 'open into a distinctive "world" of human possibilities generated in a culture' (Mittal and Thursby 2004: 1). Such concepts are particularly suited for building broader models of self, reality, and culture, and some thinkers interested in general philosophical or theoretical questions have sought to constructively build *bridge-theories* that span different intellectual histories rather than growing exclusively from only one. Methodologically this entails applying 'hermeneutical phenomenology' to more than one religious culture and describing them according to the self-understanding of the tradition in a way intended to 'allow what shows itself to be seen within religions' (Flood 2013: 10). In this way scholars can act as translators, enabling a particular culture to explain its own ideas to the world. Thus, for instance, when Frederick Smith (2006: 580, 602) uses possession traditions in South Asia to query the West's dominant notion of an 'inviolate, sovereign self' and to cast 'extreme doubt on the viability of the socially constructed individual', he is harnessing the study of South Asian culture to broader philosophical projects of understanding the self. Such work demonstrates the process by which explanations of South Asian cultures can transform organically into an application of those cultures to combined intellectual projects seeking to understand the world that we all inhabit.

## Forms of theory

Reflecting the critical scholarship that has elsewhere been brought to bear on other traditions, one purpose of the present project is to bring Hindu Studies into contemporary conversations about selfhood and embodiment, practice and materiality *in general* and the nature of theory *in and of itself*. It can be mapped against Amartya Sen's (1997) taxonomy of scholarly approaches to Indian ideas: they may take the *magisterial* approach that seeks (at best) to incorporate Indian thoughts into the superior enterprise of Western theory, or the *exoticist* approach that revels in the differentness of Indian thought without admitting its real 'rationality', or the *curatorial* approach that seeks to explain ideas authentically but never harnesses them to shared thinking. This study seeks to extend the curatorial approach into a hermeneutic search for the premises, goals and values that actually shaped the theory. But it also seeks to explain its use and meaningfulness qua *idea*. What follows adopts the model of 'a creative investigation through canonical texts' (Ganeri 2007: 5), but it also falls into the category that Roy Perrett (1998: 27) adds to Sen's list: it is an *interlocutory* investigation that aims to produce coherent and 'workable' theories for application to the world.

At the heart of many claims to the intellectual uniqueness of the West lies the idea that it somehow spontaneously generated new forms of knowledge that included the systematic gathering of empirical evidence according to 'scientific' methods meant to ensure 'truth' in the forms of generalized explanation, syllogistic logic, sceptical reasoning and a critical self-awareness of the reasoning process that results in meta-theory about the nature, assumptions and function of reason itself. Whether in Hegel's philosophical celebration of Western dialectical reasoning, or in J.G. Frazer's anthropological notion of science as the pinnacle of human thought, for centuries the idea of a classical emergence of critical theorizing has led people to believe that the distinctive rationality of the West lies in what Alain Badiou (2006) calls the 'grandiose audacity' of pre-Socratic thought and its break with all traditional forms of thinking.

But today scholars require an improved sense of what theorizing itself entails and where it can be found. A survey of different cultures yields many different kinds of 'philosophy', 'science' and other formalizations of knowledge. In the Greek context alone, reasoning followed not one but many paths. Europe's first-known theorists were perhaps the Ionian group of thinkers that included Thales, Anaximander, Anaximenes, Heraclitus and Diogenes. They were designated by Aristotle retrospectively as the Physiologoi, the 'Physicalists', because, unlike those who explained phenomena through anthropomorphic deities, they sought regular cosmological models and consistent principles embodied in underlying universal 'elements' and checked via cautious methods, using these to explain the operation of the world. These speculative models can be seen as precursors of theories about the world, but they span both creative mytho-poetic kinds of explanation, and also the systematic reasoning that is today labelled 'philosophy' (see Luchte 2011). But this is not history's only tradition of reason. As it is necessary to reconsider the format of classical philosophy, so too one may need to expand the usual Western preconceptions about styles of reasoning in order to appreciate Chinese Mohist logic and judgement (Fraser 2013), African notions of truth and understanding (Lee Brown 2004) or Buddhist deconstructive strategies (Perdue 2014).

As we will see, one form of theory found prominently in Hindu texts, cosmologies and metaphysics is *model-making*: the creative generation of explanatory schemes meant to explain the phenomena of experience. Some scholars have seen this process as central to the very nature of religion, yielding a sacred canopy of ideas that organizes the chaos of life into a meaningful *nomos* (Berger 1967), or a web of meaning that is able to domesticate the 'strange world' in which we find ourselves (Flood 2012). This can be challenging to those used to seeing theory as an instrumental science; the philosopher (and classicist) Martin Heidegger complained that theory in the West has become strongly affiliated with either the pragmatic reasoning of the sciences, or the critical theorizing introduced by Friedrich Nietzsche and later the Marxist tradition. European and American cultures have arguably lost sight of the earlier kinds of explanatory theory that took the form of cosmology or metaphysics.

But other types of theorizing than those that have become dominant in Western sciences can be acknowledged: in his histories of truth and of the various Human, Social and Natural Sciences, Hans-Georg Gadamer (2004: 4–5) noted that the modern 'scientific' ideal of knowledge is basically an *applied* one, seeking to make predictions based on 'a progressive knowledge of regularity'. The triumph of this 'new mechanics' as a useful tool led to an unfortunate but enduring mistake in Western thought in which the scientific plotting of regularities came to eventually *replace* the complexities of the lived world: mechanical truth became the primary truth. According to this reading of Western history, Enlightenment scientism obscured the diverse ways of conceiving truth that had driven earlier figures such as Leonardo Da Vinci 'in whose total genius craftsmanship, mechanical invention and artistic genius were still undifferentiably one' (80). For Gadamer and many other philosophers of twentieth-century Europe, one of the tasks of the modern West, then, was to recapture that broader vision of truth through engagement with other perspectives than that of the modern Western sciences.

In addition to the craft of coherent model-making, the views in these texts can also function as a kind of critical theory, provoking a self-reflexive awareness of one's own assumptions and unmasking the agendas that may drive more familiar claims to theoretical reason and truth. In most scholarly discussion of all of these forms of theory to date, the Western models have stood supreme, setting the criteria to which other cultures are expected to conform. But Catherine Bell (1992: 5) has given a helpful analysis of critical theory as an emancipatory activity that should seek to interrogate such presumed standards, taking both a critical and a constructive attitude:

> The critical analysis of a theoretical perspective must look not only to the logic of the set of ideas under scrutiny, but also to the history of their construction. In addition a critical analysis must incorporate a reflexive awareness of the conditions under which it operates to constitute meaningful interpretations.

For Bell, it is the genealogical contextualization of any body of interpretation – showing us how and why it sees things in a given way – that is the distinctive task of theorization. Such forms of creative scrutiny encourage us to be clearer about the goals and methods of theory, warning against univocal, unified, generalized 'straightjacket' theories. Instead one can collect and compare different interpretations, selecting preferred frameworks as cautiously – and provisionally – as a physicist does when acceding to the latest interpretation of a given set of data. More recently, Foucault ([1969] 1972) has systematized this impulse away from the continuities, generalities and totalities of 'Grand Theory', encouraging a move towards greater specificity about the limits, divisions and concretizing processes entailed in our knowledge.

But 'theory' as the West knows it has still done relatively little to take into account other cultural worlds and other goals of theorizing. The Indic tradition, however, had the cross-cultural interruption of its own intellectual tradition forced upon it by the advent of colonialism and the imposition of the Western university system. Indian intellectual culture assimilated elements of the West's epistemological, didactic, scientific, metaphysical, social and other kinds of theory, without having had the chance to develop a platform from which to engage in a dialogue of equals. This happened despite the age, richness, complexity and sophistication of its own history of theoretical reflection. What, then, in its time of crisis and its need for novelty might the Western theoretical project learn from Indian traditions of reflection? And how might India, having had so much Western thought forced upon it, choose to articulate upon the global stage its own range of distinctive worldviews and their implications for human experience?

## Multicultural hermeneutics

The 'hermeneutic' approach taken in this book – seeking to understand ideas in terms of their contextual worldview and triangulating them against alternative histories to develop bridge theories and hermeneutic 'fusions' – has a long history in the project of thinking across cultures. As the science of interpretation, *hermeneutics* is named after the Greek god Hermes who, like the Angel Gabriel in Christianity, Jibreel in Islam or the deity Agni in Vedic Hinduism, took messages between the divine and human worlds. Hermeneutic concepts are so named because they function like a messenger: delivering an insight about the meaning of the context in question (a book, person, symbol, etc.) to someone who seeks to understand it. Some of the first implicitly 'hermeneutic' thinkers were early travellers and historians who thought carefully about their methodology in describing foreign sights to those back home: the eleventh-century Muslim scholar Al-Biruni, for instance, was perhaps the first 'fieldwork-based scholar' of India and drew on primary text quotations to try to give Muslims an inside perspective; he emphasized monotheistic and transcendental ideas of the divine and offered a genetic account of the development of symbolic representations among the masses. He even called on his Muslim readers to maintain a sympathetic attitude by remembering that the Qur'an itself demands a fair hearing for other beliefs (see Sachau [1887] 1971). Al-Biruni's work shows the naturalness of tempering one's interpretation with a cautious insider understanding; indeed, in his own Muslim context he attributed this fairness of attitude to God's own exhortation in the Qur'an to 'speak the truth, even if it were against yourselves' (3–4).

In 1907 A.V. Williams Jackson, an American professor of Indo-Iranian languages, situated Al-Biruni within a long history of interpretation by compiling outsider descriptions of India in a collection that included the first-century Greek historian Strabo (who shows a healthy scepticism about the 'hearsay' of his sources), the seventh-century Chinese Buddhist traveller Hiuan Tsang, the thirteenth-century Persian geographer Kazvini as well as Early Modern Portuguese, Dutch, French, Italian and English and other missionaries, merchants and envoys. Williams Jackson (1907) speaks out of an American university culture hungry for more, and more reliable, information and declares, '[A]s I look back over the long ages of India's history and its position in Asia, I can but be struck by the thought of the ever-increasing interest in the East felt by the West, and the growing importance of a knowledge of the great historic nations of the Land of the Dawn'. This need for hermeneutic intervention has grown over the past centuries, as travel and migration have brought historically separate cultures into intimate contact.

But culture is no longer seen as a matrix of ideas that can be revealed and expressed in its entirety; like other religious cultures, Hinduism has come to be seen as a complex and multilayered multi-culture into which different voices are woven. It may be argued that a new form of 'global hermeneutics' is needed to make sense of this form of understanding that is not merely about dialogues – the one-to-one rapprochement that formed the basis of earlier hermeneutics; hermeneutics must now be concerned with multi-cultures, forums of discussion or choruses of plural perspectives that can be voiced equally and mapped alongside each other within a wider space of understanding.

The old model of hermeneutics assumed that 'I' reached out of my cultural assumptions to engage in dialogue and comprehend 'your' views, all within a dialectical relation to my tradition that meant I would necessarily transform my own cultural inheritance – 'fusing' our horizons, according to the phrase made famous from Gadamer's 1960 work *Truth and Method*. But this model envisions cultural encounter as the occasional meeting between two cultures, reaching across a border. What happens when not two, but multiple cultures become part of a conversation so that the dialogue develops into a chorus? In its 'global' form, hermeneutics might be said to take a 'Deleuzian' turn into a space of greater multiplicity, recognizing the way in which our ideas are formed not through a fusion of 'own' and 'other' cultures, but as a triangulation of *many different* cultural frameworks that exist within one's own culture, in the other 'other culture' and alongside both in alternative ways of thinking.

Time and context also transform those points of reference constantly so that hermeneutic understanding becomes something constantly provisional, multifaceted and dynamic – and the meanings that are understood in this way are not fixed, but, as Gilles Deleuze (2001: 30) describes his own form of truth, a virtual '[o]ne [that] is always the index of a multiplicity: an event, a singularity, a life'.[2] Understanding is itself a complex and dynamic phenomenon.

The hermeneutic forum of global multi-culture requires a dialectical relation that triangulates 'my' own views against not one but many parallel perspectives. Here it is less the process of fusion than the points of conceptual choice between various possibilities that come into focus: thus understanding another view also means understanding the features that liken and differentiate it from one's own and from other traditions. This means that global hermeneutics requires an acute comprehension not only of similarities but also of the specific points of contrast between cultural frameworks. It reveals each idea in relation to alternative potential formulations and the actual variant perspectives that particular thinkers have crafted. These differences define ideas, behaviours and all cultural forms in their eidetic specificity. To use classical Greece as an example, this can be seen in the decision of Aristotle to attribute properties to substances, in contrast to Plato's decision to accord to properties their own ontological autonomy as formal ideas; it is differentiating choices such as these that have shaped the pluri-tradition of scholastic thought for Judaism, Christianity and Islam alike. The same process can be seen on a larger scale, as, for instance, in the *Tao Te Ching*'s decision to prioritize not objects, atoms or substances as the basic fabric of reality, but the dynamics of energy and dialectic of ideas. The text's authors did not know of Democritus or Plato or India's King Janaka, but the direction of their interpretation shaped the future of Chinese culture, and still throws the Greek *Republic* or the Indian *Questions of King Milinda* into sharp contrast today.

Gadamer's hermeneutics can be adapted to reflect this global pluralism in a way that propels it beyond the old dialogical model. In addition to the image of dialogue as a 'fusion of horizons' in *Truth and Method*, Gadamer himself also uses what we might call 'choral' images of plural synchronous themes that together produce a new vision. Listening to the musical improvisation of a group is one example of what it means to understand plural voices simultaneously in such a way that the whole range of voices is heard in its specificity, difference and complementarity. Each voice pursues the logic of its own ideas in their distinctive 'hermeneutic identity' (Gadamer 1986: 25). Each 'has its own proper spirit' which is determined by the way it is 'patterned in various ways', differing in each case (Gadamer 2004: 107). Each has its own tempo or sense of rhythm, and by analogy the plurality of cultural views retains their difference, India from Germany, Bengal from Rajasthan, monistic followers of Śiva from dualistic worshipers of Viṣṇu and so on. But they can also be understood together as a complementary structure in which we perceive synchronically the quite different movements of alternative ways of thinking. The new 'global' notion of hermeneutics must represent a new form in which multiple partners speak simultaneously to produce something that is not communication, but a meaningful overview of many positions in their mutually illuminating relationships. Gadamer (1986: 25) uses the image of an organ playing many notes, and from this we may retain the idea of multiple voices and speak of a '*choral hermeneutics*' that produce a new simultaneous vision of many positions in relation to each other. Such an understanding is less an item of information than an artwork through which we perceive both the specificity of each voice and the shared space of possible cultural forms that they inhabit.

The wider horizon that is laid open to view by shifting from a *dialogical* to a *choral* hermeneutics tells us about the nature and possibilities of ideas themselves – in this sense it is a meta-horizon. But this does not consist in some objective understanding of each tradition from a 'God's Eye View', for that is never possible: we still understand the range of alternatives in their specificity in relation to the history of ideas that has shaped us. But now we also acquire a new meta-understanding of the *contingency* of such decisions and the concepts they generate, and their dialectical relationship within a wider landscape of alternatives. Ideas appear no longer alone, but as points on an eidetic web of concepts, continuous with alternative formulations that stand in relations of contrast, analogy or even creative complementarity. The individual worldviews are 'taken up' in the new understanding, as in the Hegelian idea of *Aufhebung* or sublimation into a higher, dialectically complex idea. This clarifies the nature of one's own beliefs: 'what we know emerges, as if illuminated, from all the contingent and variable circumstances that condition it: it is grasped in its essence' (Gadamer 2004: 114).

This eidetic web must be understood to contain not only ideas, but also values – tastes, ideals, emotions and desires – that are *part* of those ideas, and central to determining the way they are lived out. This constitutes a qualitative dimension to the vision of alternative worldviews and thought-paths, allowing us to see and compare the ideals of goodness, of ultimacy, of beauty and even of *kinds* of truth that shape each worldview. In this sense global theory requires a mapping of parallel values (including one's own) as well as of parallel ideas. In Gadamer's hermeneutics this is expressed in terms of beauty or the sense of the good that each philosopher must have in his own system of thought. But it also entails an open aesthetic sensitivity that someone seeking to comprehend multiple worldviews must show if they are to assimilate – to some extent – other values and see their relation to one's own. It is perhaps for this reason that philosophy was linked to beauty in the saying of Thucydides 'that the Athenians philosophize and love what is beautiful (*philosophoumen kai philokaloumen*)'. Understanding diverse philosophies means understanding not only alternative formulations of ideas, but also alternative formulations of value, of what is appealing and what is worthy of being sought. Indeed, Gadamer (see 1981: 141) noted that *philokalon*, 'love of beauty', might have been a good alternative word for the project of hermeneutic understanding.

At the personal level, this means seeing lives we might have pursued, in realities we might have experienced and selves we could have been. Indeed, choral hermeneutics shows us more clearly other ways that we might still think, since the contingency of ideas also implies a liberty of the interpreter to alter his or her own thought by changing course. At this point the 'hermeneutic' model of theory can be usefully augmented by Gilles Deleuze's (2001) 'virtual' model of thought, which emphasizes the constant possibility of change and new developments. This virtuality of theories consists not in their being untrue, but in their constant emergence from being only one of many options into being actualized as an idea:

> What we call virtual is not something that lacks reality, but something that is engaged in a process of actualisation following the plane that gives it its particular reality. The immanent event is actualised in a state of things and of the lived that make it happen. (31)

According to this model, the history of thought appears as a field of multiple 'virtual' possibilities constantly being made concrete through the 'event' of one thing coming to be, in place of another.

As Deleuze exhorts us to remember the field of possibilities that form a background to particular ideas and theories, so also global theory exhorts us to think *around* the theories that we know. Theory as a whole then appears as the structure of the different 'worlds' in which humans live. This 'structure of the whole can never be an objective and all-comprehending truth; the observer brings his or her own worldview into that process of triangulation. Indeed, all such theoretical understanding is necessarily a "transformation into structure" of existing forms, an art of creating new ideas that reveal the key, active elements for any discussion or "language game"' (Gadamer 2004: 100). Such multi-tradition comprehension is thus a kind of philosophy that reveals the structure of those conceptual themes with which, together, different partners are working. Gadamer's (1981: 4) 'Philosophical Hermeneutics' uses the analogy of language communities: to find an understanding that multiple communities can use is to create a new language, for 'language is not a mere instrument ... rather it is the medium in which we live from the outset as social natures and which holds open the totality within which we live our lives'. Indeed,

Gadamer argues that even dialogues between two people are actually dialogues between at least three partners: there are the two speakers and the subject matter which makes its own interventions and demands on what is said. A reciprocity is established where 'the conversation circles about the subject matter' (4).

This means deriving theory from authentic sources, and also bringing the new ideas back into relation with those sources, holding them open to constant revision and new development: it is this that constitutes the 'binding' character (Gadamer 1981: 1–2) of thinking about concepts as opposed to the applied sciences which aim at concrete results. They have to be continuously tested against their contexts, maintained in conversation so that insights can be honed and misunderstandings corrected. The resulting theory should be less like a representation *of* the culture that can take its place, than a mediating lens that allows good vision and successful interaction.

These insights into the relations that exist between different voices, worldviews or cultures can also have a critical function. Good critical theory reveals ideas in such a way that it makes them available as the basis for evaluation, rejection or incorporation, and development. But for Gadamer's 'Philosophical Hermeneutics' this was the true purpose of philosophy: a comparison of the ways of thinking that yields a wide view of the 'whole' of what ideas are, what they entail and why they concern us as they do. In such a view we understand ourselves as centres of thought within the larger landscape of ideas:

> We are ourselves encompassed in a manner that the whole would be present for us as the whole. We encounter it rather as the totality and the vastness, wherein everything is, only through adhering to what has been allotted to us, i.e. the *nomos*, whatever it may be. (Gadamer 1992: 91)

To understand Durkheim, Freud, Kant, Bhartṛhari, Abhinavagupta and Rāmānuja in terms of the choices they made, and in dialectical relation to alternative theories, means letting specific theories remind us that theorizing itself is a worldview-shaping, inherently contingent process. In a sense, this comparative understanding of theories as part of a wider eidetic web of ideas leads us to treat theorization as an *art*, creatively working with empirical observation, life experience, embodied practice, imaginative cosmology, logical structures and other theory-forming processes to create systems of thought. Hermeneutics' attempt to understand alternative histories of thought becomes part of the human project of understanding ourselves as beings who construct explanations for ourselves, as perhaps the most important of all tools for living our lives.

## Hindu worldviews as lived culture

As a hermeneutic study of selected Hindu ideas, this book will try to consider those ideas 'emically' or 'from the inside' by reference to the broader *worldviews* that underlie them. In the chapters that follow, these views will be mapped out as conceptions of the cosmos that informed influential texts, and through them shaped people's lived understanding of their bodies and minds, actions and goals. We find that ideas of the body are inseparable from ideas of the world that surrounds it – both in their metaphysical constitution and in the wider cosmological lay of the land. The ideas found in classical texts are sometimes considered to be quite separate and different from those that inform everyday lives, and this idea is illustrated by the fact that few inhabitants of Christian, Jewish or Muslim cultures have, for instance, read Luther, Maimonides or Ibn Hanifa. Worldview may be considered something lived and built from embodied experiences rather than intellectual concepts. This view assumes that for most of history 'everyday' people did not have access to texts (particularly classical ones), because literacy and education were the reserve of economic elites. But thinkers such as Charles Taylor, Michel Foucault and Alisdair Macintyre have argued that the most primary experiences of any human 'self' and its goals and values are influenced by histories of ideas drawn from older texts created by a philosophical, religious or cultural elite. Canonical ideas are disseminated in read, spoken, preached, heard, sung, watched and otherwise consumed texts – often drawn from the 'intellectual' cultures of the past as mediated through frameworks such as scripture, story or political rhetoric. Indeed, some of the first discussions of cultural worldview saw it as an inalienable fabric of: (a) ideas about a general order of existence, (b) symbols tacitly expressing that order and (c) emotions and motivations associated with those ideas that shape the everyday life of those within the culture. Worldview, then, in its original meaning, transcends the often artificial divide between intellectual and embodied culture and encompasses within itself the genealogy of lived belief in reasoned reflection.

The anthropologist Clifford Geertz (1973a) promoted the term 'worldview' as a way to approach cultures and religions. In doing so he went beyond the functionalist definitions of religion promoted by Durkheim, Freud, Mauss and others; such definitions emphasized religion as a practical mechanism of society. Geertz, by contrast, brought out the way in which

> the importance of religion lies in its capacity to serve, for an individual or for a group, as a source of general, yet distinctive, conceptions of the world, the self, and the relations between them, on the one hand – its model *of* aspect – and of rooted, no less distinctive 'mental' dispositions – its model

> *for* aspect-on the other. From these cultural functions flow, in turn, its social and psychological ones. (123; emphasis in the original)

Geertz held that ideas and practices serve not only social functions, but also cultural and psychological ones, bringing meaning to human experience, guiding and orienting individuals through life, rendering psychological events and social relationships 'graspable' and embedding in people's dispositions 'a recommended attitude toward life, a recurring mood, and a persisting set of motivations' (124). This is a view found in variant forms in the work of other thinkers, taking its inspiration from the marriage of the Human Sciences with existentialist views of humanity as concerned with fundamental and universal issues. The phenomenologist and sociologist Alfred Schütz, a follower of Edmund Husserl, argued that society involved the construction of meanings, and his work was influential on both Geertz and on Peter Berger's conception of religious culture as the construction of a *nomos*, a meaningful picture of the world that allows humans to form their identity and goals. It is also a view that echoes Paul Tillich's (1951: 61) idea of religion as something that 'formulates the questions implied in human existence', and the view that culture and religion are central to shaping human meaning and enabling human life has more recently been the focus of Gavin Flood's (2007) arguments for the 'importance of religion'.

Geertz's idea of a 'worldview' was itself inspired by an Indic source: during his fieldwork in the Hindu, Buddhist and Muslim cultures of Java, he discovered an idea that seemed odd from a Western perspective, but went to the core of what was distinctive about Javanese religion. Audiences of the popular Indonesian *wajang* puppet-dramas expressed their enthusiasm in terms of something called '*rasa*', a Sanskrit term found in Hindu texts (see Geertz's discussion in the essay 'Ethos, Worldview, and the Analysis of Sacred Symbols' (1973: 134)). In the Indonesian context, *rasa* signified both the 'meaning' of something and the 'feeling' it elicited, combining what Geertz identified as the descriptive '*model of*' way in which worldviews encapsulate the present actuality of cultural beliefs, with the prescriptive '*model for*' manner in which a worldview also sets the tone for tastes, desires, values and goals. This seamless coherence of fact with feeling, present personal experience and traditional cosmology seemed alien to the Western tendency to divide the supposedly reasoned scientific realm of empirical truth from the world of religious belief which, by contrast, was seen as mythological and emotional.

But Geertz's use of the term 'worldview' is holistic: it points to a complex, multifaceted cultural style that characterizes Hindu life as experienced through particular Indic sets of beliefs and habits. The present exploration takes that cosmological framework into which values and facts, gods and humans, mind and matter are woven, as central to understanding Hinduism. Precedents exist in the study of European culture: the excavation of worldviews has also been an important project, practiced by scholars such as Tillyard in his study of *The Elizabethan World-Picture: A Study of the Idea of Order in the Age of Shakespeare, Donne and Milton* (first published in 1942), and C.S. Lewis in his *The Discarded World* (1964). Noting the application to study of non-European cultures, Flood has highlighted the way in which Lewis brought to light a structure of European views about the world that was implicit but long-standing and pervasive:

> [I]n spite of various disagreements over intellectual matters – such as realism versus nominalism, effort versus grace – the contained, hierarchical model of the cosmos remained the backdrop of such disputes and lasted well into the seventeenth century. What is striking is that the vast hierarchy outside the human person is also found within the person as a microcosm that recapitulates the macrocosm. (see Flood 2013: 43; and Lewis 1964: 13)

Incidentally, much of what Lewis says about the medieval European world is strikingly applicable to Hindu culture. But what is central here is the way in which underlying assumptions about reality span periods and contexts of doctrine and practice. It is true that Hindu culture is more diverse (or that its diversity is more easily seen) than that of Europe, and for that reason even within the scope of this limited study we will see multiple paradigms at work in characterizing the self, reality and reason. But throughout we will see how 'religion grounds the most specific requirements of human action in the most general contexts of human existence' (Geertz 1973b: 126).

Hinduism varies profoundly in its historical and geographical range. Scholars have suggested different ways of understanding the diverse combination of different traditions within Hinduism, likening it to a banyan tree, growing from a few original stems into a multifaceted polycentric entity (Lipner 2010: 2), or a family growing from a few sources into a diverse but connected collective (Klostermaier 2007: 11), or even a 'pan of lasagna' that combines different ingredients and layers into a composite that nevertheless has its own distinctive flavour (Glucklich 2008: 5). The difficulties of trying to 'explain' a cultural form as complex as this can lead to what J.E. Llewellyn (2005: 2) has called 'the trouble with textbooks' that try to construct some kind of 'unity' out it. How, then, should one comprehend Hinduism's elusive cloud of lives, ideas, actions, traditions, institutions, objects, festivals, customs, styles, experiences and values?

In his use of the term 'worldview' Clifford Geertz (1973b) defines it as a people's 'picture of the way things in sheer actuality are, their concept of nature, of self, of society ... their most comprehensive ideas of order'. This worldview is inseparably integrated with the 'ethos' of the people, defined as 'the tone, character and quality of their life, its moral and aesthetic style and mood; it is the underlying attitude toward themselves and toward their world that life reflects' (127). While there have been excellent studies of Hindu cosmology in different traditions and periods, this book focuses on the constitution of some of the basic concepts – of self, agency, reason, ritual and reality – that circulate within the world of these selected Hindu contexts. It aims to reveal certain assumptions held by those texts, and often does so at the levels of metaphysics and of the (super)natural world. Throughout it looks for what is unseen, but nevertheless believed to be real because it is inferred as a necessary precondition – indeed, this is the classical *Sāṃkhya Kārikā*'s definition of inference, and hints at what it means to identify underlying assumptions, reasons and rationales. That means that while some of the categories examined here would be familiar to the authors of those texts (e.g. self or '*ātman*', body or '*śarīra*', ritual or '*yajña*', order or '*ṛta*', inference or '*anumāna*'), others drawn from theoretical or philosophical terminology would be less familiar (e.g. contingency, embodiment, agency, theory, *nomos*) as they seek to dig into the layer of implicit concepts that support the worldview.

This book will focus on cosmological, metaphysical, epistemological and proto-scientific ideas, as well as implied assumptions about the way in which the world works. The largely Sanskritic early Brahminical texts in the pages that follow evoke a world in which there is a fitting *dharmic* way to structure one's life or one's society and cosmos. But there is also a possibility of altering those patterns by switching between identities, adopting different paths and reshaping one's self and even one's whole world. Each individual stands within a wider continuum of beings that possess varying degrees of power or divinity – from gods, demons, spirits and ancestors, to gurus, ascetics, mediums and yogis. These other beings are rarely simply other: they stand in a 'porous' relation to the self, and may even become one-self through possession, bodily interaction, imagination or the philosophical realization of a shared identity. Just as selves can be changed, so too the 'reality' around us is replete with possibilities for becoming something new – subtle bodies, vital energies, sounds and substances, and forces of auspiciousness exist *in potentio* within the conventional environment that surrounds us. Human life involves managing the relationship with this volatile environment. Structures of ritual and ethics give a normative shape to this complex cosmos, while narratives often explore the more subversive and ambiguous paths of human agency.

These features may be widespread, but none are universal, and it is central to this book that Hinduism contains not one worldview, but many that have developed in different regional and cultural traditions, interweaving and influencing each other, sharing certain assumptions but also varying in their beliefs and forms of life. Approaches to Hinduism today must acknowledge the way in which the tradition has been constructed through 'processes of bricolage, mixture, syncretism or hybridisation' which reveal that what some purport to be an Indian monoculture is really a true multi-culture at its very core (Flugel 2005: 1). As Christianity is Western, African, and South American and Asian, so is 'Hinduism' Muslim and Buddhist, Jain and Christian and rich in indigenous traditions.

## The intellectual history of classical Hinduism

Given this complexity of what is termed 'Hindu' culture, a book like this must necessarily be selective. The focus in the following chapters is on genealogies of ideas that can be found within classical Sanskrit texts that share authorial communities, textual sources and ideas assumed as part of a common culture. These sources particularly include Vedas, Upaniṣads, Sūtras and the theoretical material found in the *Mahābhārata* and Śāstras. There is some further reference to the later Purāṇas, Tantras and scholastic theologians of the medieval period who worked with these sources. Part III also draws on contemporary sources that bear the mark of those worldviews, inscribing them onto the fabric of later Hindu life. These sources are associated with the traditions that we tend to call 'Brahminical Hinduism', but they spill across this boundary to draw on Buddhist, Jain and Cārvāka ideas, indigenous animism and shamanic practice, as well as secular dimensions of the culture. It is always risky to attempt generalized claims about classical Hindu cultural beliefs and patterns, and the goal is to use specific contexts as a window onto background assumptions that have rich theoretical implications.

In many respects 'classical Hinduism' is a fabrication of scholars, both Indian scholastic thinkers who designated a canon of central sources as authoritative, and Western scholars who read, translated and prioritized these texts in their representation of India's religious cultures. Thus classical Hinduism should not be taken to represent the views of most Hindus then or now, nor to represent the whole viewpoint of those cultures of which they are representative. Yet the conventional 'classical' sources do display a distinctive coherence as a family of texts that influenced and merged with each other over more than a millennium of Indian history.

The classical culture explored here is focused on the Sanskritic output of 'Brahminical' culture in the period from approximately the middle of the first millennium BCE to the first millennium CE. These works draw heavily on the later Vedic corpus of texts written in periods of energetic reflection on cosmology and the basic conceptual tools for comprehending the world. But the Vedic corpus that shaped the later Vedānta, Sūtras, Epics, Purāṇas and other material is a strikingly diverse body of literature. It spans the formal ritual actions of the *adhvaryu* priest and the informal spells of the *Atharva Veda* gathered much later by authors with more personal concerns, the sciences of physiology and language, the narrative and symbolic explanations of the Āraṇyakas and the metaphysical discourses of the Upaniṣads. As in the Brāhmaṇas, some early to middle period Upaniṣads such as the *Bṛhad Āranyaka Upaniṣad* and the *Kauṣītaki Upaniṣad* draw on the structure of a ritual that is to be explained as a nominal basis for arranging the text, but they intersperse *arthavāda* or discussion liberally through their ritual discourse; others such as the *Chāndogya Upaniṣad* use the mantric chants used in the rituals as the framework for speculative discussions, and still others such as the *Taittirīya Upaniṣad* use pedagogical techniques and speeches as their structural template. The Vedic tradition that is an object of inquiry here is a bricolage that developed over two millennia into a complex culture that turned again and again to its source in order to renew its identity. Following Louis Renou, Halbfass usefully questioned the idea that the heritage of Vedic culture necessarily meant a faithful correspondence to the actual corpus of Vedic texts (see Halbfass (1991: 1) on the way in which later tradition 'tipped its hat' to them), and what we see here is a set of sources that pervade later culture in a loose and creative fashion. Classical culture functioned much in the same way in which Plato, Aristotle, Marcus Aurelius or Augustine were woven into a shared European tradition, and the diverse ideas and genres of the Bible provided an ever-fruitful source for teachers and preachers as well as philosophers, poets, dramatists and artists.

The Upaniṣads provide a microcosm of this complex Vedic texture. Their composition within the Vedic culture of Brahmin clans represents the diverse expression of different associated groups who shared ideas but developed their own independent interpretations: Brahmin intellectual communities were divided in terms of professional classes or types of priest (hence the chanters, for instance, are especially associated with the *Chāndogya Upaniṣad*) as well as into related familial branches (known as *śākhā*s), whose ideas were eventually assimilated into the Vedic genres in a way that gave them a dynamic life over time, rather than any well-defined doctrinal concision. It is natural, then, that internally diverse communities developed internally diverse texts. This diversity is increased by the temporal spread of the Upaniṣadic composition over a number of centuries, from the early *Bṛhad Āraṇyaka* and *Chāndogya Upaniṣad*s through to later, possibly post-Buddhist texts such as the *Māṇḍūkya* and *Praśna Upaniṣad*s. The intellectual milieu that influenced them changed considerably over time, with dialogue partners varying from competing Brahmin families prioritizing their own kind of knowledge, to the challenging beliefs of ascetic groups and proto-Sāṃkhya ontologies, or the direct attacks of later Buddhist, Jain or Cārvāka (atheist) sceptics. Different cultural dialogues have shaped the Upaniṣads, and in many of them the situation is complicated by redaction of material from different periods into a single text.

In terms of content, this results in an extraordinary Upaniṣadic textual style of segments blended ad-hoc into sequences that may shift between different literary genres of treatise, dialogue, poetry, narrative, ritual instructions and back again in a matter of verses – making the plotting of coherent views very difficult. As we will see, different theories of self or of nature rub shoulders with each other: it is often difficult to discriminate between animist, polytheist, monotheist and philosophically monistic ideas, or different theories of self (as body, food, breath, mind or consciousness), or afterlife (in the natural world, the world of the ancestors, of the gods or of the sun). We do not have even the range of views as they were actually taught; the narratives in the Upaniṣads suggest that the versions of their ideas recorded in the texts we have were for performance in courtly contexts, to impress Brahmin patrons or to challenge other lineages vying for pre-eminence as purveyors of valued knowledge. One source of internal diversity may be non-Vedic influences on the Upaniṣads, found in aspects of Sāṃkhya metaphysics and Yogic meditation, as well as in the responses to Buddhists and other '*nāstika*' or non-orthodox groups. But importantly, even the Brahminical 'Hinduism' of the Vedas and Upaniṣads represents a range of social and religious phases which often bear little resemblance to the hot, hierarchically organized, deity-worshiping city-states that were the setting for medieval Hindu culture. The early roots of the Upaniṣads lie in the late Vedic period's 'small tribal, pastoral societies of the Eastern Panjab' which Witzel (1996: no page number) describes as being 'without or with only an incipient caste system, a pre Hindu religion, a cold winter, no real monsoon, without cities, and with an economy based on cattle herding'. But the philosophy that began in that tribal, pastoral society came to fruition in sophisticated Upaniṣadic texts that incorporate narrative frameworks about Brahmins and kings. From the sixth to fourth centuries it was a new world that provided the background for the Upaniṣads, with 'craft specialization, monumental architecture, rapid rates of population growth and agglomeration … [and] the first emergence of a state level political organization' (Erdosy 1988: 116). While the rise of kingdoms and courts was a major factor in shaping the discursive culture seen in the Upaniṣads, Erdosy (1995: 84) warns against taking the texts' depictions as a truthful portrait of the majority of north Indian society; rather, they point to a social sphere that Brahmins of certain classes had come to see as part of their cosmopolitan identity. Indeed, the horse sacrifice that begins the *Bṛhad Āraṇyaka Upaniṣad* was a rite designed to confirm the territorial boundaries of a king, and it signals the way in which the priestly class had woven together both secular and sacred ideology into its new theory-rich Upaniṣadic versions of Brahminical ritual. The relation between Brahmin culture and that of the ruling Kṣatriya class has been a topic of particular scholarly debate, with consensus settling on a relationship of patronage and performance that essentially reiterates Jan Heesterman's (1993) theory of a symbiotic culture of priestly authority and sovereign power (Olivelle 1996b: xxxv; Black 2007: 12–16). Brahmins sought the protection of Kṣatriyas and won their support by displaying their own knowledge through both ritual and debate in the courts of the regional rulers – particularly as certain groups moved East towards the eastern Gangetic Kosala-Videha region and more unfamiliar territory (see Witzel's (1987; 1997) theory of a gradual movement eastwards). Yet this regionalized world of trade and travel was united by the growth of shared languages such as Sanskrit, and the predominance of 'court and craft rather than village and agriculture' (Olivelle 1996b: xxix) so that a multi-culture in creative competition is represented. The ideology of performance in circumstances of pluralization and change is central to understanding the development of these theoretical sources, as well as of the later epic literatures and the theological treatises that were forged in the arenas of inter-sectarian debate. It was in recognition of their own embeddedness in a larger world of ideas and communities that early Brahminical communities crafted the texts we read today.

Yet there is great coherence between these sources and the families of commentaries, narratives (*itihāsa*) and teachings (*sūtra*s) or songs (*gītā*s) that grew around them. It is clear that even at the earliest stages the recorded texts drew upon a 'common stock of episodes and teachings' (Olivelle 1996b: xxxiv), and this recycling of material continued for millennia, sometimes through formal commentary or citation, and sometimes through creative elaboration in new explanations, stories and images. The very process of gathering and formalizing texts created theoretical frameworks that lent them greater coherence; this can be seen in the development of a science of grammar that initially ensured the correct capture and preservation of the Vedas, but would also provide fuel for innovative interpretation of sources such as the *Māṇḍukya Upaniṣad* and of language itself. Practical mechanisms for ensuring unity came to provide material for further theorization about the coherence of the classical Sanskritic heritage of the Vedas.

But above all it was the internal *ideology of unity* that lent a genuine conceptual coherence to the immense body of ideas that populated 'classical Hindu' texts. This self-perceived unity has become a topic for debate in relation to the early-modern period (see Nicholson 2010), but it begins much earlier with the idea that those literatures in the Vedic tradition which saw themselves as revelatory in a broad sense were really the expression of a shared source. The Vedas came to understand themselves in terms of a story about their own origin that expanded with the telling over the centuries. The texts recited, taught and shared were not simply ideas that some particular person had come up with; they were seen as manifestations of a prior principle of truthful order, *vāc*. They had been heard by *ṛṣi*s or sages with a particular ability to perceive this hidden reality whose visionary skills often coincided with those of word-craft, so that a sage might also be *kavi* or poet, blessed with the combined powers of perceiving and communicating to others. This framework, a primeval history of humanity's relationship with reality, is retold in more elaborate forms in later texts. By the epics and purāṇas the *ṛṣi*s form a known community of pure, meditative figures who shine like the sun (*Mahābhārata* 1.1.14-16), and many of them are established authorities, celebrities even, like the sage Vyāsa, who is the narrator of the *Mahābhārata*, or his son Śuka, who was famed for his achievement of liberation and also as the source of the *Bhāgavata Purāṇa*. Such sages acquired a setting – the Naimiṣa forest which is depicted as a beautiful utopia of flora, fauna, Brahmins performing well-ordered rituals (*Brahma Purāṇa* 1.4–12) and sages enjoying perfect self-control (*Vāyu Purāṇa* 1.11–12). To this transhistorical setting come bards (*sūta*s) who acquire extraordinary wisdom that can be gathered in verse form and returned to the humans in the mundane world, dispensing the stories they have collected in a way that thrills their listeners (1.13–14). In many cases the source of the bard's words are the narration of a deity – Brahmā or Śiva, for instance – himself, as in the Tantras. In this worldview, super-normal truths flow freely out of the past or from hidden levels of reality into human awareness. The challenge is less how to acquire such 'higher' knowledge, than what to do with it.

Thus the classical worldview included a setting in which elevated persons have access to timeless truths of both historical and theological–philosophical character, truths with which the average person could connect through the intercession of bards not so different from those who would have sung familiar stories in each local village. These stories provided the causal rationale behind the 'common stock of episodes and teachings' that continued to proliferate over the ensuing centuries, making them natural parts of the landscape of ideas and what is more, making them available, in a realm beyond history, for further use.

Gavin Flood has used the term 'imaginaire' to speak of Hindu cultures (ascetic cultures in 2004: 25; and Śaiva ones in 2009: 200) showing how ideas were passed down through multiple generations in such a way that they formed a shared language of ideas, a cultural memory. He links it to worldview, defining an 'imaginaire' as 'a possible world or horizon that the reader, receiver or community of receivers learn to inhabit' (Flood 2004: 26). The idea draws on Gilbert Durand's (1984 [1964]) development of the imaginaire in texts such as *L'Imagination Symbolique*. Durand was an associate of Carl Jung and was also involved in the tradition of French Structural Anthropology that shared some of the constructivist views of phenomenologists such as Schütz and anthropologists such as Geertz. An imaginaire signified a cultural archive of ideas used generatively as a resource for 'le dynamisme créateur' (76) of thinkers expanding the cultural product of any age. This idea seeks to treat the way in which conversational, didactic and literary discourse across traditions, as well as bardic cultures, technical treatises and consumption of texts through art and mythology, provided a cultural memory that in its own turn served as a world to 'inhabit'.

This does not express a claim that Sanskritic culture is the 'real Hinduism', or that Hindu culture is the 'real India'; this project presents a genealogy of classical Sanskritic ideas only in order to form a sounding board against which Tamil, Bengali, and other cultures could also be persuaded to yield up their own implicit theoretical frameworks for scrutiny and comparison. This is but one account of some selected theoretical frameworks underlying selected strands of the culture; other genealogies, narratives and theories doubtless wait to be excavated from these and other materials.

On a cautionary note, many historians and philologists would question the ambition to excavate broad-scale theories and paradigms from texts on which scholars have not yet had the last word, texts that are still emerging from history. They are right, insofar as we can only make provisional suggestions for ways of understanding. But they are wrong in thinking that we should not try and formulate an idea of the underlying assumptions behind those texts; we know as little about many ancient Greek texts, and yet Classics has been an unfailingly rich resource for intellectual history, philosophy, literary theory, aesthetics and other disciplines of the Humanities for centuries. Theory-sceptics are also wrong in suggesting that one could do anything other than the merest recording of historical facts, without speculating on the assumptions that underlie their sources. Even to cite a text's thoughts on *ātman, anumāna, dravya, śarīra, dīkṣā* or *sampradāya* in the most modest way is to raise questions about cultural understandings of identity, reasoning, substance, body, authority or tradition. The key is to remember that these translations into worldview can only ever remain provisional – but perhaps no more provisional than the theories of totem, gift, purity, mimesis, liminality or the sacred that were developed by Durkheim, Mauss, Daly, Girard, Turner and Eliade, respectively, and which have dominated theories of culture and religion.

Of course, one must remember that a worldview and its ethos, as held by people within a religion, does not necessarily fit the reality of history. The way in which one sect describes itself or other groups is not necessarily how things were from the perspective of historical events observed by onlookers. Furthermore, there is both explicit theory that presents itself as part of a systematic culture of explanation of knowledge, and also implicit theory that presents broader frameworks as part of the underlying rationale of an idea without explicitly presenting itself in that way – as the Renaissance historian Marc Bloch put it, '[T]o understand the attitude of the medieval vassal to his *seigneur* you must inform yourself about his attitude to his God as well' (cited in Geertz 1973b: 362). The former explicit kind of theory is more likely to derive from educational cultures, and so from intellectual elites and upper classes; as such, it represents traditions of reasoning and social identities associated with the cultivation of that specific activity. Philosophers and philosophy, the 'intelligentsia' in some form, educators and critics may all be producers of explicit theory that holds to the importance of specific ways of thinking, supported by shared reasons and reasoning.

But the implicit kind of theory is more likely to arise in the culture at large, within a discourse that may be unattached to systematic disciplines of knowledge. Implicit theory that lies beyond the range of classical text has become important for scholars studying cultures that have not cultivated explicit traditions, but which preserve ways of understanding, analysing and communally applying good thinking through other forms of tradition. The search for systematic speculative traditions in non-literate African cultures, for instance, has been a fruitful ground for discussions of implicit reasoning, finding that where reflection was not recorded in fixed texts, nevertheless,

> we have fragments of their philosophical reflections and their views preserved and transmitted to us through channels other than writing such as mythologies, formulas of wise-sayings, traditional proverbs, stories and especially religion ... Apart from mythologies, wise-sayings, worldviews, knowledge can be preserved in the social-political set-up of the people. (Omoregbe 1998: 5)

Omoregbe's list here is aimed at African cultures; but with Hindu cultures in mind, one might add that theoretical ideas can also be encoded and transmitted in ritual and liturgy, songs and recitation, cosmologies and lived geographies, as well as in the grammars and terminologies that are used on a regular basis throughout any given community. In light of this larger pool of possible theoretical material, Henry Odera Oruka (1990) argues for a distinction between professional philosophy on the one hand – highlighting the contexts in which topic-focused reasoning took place as part of a professional tradition – and ethnophilosophy or sagacity on the other (i.e. beliefs assumed by a community, or insights expressed by individuals for the community, whether through chieftains, individual teachers, poet-bards or ascetics). In India the latter sources arguably vary much more widely than did the trained elites of Brahmins, nobles or ascetics who were so often responsible for Indian philosophies and sciences. They include the unnamed and probably multiple authors of the *Rāmāyaṇa*, *Mahābhārata*, Purānas as well as the vernacular poet-saints, local gurus and paṇḍits, and unrecorded teachers who contributed to yogic, tantric and other traditions.

Thus implicit theory speaks for those who stand beyond the margins of explicit traditions of 'professional philosophies and sciences', and it often reflects a wider spread of influence. The texts of Indian Sanskrit-speaking elites are paralleled by other sources of theory that include cosmological narratives, practical sciences, vernacular songs and even unwritten regional practices. All of these help to generate theory as the modern academy understands it. J.N. Mohanty (1992: 10), the Indian Husserlian philosopher, described 'rationality' as reasons that 'operate first of all in the life world of the community concerned, then in the higher order decisions by the scientists, law-givers and artists, finally in the theoretical discourse of the philosophers'. His sketch of theory's uptake into different fields provides a helpful reminder that theory in a given culture potentially extends far beyond the kind of highly specialized academic usage that characterizes contemporary Western philosophy, critical theory and science.

Worldview is always a complex phenomenon, and anyone who tries to describe a worldview runs the risk of reducing the details to generality; one could even say that every individual has his or her worldview, varying to a greater or lesser degree from that of other members of the culture. Thus every description of a worldview is only provisional – just as philosophical histories of the West by thinkers such as Friedrich Nietzsche, Bertrand Russell, Martin Heidegger, Charles Taylor and Michel Foucault have constructed historical narratives in order to highlight certain typical assumptions. So too any construction of theory based on Indian history is also the writing of a narrative that weaves together patterns in the culture itself. But in order to avoid the imposed caricatures and forced limitations of Orientalism, scholars must acknowledge that, as J.L. Brockington (1981: vii) put it, 'what has been passed over in silence is just as much part of the rich fabric of Hinduism'.

# PART ONE

# The art of embodiment: The self made of matter

# 2

# Theories of self in classical Hinduism

Although it is the concept of a 'core self' that has claimed centre stage among both Hindu theologians and contemporary scholars – usually seen as an immortal soul hidden within us like a treasure waiting to be discovered in a cave (see Ganeri [2007] 2012: 21), nevertheless it is the self embodied in matter, energy, ideas, emotions and action that dominates Hindu life and literature. In what follows we will see ways in which certain classical Hindu contexts depict the self as *a part of* reality, embedded in the different strata of the cosmos. As a conscious agent, the self is interwoven into multiple fabrics that constitute the universe; it can expand and contract according to the ideas that it encompasses. Its agency plays out in the 'mental' fabrics of consciousness and reason, as well as in the 'material' fabrics of the elements, energies and structural relations that shape the natural world.

Scholars have highlighted at least three approaches to selfhood in classical Hindu sources. We see:

- a 'pure self' that is unaffected by **any** association with the world,
- a 'core self' that may interact with the world but stands in counterpoint to it, and
- an 'open self' that is deeply engaged in the world and continuous with it.

These ways of analyzing Indian approaches do not exhaust the source material, but they do suggest that early thinkers were concerned about how humans should understand themselves in relation to the world at large ... a world of which their own bodies were an integral part. One interpretation of these ideas is that they were symptoms of an early concern about 'reductionism' – the idea that humans can be reduced to the material constituents of the environment and nothing more. Another interpretation, however, is that they express a tension between those who aimed at a passive state of selfhood, liberated from action and the whole narrative form of day-to-day life, and those who sought a more constructive state of engagement with the world. Thus the competition between different models of the self was fraught, for it also entailed a choice between different ideals for human existence.

The West has come to see the self as a concept with a complex history, despite the fact that it is arguably the most intuitive and universal idea that is employed in day-to-day life. Charles Taylor's influential 1989 study of the 'sources of the self' attempted to uncover our implicit 'understandings of what it is to be a human agent: the senses of inwardness, freedom, individuality, and being embedded in nature which are at home in the modern West' (ix). By giving a detailed genealogy of the idea in Western sources, it provided a model for other possible accounts of the self in other cultures. In the study of India, the result has been a prolific but somewhat piecemeal scholarship on identity, body, mind, experience and agency, variously outlining the self as an indexical form of identity aligned with a tradition-constructed embodiment (Flood 2006), a multiform centre of shifting forces and identities (Smith 2006), or a coordinated 'performance' of unified memory, disposition and desire (Ganeri [2007] 2012). Dominik Wujastyk (2009) and Barbara Holdrege (2015: 11–16) have charted this very multiplicity of bodies and noted that the body also serves as a nexus of numerous systems and purposes, as 'the vehicle for the maintenance of the social, cosmic and divine orders ... an instrument of biological and socio-cultural reproduction' (Holdrege 1998: 341). These and other scholars have tried to sift through the extraordinary range of theories to be found within Hindu cultures, all seeking to identify the distinguishing characteristics of selfhood that are most 'at home in India.'

Terminologically, the body could be many things in the Sanskrit literatures of classical Hinduism – *deha, kāya, śarīra, liṅga, vigraha, mūrti, vapus, tanu, pudgala* and other words. This wide range of terms depict the body in various ways: as a physical form, a tool of interaction, an aggregation of parts, a material manifestation of an underlying reality and so forth; the range indicates that the idea lies far from the simply 'material' model of the physical body that is generally associated with modern medicine and physics. Indeed, a number of the Sanskrit terms do not take their meaning primarily from reference to the physical body of everyday experience, but from more abstract notions; they can denote material entities understood as an assemblage of elements (*kāya*), or that which 'marks' out a thing (*liṅga*) and individualizes it as a graspable object (*vigraha*), or materializes it in physical form (*mūrti, piṇḍa*). What in most

European cultures is known merely as a 'body', then, is something that, in the Indian context, touches on wider questions about the nature of physicality, individuality and the material world. As we will see, the concept often centres on a primary meaning as that assemblage of materials through which an entity has its own individual reification as one being in a world of many others.

This materialization can take many forms, however; the wide range of different embodiments available to human persons has led Dominik Wujastyk (2009: 191) to speak of the 'many bodies of India'. These include the 'ritual' body found in the Vedas which is homologized with the cosmos; the Jain 'apophatic' body which has moved along the spectrum from karmic imprisonment to unqualified purity; the Buddhist processual body which is a 'bundle' of elements in constant flux; the yogic–tantric body with its chakras and tubes along which *prāṇa* or life-breath flows; the 'wrestler's' body of vital, vulnerable pressure points; the Āyurvedic body which charts the mechanisms and movements of the humours; and also potentially the erotic body, the gendered body and even the specific conceptions of the body imported from Persia, European medicine and so on. Barbara Holdrege (2015) has also developed a taxonomy of different culturally constructed kinds of embodiment in the brahminical and tantric, classical and medieval worldviews: these encompass 'divine', 'cosmic', 'social' and 'human' conceptions of the body, and also a set of what Holdrege calls 'processual' bodies conceived in terms of religious traditions of ritual, ascetic, purity, tantric and devotional self-transformation (15–20). Thus, far from revealing a single genealogy, questions about the nature of self and body in India have provided an arena for many possible theories.

## The self as 'pure' consciousness

The range of theories of the self proposed by Hindu, Buddhist, Jain and Cārvāka philosophies produced a sophisticated Indian dialogue about what it is that constitutes the 'core' of the human person. The Upaniṣads give voice to this debate through a fascination with the idea of the '*ātman*', a term for self used in a range of ways, but often given the special sense of an 'identity' or 'essence'. When applied to the human person, knowledge of one's essential identity undercuts the contingencies of normal perception and reveals the most abiding self. In addition, certain texts describe this core self as immortal and impervious to the pains of life. It is something that we already possess, but rarely glimpse, and it is this model of an elusive but precious identity which has been consistently depicted as the distinctive 'Hindu' theory of selfhood, and characterized by scholars as 'the inmost truth of man' (Hiriyanna 1993: 56). Surendranath Dasgupta (1922: 47), in his voluminous account of Indian philosophy, explained such ideas as seeking 'a constant and unchangeable essence in man as was beyond the limits of any change ... described as pure subject-object-less consciousness'. Thus while the word '*ātman*' in its simple primary meaning as 'self' formed part of conventional everyday discourse about oneself and one's spiritual life, it also carried religious and metaphysical meanings that allowed it to serve as a central theme of Hindu soteriological thinking.

One approach to this core identity was to see it as something utterly divorced from the fabric of the world because of its unique constitution as 'pure' consciousness, unsullied by bodily or mental particularities. Certain early texts lend themselves to this view. The *Kena Upaniṣad* hints at the idea of a self that is different from what is known and unknown, and cannot be expressed through speech, sight or even the mind (1.3–6); and the *Māṇḍūkya Upaniṣad* describes not one but two forms of non-normal consciousness: in the first state one 'entertains no desires or sees no dreams' and becomes 'a single mass of perception; consisting of bliss, and thus enjoying bliss; and having thought as his mouth' (5), and in the second one becomes a being 'whose essence is the perception of itself alone ... without a second', lying 'beyond the reach of ordinary transaction; as ungraspable; as without distinguishing marks; as unthinkable; as indescribable' (7). These ideas had relatively little impact on the immediate tradition of classical Vedāntic thought found in the *Bhagavad Gītā* and *Brahma Sūtra*s, but they shared an ideal of unadulterated awareness with other schools that developed over time, including the Nyāya's school's ideal of achieving a 'passive state of self in its original and natural purity unassociated with pleasure, pain, knowledge, willing, etc.' (Dasgupta 1922: 366). Later, the medieval schools of non-dual 'Advaita' theology also developed this idea in different ways, sometimes holding it to be a single self (*ekajīva*) behind all subjectivity, onto which multiple forms and manifestations are erroneously superimposed (see Timalsina (2009b) for a discussion of some of the different '*abhāsa*', '*avaccheda*', '*pratibimba*' and '*dṛṣṭisṛṣṭi*' doctrines).

An important locus in which the idea of an impassive spirit at the core of the person was worked out in greater detail was in the Sāṃkhya school's doctrine of a pure form of consciousness. Reality, with all of its empirical diversity, was attributed to the sphere of *prakṛti* or created reality (*prakṛti* literally, 'pro-creation'), a quite different sphere of *puruṣa* or pure consciousness was counterposed to this and believed capable of existing in a state of total isolation from the reality of experience. In this state of absolute 'isolation' from any environment, *kaivalya*, 'one dwells in pure translucent consciousness ... radically emptied of all content' (Larson 1969: 208). This idea – so counter-intuitive given the pervasive presence of conceptual content in all human experience – may have been a response (or a precursor) to the Buddhist idea of *nirvaṇa* which held that a complete cessation of selfhood is possible. Such theories made a basic philosophical assumption that conscious awareness is able to be separated from its content (ideas, perceptions, emotions, etc.), or to put it in modern phenomenological terms, that consciousness can exist without any intentional relation to a particular focus or object. Gerald Larson (1969: 230–3) has suggested that, in the Sāṃkhya case, this may also have been a natural logical development of Indian conceptions of non-being, which held that consciousness could exist without its particular present forms and modifications.[1] On this model, forms of ontological purity (e.g. as of a medium without its modes, or a witness without its objects) were conceived as possible in India to a degree never fully entertained in European reflection. It is perhaps for this very reason that such ideas of a 'pure self' became so popular in later European conceptions of Indian thought.

The idea of a core self was all too easily identified with the European idea of a soul by Western-educated thinkers such as Swami Vivekananda, a nineteenth- to twentieth-century thinker who followed the lead of particular texts (the *Kaṭha Upaniṣad* and the development of its ideas in the *Bhagavad Gītā*) in emphasizing that the *ātman* is what survives death and all changes. It was in this sense that self formed a non-contingent core for Vivekananda, and this tied into his typical Advaitic tendency to see only immutable and non-decayable realities as real. To the philosophical question, 'In this body which is an aggregate of molecules of matter, is there anything which is real?', Vivekananda (1999: 79) suggested that the idea of an 'infinite Unit [which] is unchangeable, immovable, absolute' offered an answer, describing 'the Real Man' at the heart of the person. His view was supported by influential Indian thinkers such as M.K. Gandhi. Others saw a parallel with European philosophies in the fabled 'tendency of Indian philosophy ... in the direction of monistic idealism' (Radhakrishnan 1957: xxv), supported in some measure by texts insisting that one should see the self in all beings, and all beings in the self (*Īṣa Upaniṣad* 6).

A fair measure of historical retrospective interpretation also took place among those who read earlier texts through the lens of later medieval thinkers; Paul Deussen, one of the only scholars to have tried to derive a single coherent philosophy from the whole diverse corpus of the Upaniṣads, took the view that the Advaitic non-dualism found in the work of sixth- to tenth-century thinkers such as Gaudapada, Śāṃkara or Abhinavagupta was present in the earliest stages of the Upaniṣads' composition before being gradually dissolved into more theistically inclined theories. For Deussen (1908: 398), these early Brahmin authors discovered insights that would lie at the heart of European idealism almost two thousand years later. This was a neat historical reading, but others have warned against over-reliance on the commentaries written by later thinkers such as Śaṃkara (e.g. Nakamura 1973: 79), and Deussen's view was given a thorough historical critique by Max

Hunter Harrison (1932: 90–3) in the 1930s, and by most scholars who have addressed the issue in his wake. The *ātman*, as it appears in classical texts, could not be so easily assimilated to a single model, and particularly not to the pure consciousness idea that later became most famed outside of India. In fact, the pure awareness described in later sources, or in the Sāṃkhya texts, was by no means unambiguously represented in the Upaniṣads. Indeed, other 'embodied' notions of the self – identified with the world, imagination or active agency of personhood – received as much attention in classical sources.

## The self as the core of personhood

Other views disagreed that the self must be a 'pure' disembodied being that is separate of the world, but did hold that it must serve as some sort of *core* – a centre or anchor - for the embodied world of change that surrounds it. Discussions of the nature of the self were confusing partly due to the range of meanings encompassed by the term '*ātman*'. It could signify both 'the spiritual self or the inmost core of a human being', but alternatively it could also refer to the 'living breathing body' (Olivelle 1996b: xlix). Accordingly, some commentators have highlighted the diversity of different forms that this 'core' idea could take, presumably reflecting the varying positions that existed among the communities who authored the source texts themselves. William Beidler (1975: 104–109), for instance, suggested four different ways in which the Vedāntic texts explained the 'real potentialities' of the self: (1) as 'that most immediate sense of self to be had in superficial observation of our day-to-day experience' (as seen in the *Kena* and *Aitareya Upaniṣads*); (2) 'a unitary cosmic self, a transpersonal being permeating all creation' (e.g. *Muṇḍaka Upaniṣad* 1.1.5); (3) 'consciousness which is self-absorbed, self-sufficient, and void of all action in the universe' (as seen in the *Māṇḍūkya Upaniṣad*'s description of the state of 'deep sleep'); and (4) a synthesis of all of these states in one multiform conception of the self that Beidler associates with 'panentheism'. Beidler's account is significant in that it opened the way to pluralistic accounts of the self in Hindu classical traditions: the core could be many things even within a single text, and much of the creative thinking of the tradition could be seen in terms of attempts to combine or develop these.

In this sense, early thinking about the self could be seen as a forum collectively organized around producing theories of an inner core that is 'hidden' and to be sought. That forum explored a range of different models, alluding to them in the Upaniṣads (which are often teaching exercises intended to help teachers explain this or that account of the self), and often formalizing particular theories in the later genre of Sūtras and Kārikās. One of the defining themes of discussions about the topic seems to have been its dialectical relation to the changing, temporary, dependent features of the world, and with this, of the mind and body. Self in the philosophically interesting sense that inspired discussion was a fundamentally *relational* concept, dialectically defined in counterpoint to those things that are dependent on, or under the control of, other things. As we will see, it was the chain of causal and ontological power relations that drew the line between core and contingency, self and body.

Thus, for instance, one meaning attributed to this self is that it is the centre of perception insofar as it is the origin of sight, hearing, speech and so on (e.g. in the *Kena Upaniṣad* 1.1–2, or in *Kaṭha Upaniṣad* 4.1). In other texts this perceptual 'source' self is generalized to all selves, forming the hub not of one person but of all (see Ganeri 2007: 13–38). Other texts depict this self as 'core' in the sense that it has access to the different spheres and strands of the universe; thus Arvind Sharma (2000) noted that the Upaniṣads situate the self at the heart not only of the body, but also of the world, citing the *Bṛhad Āraṇyaka Upaniṣad* 2.1.20's depiction of it: 'as a spider moves along the thread, as small sparks come forth from the fire, even so from this Self come forth all breaths, all worlds, all divinities, all beings'. On this account, when the texts claim that its secret meaning is the 'truth of truth', this statement carries quite a technical meaning (52).

Whatever the nature of the self, it is generally described as something that militates against finitude in all its (spatial and temporal) forms: it lies beneath the changing levels of material reality as something more permanent, and spans particular entities, principles or elements as an underlying generality. As we will see, one of the defining features attributed to it, and developed in later texts concerned with ethics and action, is its ability to eschew the automatic drives that govern material reality. The core self has the power to take some control over the more contingent levels that are dependent on it. This is a theme bound up with the growth of yogic cultures of control and discriminating action. The idea of a core, then, repeatedly signifies that which avoids the limitations of worldly being, such as contingency and forced change, but which also has some kind of central access to the widest range of world – from minds to matter.

## The open self

Another important approach to the self notes the importance not of its *contrast* to the environment, but rather of its *intimate relationship* with it. Scholars of both text and contemporary ritual have emphasized that the non-dual, disengaged, pure form of selfhood is not the one that most Hindus experience and negotiate in everyday life. The person who feels himself or herself to be present in both philosophy and practice is the *embodied* self, a being characterized by reason and affects, flesh and energies, empirical observation and reflexive self-awareness. This self is deeply embedded in the physical world and the quotidian power struggles that take place in the landscape of thought, nature and society. The dazzling array of Indian discussions on this embodied form of personhood is distinguished by the way in which the discussions acknowledge the inner complexity and the dynamic plasticity of embodiment. Numerous elements coexist within Hindu understandings of the body, varying from text to text in their precise constitution. All are characterized by constant change, and early classical philosophy depicts this complex array of bodies as functioning simultaneously at different levels, subject to *internal* relation and interaction. Each person can be, as Frederick Smith (2006) has pointed out, a community in his or her own right.

Beidler (1975: 17) distinguished this embodied self from the core self by separating the idea of the *ātman* from the *puruṣa*, defining the latter as 'the self on the most basic level of physiology and psychology'. His distinction is not always followed by the texts in this clear-cut way, but it does point to the existence of a conceptual differentiation between the core *ātman* and the embodied conception which is generally depicted as an amalgamation of various constitutive elements such as mind, imagination, discernment, insight, memory, speech, life-breath, perceptions, ego, the elements, sense faculties, energies such as *tapas* (heat) and fuels such as *anna* (food), all caught up in a constant course of transformation.[2] It is this self that makes, perceives and interacts, reaches decisions and reaps results; and it is this self that must be *a part of the wider world* in order to act in these ways. The body, then, is necessarily open to the environment, and through movement, the exchange of substances such as food and water, energies such as heat or life-breath, actions and even perceptions and consequent ideas about the environment, the embodied self shares causal connections of different kinds with the world beyond it.

Numerous scholars have rethought Hindu conceptions of selfhood along these lines, emphasizing the variegated and active embodiment of the individual, in contradiction to the ideal of an undivided core. McKim Marriott's (1976) anthropological study of bodily 'transactions' questioned the boundaries between self and world in such a way as to counter Western concepts of 'dualism' with the Hindu tendency to acknowledge 'diversity'. He was inspired by his reflections to coin the term 'dividuals' (rather than individuals): persons understood as composite beings who participate in their environment to the extent of sharing aspects of their essential identity with it. Shortly after Marriott's work others began to note the transactional character of Hindu selfhood in areas such as ritual and social interaction, and in yogic and Āyurvedic models of the body (Zimmerman 2011). Frederick

Smith's (2006) study of possession led him deep into philosophical questions about the nature of the self, and he found himself interrogating the notion of identity alongside the wide range of texts, classical and modern, that were his sources. Depictions of possession in Indian contexts considered the possibility of different forms of self:

> Is there a true self (assuming for the moment that this is a viable concept and can be located) contaminated or camouflaged by possession states, spirits or deities? Is the self a singular, stable, undiluted entity? Or is it a referential, undiluted entity? Or is it a referential, explanatory convenience, an individualised composite construction, and thus unrealisable beneath its layerings ... if the latter, is such possession a random or occasional component in a mutating multiform self, and if so can we really call this a 'self' rather than a 'person'? Or – another possibility – is possession merely a trope, a significator for an essentially plural or composite self? (9)

The answers to these questions clearly vary according to genre, school and period of thought. But the openness of the self to transformations that involve exchange with other entities has become a central theme of scholarship, resulting in what Arno Bohler (2009: 128) calls a 'bright, vast and open' conception of the body in Yogic textual sources. In later devotional 'bhakti' literature, David Haberman ([1988] 2001: 4) speaks of the way in which the cultivation of emotion leads humans to realize their 'malleable nature' in which 'a wide and seemingly endless range of possible realities' becomes open to each individual person.

The following section will explore the embodied self not only as an individual configuration of agency, but also as something 'open' that mirrors Hindu conceptions of *reality* per se. Em-bodiment is reinscribed as en-worldment, the embedding of the individual in a multiverse of elements and energies, physical and mental materials and transitioning levels of being. Indeed, the 'muti-verse' and the 'multi-self' necessarily correspond to each other because they lie on a continuum of materiality; they are both made of the media in which agency, thought-acts, ritual performances and practice have their being. Thus as conscious agents, we are interwoven into the multiple fabrics that constitute the universe.

One illuminating feature of these sources is the way in which they envision materiality itself. In contrast to the modern Western notion of matter, which is popularly seen as a self-explanatory collection of basic constituents (atoms, particles or waves, for instance), these sources suggest that Indian matter was seen as variable across a matrix of different fabrics, including structured aggregation and modal change. Both 'mental' fabrics of reason and the 'material' fabrics of concrete objects were 'shaped' in this way, and it is through this material embodiment that human agency manifests. We will see that what defines the self is not simply a single entity called the *body*, but rather a complex and variable configuration that is united under the cohering governance of a 'core' will or *agency* that 'witnesses' each case of embodiment and creatively directs it. The textual record shows that with awareness of the nature of the person came awareness of its variable changefulness and ultimately its plasticity; gradually the shaping of selfhood became a recurrent theme in early thought and a foundation for Hindu soteriologies.

# 3

# Bodies made of elements and structures

Classical literatures such as the Upaniṣads are a rich resource of ideas of the body, locating it within reflection on the wider constitution of the natural world as a whole. In such texts, the self is woven from a multilayered fabric of elements such as earth, wind, fire, water and ether, vital substances such as breath and food, energies, various biological systems, sense organs and mental faculties, as well as the 'subtle' materials of energy and imagination. All of these furnish a multilayered structure that constitutes the 'body' of the self.

## The elements of the Upaniṣadic body

Some of the earliest attempts to list the materials that make up the world and its constitutive objects are seen in the numerous catalogues of elements, varying subtly, which are scattered across the early Upaniṣads. Later texts such as Buddhist and Cārvāka (atheist) literatures, as well as the early philosophical material in the *Mahābhārata*, point to the existence of various cosmologies developing among different groups, in different regions, and upheld by different lineages of Brahminical culture around the middle of the first millennium BCE (see Bhattacharya (2012: 610–11; 2001: 19–22) on the competing candidates for a primal essence or *svabhāva* that are discussed in early philosophical literature). There appears to have been a competition to produce the perfect list of the elements that make up the world within classical intellectual culture.

The *Bṛhad Āraṇyaka Upaniṣad* contains many such taxonomies of materiality, and its very first image – of the Aśvamedha sacrifice involving the offering of a horse to the gods – treats the biological body as a microcosm of all of the world's elements. The sacrifice of animals to the gods in Vedic ritual was not just a process of bartering with the Gods. It provided a medium for reflecting on the symbolic significance of the body and its relationship to the constitution of the world as a whole. An evocative, almost poetic list associates the horse's body parts with important features of the natural world:

> The head of the sacrificial horse, clearly, is the dawn – its sight is the sun; its breath is the wind, and its gaping mouth is the fire common to all men. The body (*ātman*) of the sacrificial horse is the year – its back is the sky; its abdomen is the intermediate region; its underbelly is the earth … its flesh is the clouds, its stomach contents are the sand; its intestines are the rivers, its liver and lungs are the hills; its body hairs are the plants and trees … when it yawns, lightning flashes; when it shakes itself, it thunders; and when it urinates, it rains. Its neighing is speech itself. (*Bṛhad Āraṇyaka Upaniṣad* 1.1.1)

This passage exemplifies the cosmological mode in which much of the Upaniṣadic genre would go on to reflect on the nature of the body, associating it as much with the natural materials of the universe as with conceptions of a soul or thinking 'person' within it. As we will see, much of the Upaniṣadic discussion of selfhood actually consists in models of this natural constitution of the body and mind, seeking to analyse their constitutive ingredients, structure, substrate and also the agency that unites them into a coherent whole.

Lists of the different components of nature are given at various stages in the Upaniṣads' Brahminical teachings about the nature of the self and of the world. This opening passage of the *Bṛhad Āraṇyaka Upaniṣad* alone includes vital energies (sun, wind, fire, breath), temporal modes (seasons, months, fortnights, days and nights), the spheres into which the cosmos was thought to be spatially divided (sky, intermediate region, earth, the quarters, the zenith), natural processes (such as lightning, thunder, rain and the rising and setting of the sun) and natural features (clouds, sand, hills, rivers and plants). In addition, even more elusive 'elements' of reality are also included in this passage, such as speech itself and the ideas that it expresses. The next verses link the medium of the horse's body to another story in which death assumes a body that gives rise to a succession of natural elements such as water, earth, fire and wind (1.2.1–3). The text seems to equate the process of embodiment with the generation of the constituents of the universe, and the message repeated again and again is that an understanding of the true constitution of the self is a particularly important kind of knowledge. It is by knowing 'the person whose abode is the earth, whose world is fire, and whose light is the mind', who is 'none other than this bodily person', that one 'truly knows' (3.9.10).

Such lists fill the Upaniṣads, stretching from their earliest portions through to the later texts that may have been composed in conversation with sceptics such as Buddhist and Cārvāka atheists, and potential allies such as the exponents of early versions of Sāṃkhya and Vaiśeṣika philosophy. *Bṛhad Āraṇyaka Upaniṣad* 3.7 asks about the different media upon which the self is 'strung', and lists earth, water, fire, the intermediate region (*antarikṣita*), wind, sky, sun, quarters, moon and stars, space, darkness and light as materials of self situated in the 'immortal' (*amṛta*) realm. Breath, speech, sight, hearing, mind, skin, perception and even semen, that source of corporeal life, are materials that make up the body (*śarīra*) on the level of beings (*bhūta*). In the *Bṛhad Āraṇyaka Upaniṣad* alone, which is probably the earliest of the Upaniṣads but also one with a particularly wide period of composition, this theme is revisited repeatedly. Standard elements include earth, fire, sky, sun, waters, moon, breath (see 1.5.11–13; 1.5.18); to this list others are added in different passages, such as lightning and space (2.1), darkness and light (3.7) and the stars (3.9). This is clearly a period that predates the later formalization of the elements into five standard '*mahābhūta*s' or great elements (fire, earth, air, water and space) for those are seen in continuity with a wider range of natural features. These natural elements are either seen as materials of the world (e.g. space, earth, fire, water, darkness, light, etc.) or as important features of the cosmos itself such as the sun and moon and stars which are themselves sometimes associated with elements such as fire and water. In some lists, subjective realities such as bliss stand alongside externally perceived entities such as the sun and moon: the *Taittirīya Upaniṣad* lists food, life-breath, mind, understanding/perception and bliss (2.1–5, 3.1–6). It is important to note that the boundaries of 'inner and outer' phenomena are permeable: other criteria are more central to the project of identifying the constituent elements of reality.

It was common for the lists of natural elements to turn into lists of bodily constituents such as breath, speech, sight, hearing, mind, skin, perception and the life-giving substance of semen (see *Bṛhad Āraṇyaka Upaniṣad* 3.7). Consonant with this holistic approach to cosmology is the way in which the *physical* elements are mixed with what in the West would be considered *mental* ones. The five senses, and particularly the vital powers of breath, speech and mind (e.g. 1.5.3–7), and sometimes semen (6.1) are key constituents of the person. These personal bodily elements were also linked to the external sphere of nature, with the senses, vital energies, mental organs and capacities often coupled with those external features of the world that they make accessible to individual minds. One passage lists these mental elements as 'graspers' and 'over-graspers' (*graha* and *atigraha*): the out-breath 'grasped' by the in-breath yields awareness of odours, and similarly speech is grasped by words, the tongue by flavours, hearing by sound, the mind by desire, hands by action and skin by touch (3.2.1–9). 'Grasping' seems to signify a relation of control or influence that links different elements: in this text it is sound that grasps the ear, desire that grasps our minds and words that grasp our speech and demand expression through it. Awareness, combining both the sensations and their objects, then, is also considered an important material of the world and the self; indeed, the conceptual coupling of features of reality alongside the sense organs that grasp them is so common that some scholars have argued that the analysis of world elements may have *derived* from the subjective organs of perception, or at least evolved in tandem with them (see, for instance, Lyssenko 2004: 32; Gaur and Gupta 1970: 52; see also Mikel Burley's (2007) 'subjectivist analysis of classical Sāṃkhya).

These analyses of 'mental elements' do seem to reflect the process of empirical self-observation and may have been associated with the rise of yogic meditation, pointing to a 'phenomenological turn' taken very early in Indian thought. Those Upaniṣads most closely associated with Yoga and Sāṃkhya clearly advocate that one should remember to look 'inwards' as well as outwards, and advise that the knowledge resulting from inward observations is more lasting than the impermanent sensations received from the outside world. Thus, the *Kaṭha Upaniṣad* (4.1–3) analyses sensations that reveal the external world, and advises greater attention to the contents of thought and awareness:

> The Self-existent one pierced the apertures outward,
> Therefore, one looks out, and not into oneself.
> A certain wise man in search of immortality,
> Turned his sight inward and saw the self within.
>
> And enter the trap of death spread wide,
> But the wise know what constitutes th'immortal
> And in unstable things here do not seek the stable.
>
> Touches and sexual acts –
> That by which one experiences these,
> By the same one understands.

Ultimately, while the text deems attention to the underlying 'experiencer', the 'self', to be most important, it also highlights the different constituents that make up experience along the way. It does seem to be the case that empirical investigation was understood to apply just as much to the sphere of internal things ('thought') as to that of external ones ('world'), and inward viewing revealed the five sensory elements of form, flavour, scent, sound and sensation to be as necessary pillars of reality as the five physical elements of earth, air, fire, water and space.

Other Upaniṣads give varying lists of the constituents of the experiencing 'inner body' of the self, such as the mind (*manas*), intention (*saṅkalpa*), thought (*citta*), deep reflection or insight (*dhyāna*) and perception (*vijñāna*) found in the *Chāndogya Upaniṣad* 7.8.1–15, or the heart (*hṛdaya*), mind (*manas*), awareness (*saṃjñāna*), perception (*ajñāna*), discernment (vijñāna), cognition (*prajñāna*), wisdom (*medha*), insight (*dṛṣṭi*), steadfastness (*dhṛti*), thought (*mati*), reflection (*manīṣā*), drive (*jūti*), memory (*smṛti*), intention (*saṅkalpa*), purpose (*kratu*), will (*asu*), love (*kāma*) and desire (*vaśa*) that are listed in the *Aitareya Upaniṣad* 3.1–2. The *Kauṣītaki Upaniṣad* 3.8 affirms the interdependence of mental and physical elements even more explicitly, telling us that the different 'particles' (*mātrā*) making up intelligence and the external world necessarily exist in correlation to each other, since if mind and world were in isolation 'from either of them independently no image [of the outside world within the mind] would be produced'. These lists of ingredients subject the mental self, which is often seen in the West as the core person, to the same constitutive parts-based analysis that is normally applied to the material body.

But such mental bodies did not have to be bound to physical ones; from the Upaniṣads onwards it was assumed that bodies made of the imagination are as useful as bodies made of flesh – and probably more so, given their freedom from the restrictions of the solid world. As the corporeal self participates in the physical, so the mental self can act and interact in what Shulman (2012) calls the 'mind-born worlds' of the imagination. In practices dating from Vedic ritual culture, imagination was seen to possess a semi-material reality that could be shaped, used and also dissolved. The post-Upaniṣadic classical Sāṃkhya philosophy expressed in the *Sāṃkhya Kārikā* similarly developed an account of the elements that make up the body, including those that constitute consciousness: awareness (*buddhi*), ego (*ahaṃkāra*, a kind of *abhimāna* or conceptualizing oneself) and mind (*manas*). These together form the 'inner-instrument', as Burley (2007: 171) calls the *antaḥkaraṇa*, and are continuously connected with the *indriyas*, commonly translated as sense organs (*buddhīndriyāṇi*) that facilitate the perceptual contents of consciousness (the eye, ear, nose, tongue, skin), as well as the organs of action (*karmendriyāṇi*: the voice, hands, feet, and excretory and sexual organs). Both the mental and material constituents form a continuum that differs strikingly from the Cartesian mind–body dualism that is so familiar to the West (75–9). But here the body is not merely an aggregation of materials; it is also made of points of transition, the organs of sense and action that facilitate *interaction* with the surrounding environment. The 'open-ness' of the mind to its environment of the body, and of the body to the environment of the physical world which is its 'outer body', is here shown in technical detail.

Thus both physical and mental realities, woven together, constitute the natural world of elements which includes even more abstract features of the world such as name, form and action (here in the *Bṛhad Āraṇyaka Upaniṣad* 1.6.1), or structural features of arising, sameness and foundation that characterize existing things (expressed symbolically through the *uktha*, *sāman* and *brahman*; 1.6), and even *dharma* or natural order, truth and humanity (2.5.11–15). Later texts list cite still more abstract concepts such as inherent nature (*svabhāva*), necessity (*niyati*) and chance (*yadṛccha*), along with more familiar elements (e.g. *Śvetāśvatara Upaniṣad* 1.1–2). These lists demonstrate that thinkers of the time were engaged in wide-ranging analysis of nature, and addressed it in a way that did not automatically discriminate between body, world and mind, nor even between concrete and abstract realities. The materiality of the natural world consisted in a wide-ranging, multifaceted texture which ill accords with the substantialistic approach to natural materials that Europe eventually adopted in its scientific and philosophical concepts of matter. In many respects the material world envisioned by the authors of the Upaniṣads across families, traditions of thought, regions and arenas of discussion spanned a range of materials that were as diverse as the different metaphysics of atoms, ideas, substances and change considered by the followers of Democritus, Pythagoras, Aristotle or Heraclitus in classical Greece. They produced a picture of reality as a fabric woven of many threads, and the early Upaniṣadic imagination locates the human person at the centre of this fabric, attached to each thread and thereby to the furthest reaches of the physical and mental universe.

Importantly, in these texts the natural constitution of the self as a composite of pre-existing materials does not have to be taken as the basis for a naturalization of the human person into a mere aggregation of parts. This had been the typical strategy of Buddhist and Cārvāka atheist thinkers who sought to dissolve Hindu claims to a coherent core self or soul. Rather, understanding the body as a material form made of natural elements provides a crucial link between the human self and the cosmos as a whole, incorporating understanding of the body into the broader project of cosmology and metaphysics. The bodily person is shown to possess connections with the cosmos that can transcend the bounds of the individual body with its finite mortal character. Being embedded in the natural world was considered one way of transcending finitude and death. In addition, as Olivelle (1996b: l) notes, the elements were not seen as inactive, dull substances, but as vital principles possessed of their own character and energy; the *Aitareya Brāhmaṇa* even includes bodily vitality (*asu*) identified with the intermediate region in the cosmos (*antarikṣan*) as one of the elements. Indeed, far from being 'merely' material these elements are 'deities' (*devatā*, or 'cosmic powers'; see Werner 1978). In listing functions that animate both the human body and the physical world it includes the mouth, speech, fire; nose, breath, wind; eyes, sight, sun; ears, hearing, directions; skin, hairs, plants; navel, inhalation, death; penis, semen and waters (*Aitareya Upaniṣad* 1.4) and classifies all of them as *devatā*, signifying that they are vital, life-giving, animating forces within the body and within nature at large. It should not be assumed, then, that 'elements' are seen as merely inert matter. The energetic and effective quality of fire, air and other elements are essential to their character.

The human state of being embodied in these elements was not necessarily viewed as a problematic imprisonment of the soul, as in the doctrine of rebirth that developed. Embodiment within nature could also be seen as a form of participation in the matrix of powerful, energetic phenomena that drive the universe itself. Indeed, rather than seeing the human being as contained within the cage of the elements, one pre-Upaniṣadic passage describes these natural cosmic 'deities' as contained within the human person like cattle in a pen (*Atharva Veda* 11.8.32). According to this model it is the elements of nature that wait to be released from us, rather than we who must be released from them. In this light, one can see why the cataloguing of natural elements, and their role in both body and cosmos, plays such a central role in the Upaniṣadic texts: they are central to the project of connecting humanity with the cosmos in its widest reach. They point to a level of human existence able to transcend the limitations of the body, and address a sphere of natural power and vitality.

## The importance of structure

As in early Greek natural philosophy, however, it gradually became clear in early Indian thought that any theory that the world is composed of elements naturally provoked an underlying question that could be seen as shifting the sphere of inquiry from physics to *metaphysics*. What is it that binds these diverse elements into the complex aggregates that we know as objects? What provides the pattern or template that gives each object its own distinctive nature, over and above the common elements that it shares with the rest of the natural world? What, in short, accounts for the structuring of elements into entities such as the self, each with its own defining characteristics? Later this problem would play an important role in Buddhism's challenge to Hindu ideas, for early Sarvāstivāda Buddhists argued that there is no cohering 'self' but only the aggregation of parts. Early Hindu texts and schools of thought responded by giving various accounts of the identity of aggregated *structures* such as the embodied self.

In the Upaniṣads a proper structural arrangement is assumed for the body as for the cosmos. Hints of this structuring principle can be found in the account of the horse sacrifice at the beginning of the *Bṛhad Āraṇyaka Upaniṣad*: the homologies that are asserted between the body parts and the universe outline a number of naturally occurring structured systems that make a whole, including the functions of the limbs, senses and organs, and the structures of sky and landscape, directions, time and weather (see 1.1.1). The observation of such cases of naturally ordered complexity seems to have inspired a conception of a 'whole' that is defined by functional complementarity, that is, the holism of *systems*. The whole system of symbolic equivalences and homologies that came to underpin the Vedic sacrifice, and that was gradually outlined in the Brāhmaṇas, Āraṇyakas and Upaniṣads, assumed a notion of natural order that defined both self and world. A passage in the *Chāndogya Upaniṣad* equates the ordered aggregation of the mind's elements (speech, breath, sight and hearing) to the ordered structure of the natural elements (fire, wind, sun, quarters; 3.18.1–2), seeing the same principle at work in both. Even more explicitly *Bṛhad Āraṇyaka Upaniṣad* 1.3.12 explains that the natural elements are merely the deathless or unlimited form of the familiar bodily elements: speech when 'freed from death' becomes fire, breath becomes wind, sight becomes the sun, hearing becomes the quarters and mind the moon. Their relationships of shared qualities bind them into a structural relation of equivalence.

What makes a coherent system out of these constituents is their ability to form what the *Taittirīya Upaniṣad* calls 'large-scale combinations' (*mahāsaṃdhā*), ordered aggregates which – in the Taittirīya – are modelled on the ability of language to create meaningful wholes (see 1.2 on the principles attributed to phonetics). In this text, precise order is what counts – as earth and sky are united in space and linked by the wind, so too are fire and sun united in the primeval waters and linked by lightning, the teacher and pupil united in knowledge and linked by instruction, the mother and father united in the child and linked by procreation and the lower and upper jaws united in speech and linked by the tongue (1.3.1–4). These precise combinations focus on structures of association that allow parts to form a new complex whole. Here it is not only systematic function that shapes the whole, but the emergence of new possibilities from those relations. This text praises knowledge of this hidden structural 'grid' that give order to reality (it even gives a detailed table of elemental equivalences in body, mind, elements, breath and cosmos; 1.7), and it is said to be linked to the "rule of substitution" that a student should seek to learn.

The *Kauṣītaki Upaniṣad* is also much concerned with outlining the proper connections and combinations of things in relation to sentient beings, positioning mind as a central cohering feature of the senses and vital functions (3.2–3) and countering the idea that the self and its relation to the world are really characterized by diversity; the world, intelligence and vital breath are coherently linked like the rim, spokes and hub of a wheel (3.8). The text is also adamant that the collection of elements described here is strikingly flexible in its formation, for it can be unified within a single medium, as the mind and its senses do when we sleep, and then expand back outwards again into a dispersed, larger structure. What controls this process of expansion or contraction, giving shape to the diverse parts, is the self which the Kauṣītaki describes as being like a 'chieftain': 'To this self (*ātman*) cling these other selves (*ātman*), as to a chieftain, his own people. It is like this – just as a chieftain makes use of his own people, and his own people make themselves useful to a chieftain, so this self consisting of intelligence makes use of these other selves' (4.20). *Ātman* here more explicitly seems to mean an entity or element made of other 'selves', brought together in coherent cooperation.

It is tempting to read these images of structured self as developments of the older Vedic idea of cosmic order, *ṛta*, as a precursor of the developing socio-ethical notion of *dharma*. But it is also important to see here that these Upaniṣadic sources have their own philosophy of the unity of aggregated parts into complementary structures. Here, as opposed to the Buddhist and Cārvāka views that see such unity as a mere conventional arrangement, a sort of coincidence possessed of no autonomous ontological status as realities, certain authors of the Upaniṣads explored the view that structure is characterized by certain positive features:

**a)** It is functionally positive, enabling entities and systems to exist in their own right. Thus, in contrast to Buddhist and Cārvāka views, they were seen to possess an intrinsic value. The structures of physical cosmos, biological processes, mind and sensation, language and time, all make possible the features of the world we know. Where reductionist systems assumed the constituent parts to be most basic and non-dependent, this trend in Hindu thinking upheld the intrinsic value of multipart wholes, taking them to be even more basic and ontologically non-dependent than their constituents. The parts could be seen as derivations from the whole, rather than the whole being dependent on the parts. For if the parts possessed the ontological virtue of being 'simple' non-composite units, the wholes possessed the value of pervading and outlasting their parts, and thus appearing more stable and durable.

**b)** The functional coherence of these structures reflect an idea that the elements of nature possess intrinsic characters, innate dispositions that define them. Sight, sun and visible appearance are linked by their own natures, and combinations are not mere coincidence, but the manifestation of functional structures. In other worlds, the large-scale combinations that Buddhism rejects because they are dependent can be seen in this Hindu perspective as equally primary realities of which individual elements are only aspects. According to this model, the structured body is no less real than its elements, and the identification of Being with the classical ontological features of simplicity (non-complexity) and aseity (non-dependence) is rejected.

**c)** These structures are not necessarily fixed, but have the capacity to be altered, reconfigured, condensed and expanded by an intelligent agent able to recognize and assume control of them. There is a recognition among the authors of these texts that structures are innately variable, and this allows a highly *constructive* view of the elemental body. As we will see, this will have considerable implications for our understanding of embodiment and agency.

The materiality of structured elements – of bodies then – is real and shaped by both the natural functions of the elements and by the guiding intercession of any intelligence able to direct them.

With the development of multiple philosophical perspectives in the classical period leading up to the various Sūtras, it became clear that elements-based philosophies potentially created certain problems. They threatened to elevate the elements themselves as the most fundamental units of existence, while demoting other entities to subsidiary and dependent forms of being; this perspective led to Buddhist and Cārvāka rejections of the genuine existence of the self, and inspired the Vaiśeṣika school to craft a direct riposte by positing that *samavāyi-kāraṇa*, a form of 'cohering causality', exists, through which the different categories of elements complement each other to shape the world we know. As Lyssenko (2004: 37) puts it, '[F]or Vaiśeṣika, its governing model concerning the body is an additive whole, a whole (*avayavi*) that is a collection of its parts. That is why, the Vaiśeṣikas sometimes designate the human body as a *piṇḍa*, a mass, or a ball, an agglomeration or a collection of homogeneous particles'. To resolve the problem raised in classical debates about aggregation and identity they were forced to emphasize the necessity of an external agency, an efficient cause of that agglomeration. In relation to the world, this causal agent was *Īśvara* or god, while for the body it was the self. But in both cases, the elemental view of material reality made it necessary for there to be an agent at the heart of the material world: the Vaiśeṣikas were thus carrying on a line of thought that had already played an important role in earlier classical thought about the relationship of agency to embodiment. But where the Vaiśeṣikas came to emphasize the creative control of god over the elements of the world, the Upaniṣads celebrated the creative control that any self can potentially exert over mental and physical embodiment. The continuity of body and world meant that this control had the potential to extend beyond the conventional bodied self. Through ritual – as we will see – the self wielded a creative control over the universe as well.

## Structuring the universe

Buddhist thinkers had provoked an anxiety that the self could disaggregate and become unstructured with no remaining continuity with the structure that had defined it. This in turn inspired a parallel fear for the universe itself, for all material reality seemed subject to the same danger – a threat that took on concrete form in later cosmologies (in texts such as the Purāṇas) which held that the universe does indeed dissolve at the end of each world-cycle.

Thus the vision of an ordered cosmos seems to have existed in tense counterpoint with the fear of a disordered one: Vedic hymns are frequently concerned with reinforcing the structure of the natural world through precisely ordered ritual actions. In the mantras, or verses that form a poetic accompaniment to the sacrifices, order is a common theme, and various hymns speculate on the sources of order in the natural world or describe gods such as Varuṇa and Indra creating order – physical, social or ethical – out of chaos (see Horsch 2004). The twentieth-century historian Louis Dumézil (1968–73) had tried to explain this Vedic fascination with order in terms of what he called the 'trifunctional hypothesis'; he argued that Indo-European cultures tended to classify society and other spheres of knowledge into a tripartite order broadly concerned with religious legitimacy, temporal governance and agricultural fertility. Dumézil's thesis was criticized, but Jan Gonda (1976), a twentieth-century Indologist, argued that the tripartite template for ordering the universe should be seen as the result of an even more basic cultural tendency to incorporate a clear structure into any form of 'weltanschauliche' (worldview) speculations. Subsequent attempts to explain Vedic cosmology and ritual have often returned to the theme of creating an ordered cosmos through attention to structure. Charles Malamoud (1998) emphasized the way in which ritual instructions function on the basis of basic categories of meaning such as 'continuity and discontinuity, repetition and difference, "principal" and "remainder", perishable and permanent, immediate and deferred, fullness and emptiness, implicit and explicit'. They are 'universal categories, all' he claims, 'but unique in India, inasmuch as they come to be arrived at in the course of speculation on the sacrificial act' (4). In Vedic culture it was ritual as an embodied intervention in the materials of the cosmos that provided a practical framework for conceiving and creating structure in the world.

This explained Brahmin communities' interest in 'classifying the universe', as Brian Smith (1994) puts it in his analysis of the different categories into which early Hindu texts tried to organize the known world. Concerns regarding understanding and correctly bringing order to the material world were motivated by a fear that material reality would fall into one of two extremes: either reality could condense into excessive sameness (*jāmi*) like clay pots pressed into a single homogenous lump, or it could separate and disperse into excessive isolation (*pṛthak* or *bahutva*) as a completely diverse chaos. Smith identifies analogy or resemblance as the idea seen by Vedic authors as the proper balance between these two extremes, linking things into stable structural relations and forming a basis for the conceptual categorization of the universe into meaningful forms. From an insider perspective, Smith (1998: 53) argues, the meaning of Vedic ritual action pivots on this 'metaphysics of resemblance'.

The fear of disorder was balanced by a certain optimism about the presence of order which is striking against the broader background of Ancient Near Eastern cultures that feared the prevalence of chaos, often evinced in the recurring mythological image of dark and primeval 'waters'. By contrast, in its attention to *ṛta* or order, the Vedic worldview had maintained a belief that the world is inclined to take the form of a coherent cosmos, rich in internal structures that make it exist and function. As Mahony (1997: 104) notes, the poetic eye of the early Vedic authors saw the environment of ancient Hinduism in an observant and appreciative light.

> Looking out over the earth's broad expanse, up into the skies and the heavens above them, Vedic poets saw a powerful and mysterious play of being. The sun rose in the morning seemingly out of nothing ... bringing form to a formless world and impelling sleeping creatures to begin the new day ... Based on the principle of *Ṛta*, the world in all of its complexity revolved like a smoothly turning cosmic wheel.

Optimally, this idea – evoked in poetry, myth and later narratives – provided an ideal for the ordered status of the cosmos, society and the human person itself: pleasing, functional, peacefully inclined not only to function but in doing so to generate a succession of emergent realities such as biological life, community and culture, and the various states of imagination, understanding and emotion. These auspiciously fruitful structures attested their own value; they increased the meaningful content of the world and made new possibilities available – the very gifts for which the Vedic gods were so frequently thanked in the Ṛg Vedic hymns.

One of the texts to make most influential use of this Vedic counterpoint between order and chaos some centuries later was the *Mānava Dharma Śāstra*. It wove together ideas on social order from the earlier *Dharma Sūtras*, with a range of Vedic hymns to create its own intriguing cosmogonic narrative. The point of the new version was to highlight the naturalness of order as an intrinsic defining feature of all things, as well as its desirability as a principle that underpins the surrounding cosmos through life-enabling structures such as the elements, seasons, biological growth and the communal structures of society. It thus sought to ground the aesthetic of an ordered society in a theory of natural laws and innate dispositions:

> Manu was seated, absorbed in contemplation, when the great seers came up to him, paid homage to him in the appropriate manner, and addressed him in these words: 'Please, Lord, tell us precisely and in the proper order the laws of all the social classes, as well as of those born in between, for you alone, Master, know the true meaning of the duties contained in the entire ordinance of the Self-Existent One, an ordinance beyond the powers of thought of cognition.
>
> . . .
>
> There was this world – pitch dark, indiscernible, without distinguishing marks, unthinkable, incomprehensible, in a kind of deep sleep all over. Then the Self-existent Lord appeared – the Unmanifest, manifesting this world beginning with the elements, projecting his might, and dispelling the darkness. (1.1–3, 5)

This excerpt, taken from the framing narrative that surrounds the main body of teachings, makes the argument that social structures are grounded in the natural order that was established in the first moments of creation as part of the very fabric of the cosmos. It lays claim to an intuitive conception of right order, using the phrase *yathāvad anupūrvaśaḥ* to express the idea of that which is explained 'in its proper order', and this is further compounded by attributing the order of things to the 'ordinances' (*vidhāna*) of the self-existent first whose privileged knowledge is inconceivable (*acintya*) and unperceivable (*aprameya*) to normal minds. The text constructs a counterpoint between natural order and the prior state of chaotic formlessness, borrowing images from Vedic cosmogonic hymns to evoke a state of darkness without distinguishing marks (*alakṣaṇa*) in such a way that it resists insight (*aprajñāta*), logical comprehension (*apratarkya*) and direct knowledge (*avijñeya*). The conception of order evoked here spans the ontological and epistemological spheres so that chaos becomes synonymous with inconceivability and cosmos with comprehension.

The passage goes on to describe the order that is laid out, giving its own list of the 'elements' of the cosmos:

> In the beginning, through the words of the Veda alone, he fashioned for all of them specific names and activities, as also specific stations.

> Time, divisions of time, constellations, planets, rivers, oceans, mountains, flat and rough terrain, austerity, speech, sexual pleasure, desire and anger – he brought forth this creation in his wish to bring forth these creatures.
>
> To establish distinctions among activities, moreover, he distinguished the Right (*dharma*) from the Wrong (*adharma*) and afflicted these creatures with the pairs of opposites such as pleasure and pain. Together with the perishable atomic particles of the five elements given in tradition, this whole world comes into being in an orderly sequence. As they are brought forth again and again, each creature follows on its own the very activity assigned to it in the beginning by the Lord ... whichever he assigned to each at the time of creation, it stuck automatically to that creature. (*Mānava Dharma Śāstra* 1.21, 24–29)

This innate nature of things, reaching from moral to natural to metaphysical levels of reality, is something that 'sticks naturally' to each creature which follows it 'on its own'. The text goes on in a long passage to describe the constitution of the universe with considerable relish, giving a place to gentleness and cruelty, man and woman, gods and other supernatural beings, lightning bolts and rainbow streaks, monkeys and fish and other diverse aspects. Interestingly the passage returns at its end to a reminder that this should all be seen as part of the body of the self-existent first being – into which it returns periodically so that the whole cosmos is restored to its primeval foundation on a regular basis (1.54–57). Order here appears as the benevolent bestowing of intrinsic natures on individual things, allowing beings to exist and live within the enabling space mapped out by these 'distinctions'. As distinctions made by the first being, they prefigure the distinctions made by the earliest seers and poets in creating the texts of the Vedas, and they establish the template for those who seek to establish order through their discriminating understanding of the world, and their actions. The process of differentiation, identification, classification and understanding of the dispositions and relations of things is figured as a life-giving principle that allows mercurial bundles of elements to become united in the teeming system of selves that is 'the world'.

# 4

# Bodies made of substances and modes

While the structural unity of the elements was one important way in which the natural world could be interpreted, a second paradigm for thinking about materiality became equally, if not more, important in Vedānta, in Sāṃkhya and in the diverse traditions influenced by them. It highlighted the way in which material objects change by transitioning through different states or modes. One sees different modes of being in most entities, sometimes altering their apparent nature considerably, such as when milk becomes curd or cheese, a bundle of thread becomes a piece of cloth, a seed becomes a tree and an embryo becomes an adult. But at a fundamental level each is inevitably underpinned by a more basic, pervasive and persistent identity. That deeper level – whether defined as the substance of which different forms are made, or the necessary prerequisite factor that enables them to exist, or the enduring property that pervades the diverse forms and mutations – could be taken to indicate the essence or 'true' identity of an object. It is on this premise that much Hindu classical literature claimed to reveal the true nature of things. Where embodiment in structured elements represented the consequences of older Vedic paradigms of thinking about natural order, the 'modal' form of embodiment as the manifestation of changing qualities in a single substrate was the basis not only for much Sāṃkhya metaphysical reflection, but also for the development of new conceptions of a pervasive level of reality, as well as conceptions of divinity that contributed to the concept of *brahman* as it was outlined in the Upaniṣads.

The idea of an underlying deeper level – an element beneath the elements, as it were – is a common theme in the late Vedic material, and it provides a distinctive idea of unity. The essential impulse behind this approach is expressed in a hymn in the *Bṛhad Āraṇyaka Upaniṣad* which suggests hopefully that the mortal material self, so like a tree with its trunk and limbs, is grounded in some underlying root from which it can spring forth again when it has been 'cut down'. The resulting verses provide a clue to the way in which the search for a cohering level of self was bound up with anxieties about death:

> Man is like a mighty tree –
> That's the truth.
> His body hairs are its leaves,
> his skin is its outer bark.
>
> His flesh is the sapwood; his sinews are the fibres -
> That's certain.
> His bones are the heartwood;
> and his marrow resembles the pith.
>
> A tree when it is cut down
> Grows anew from its root; from what root does a mortal man grow,
> When he is cut down by death?
>
> (3.9.28)

This hymn draws a compelling analogy between the development of a human person and that of a grounded organism that has deeper roots which are not destroyed at its apparent death. By implication, if the 'roots' of the human in a persistent underlying level can be discovered, then the continuance of the person can be ensured – at least according to the author of the hymn. But the roots must be of a special sort, able to generate not merely a part, but the *whole* of the person anew; they must, in some sense, contain the 'essence' of the whole entity. It is this search for a deeper level, and particularly one that contains the whole, that accounts for the hierarchical arrangement of so many of the lists of elements in the Upaniṣads: again and again they are organized in terms of their ability to pervade, provide a foundation for, outlast, assimilate or serve as an equivalent to the other elements. If one can find it, the deepest level is the one that can carry the others 'beyond the reach of death' (1.3.11–16).

Where the 'structured' model of the self saw death as a disaggregation of the parts that constitute the body, this 'modal' model sees death as the ending of one form or aspect of a being, while at another it may persist. This underlying level thus takes on special importance as the most persistent part of the self and of all beings (both material and, as we will see, mental), providing a locus for their changes while anchoring them to a single identity. Some texts prioritized particular elements over others on the basis of some underlying quality that was accorded particular value, such as lightness, pervasiveness or vitality. An example of this is seen in the *Kauṣītaki Upaniṣad*'s (2.1) argument that *life-breath* is the foundation (*brahman*) or sovereign of the body:

> 'Brahman is breath' – that is what Kauṣītaki used to say. Now, of this breath that is brahman – the messenger is the mind; the guard is sight; the crier is hearing; and the maid is speech.
>
> And, indeed, anyone who knows that the mind is the messenger of this breath that is brahman comes to possess a messenger.

Here the elements of self are arranged to present one among them (breath) as the sovereign controller and anchor of the others. In connection with this idea that the life-breath is the essence of the self, this Upaniṣad also outlines a system by which a father who is dying can effectively transfer himself to his son. He should systematically deposit the elements within him of speech, breath, sight, hearing, taste, actions, pleasure and pain, bliss, passion and procreation (*ānandaṃ ratiṃ prajātiṃ*), movements (*ityā*), mind (*manaḥ*) and intelligence (*prajñāṃ*) into the son's body; but if the father is too ill or close to death to list all of these, a brief reference to the one element to which all are tied, life-breath (*prāṇa*), will do. This idea is linked to the belief that certain faculties of the self may be 'captors' of others which are controlled through them (2.3). Similarly, one passage in the *Chāndogya Upaniṣad* calls this underlying level the 'gatherer' (*saṃvarga*; 4.3) and bears out the unity of body and nature by equating it with the wind 'among the deities', and with the breath 'among the vital functions'. In the different passages describing a 'gatherer', able to assimilate the diverse elements into itself, it is seen as a natural and necessary feature of any composite thing; as the Brahmin Yajñavalkya points out, if the different constituents of the body were ultimately grounded in something outside of itself, then that external foundation could be destroyed: 'dogs would eat it, or birds would tear it up' (3.9.25). There must be a foundation that lies within the entity itself.

In such cases a hierarchy of elements emerged, based on the way in which some are dependent on others. In a passage that calls itself the 'dying of the deities', the hierarchical arrangements of the body's faculties, centred around breath as a core, is paralleled by the hierarchical arrangement of cosmic elements around the wind as an undying element:

> Next, the 'dying around of the deities'. The brahman shines forth here when the fire is burning; but when the fire stops burning it dies, and its radiance goes to the sun, and its lifebreath to the wind. The brahman shines forth

> here when the sun is shining; but when the sun stops shining it dies, and its radiance goes to the moon, and its life breath to the wind . . . Now, when they have entered into the wind, when they have crept into the wind, all these deities do not lose their self-identity, but emerge from it once again. (*Kauṣītaki Upaniṣad* 2.11)

Again the paralleling process returns to the body, making exactly the same argument with regard to speech, sight, hearing and thinking, and summarizing it all with a 'proof' based on the idea that one may speak, see, hear and think while remaining physically prone, but it is breath that revives us to life again (2.12–13). Breath here clearly functions as one model for *brahman* (see Connelly 1997). But such arguments also remind us that *ātman* or *brahman* were not automatically assumed to be a non-material core – it could simply have been the most basic of many natural 'fabrics' on which the others were dependent. But wherever *brahman* was identified with the most basic or pervasive element, its defining feature was that it served as the foundation of the natural world and of the body, the 'root' that remained undisturbed when all else changed. In such cases the realization of *brahman* was about resorting to a deeper identity in order to access a level of selfhood that could outlive the volatile shifts and changes of one's body. In these modal views of reality, *brahman* represented essentially a natural conception of the 'deepest level' of any given case of embodiment, be it the embodiment of a person, a thing, a system in nature or the cosmos as a whole.

## Transformations in nature, energy and substance

On a broader scale, this idea of a root or level that underlies change provided the basis for many Indian philosophical views that the cosmos as a whole must be ontologically dependent on a deeper 'ground'. As in Western scholastic thought, contingent and changing things ultimately came to be seen as ontologically 'needy' and necessarily dependent on more basic, unchanging and self-existent realities, seeking what in philosophical terms is called a 'fundamental ontology', a basic level of existence. Successive generations of Vedāntic philosophers devoted vigorous debates and treatises to the nature of such foundational realities. But this philosophical dimension of reflection on the ground of modal transformation was also augmented by another way of understanding identity in change, based on empirical observation of the natural world. Much as Aristotle identified the telic transformation of things into predetermined forms (as of the seed into a tree) as a central pattern in nature, so also certain Indian classical texts identified the transformation of energies and substances as a basic modus operandi of the natural world. In this view, it was not structures but changes that mattered.

Transformation and the power to initiate it had been a theme of Vedic thinkers from an early stage of Hindu cosmological reflection. A number of Ṛg Vedic accounts of the origin of the universe describe the 'inner transformative power' of the gods in terms of the energy of *tapas* or heat. The idea of *tapas* seems to be modelled on actual fire and its capacity to transform matter into new states: liquid into gas, solids into ash or mere smoke and so on. This transformative capacity, re-envisioned in the abstract concept of *tapas*, encompassed other processes of warming, cooking and energetic changes of state. Vedic ideas of a creator–being frequently referred to its special power to transform itself into new forms, describing it as a kind of *tapas*, as in *Ṛg Veda* 10.72.3 which explains it as 'the swelling creative power' from within which aspects of the universe emerge. This transformative capacity in things is basic to the notion of the natural world as an organic process that takes place in all elements and bodies, minds and other 'subtle' forms of existence. All of nature can be seen as a process of transformation:

> Prajāpati wished 'May I be propagated, may I be multiplied'. He practised *tapas*. Having practised *tapas* he emitted these worlds: the earth, the atmosphere, and heaven. He warmed up these worlds, and when he did so, the bright ones [that is, the luminous deities] were born. Agni [fire] was born of the earth, Vāyu [wind] from the atmosphere, Āditya [the sun, light] from heaven. (*Aitareya Brāhmaṇa* 5.32)[1]

Cosmological speculations in the Vedas and Upaniṣads often refer to the vital elements such as breath, or sunlight, as raw materials of nature, transformed through the natural processes of biology and climate. In the Upaniṣads food (*anna*) is one of the early candidates for an account of *ātman*, understood as a substrate of reality insofar as it is that medium that undergoes change, is processed, takes on new forms and always returns to its own basic nature:

> From this very self (ātman) did space come into being; from space, air; from air, fire; from fire, the waters; from the waters, the earth; from the earth, plants; from plants, food; and from food, man. Now, a man here is formed from the essence of food.
>
> From food, surely, are they born;
> all creatures that live on earth.
> On food alone, once born, they live;
> and into food in the end they pass.

For food is the foremost of beings,
so it's called 'all herbs'.

From food beings come into being;
By food, once born, they grow.
'It is eaten and it eats beings.'
Therefore it is called food.

*Taittirīya Upaniṣad* 2.1–2

Despite the progressive transformation from more subtle to heavier materials, the passage nevertheless asserts a continuity between food, the most basic level, and the different forms that it takes. Where food was seen as a *material* undergoing change, fire was seen as a *catalyst*. Its capacity to transform that which it burns was interpreted as an ingesting process that takes in and changes substances into invisible yet still more powerful forms such as heat or bodily energy. Laurie Patton (2005) has noted that not only fire, but the image of fire in mantras, and the ritual forms to which those mantras are applied were attributed the power to transform the environment. In such cases rituals involving fire and similar 'digestive' processes aided the human individual to become an 'individual eater who digests with the power of fire and the gods – all on his own' (116).

Where the *Taittirīya Upaniṣad* speaks of transformations in energies, the *Chāndogya Upaniṣad*'s sixth chapter repeatedly evokes the transformation of a substance into new forms, and was taken as one of the sources for what became known as *pariṇāma-vāda*, the doctrine of reality as transformation of an underlying substrate. In an influential passage it likened reality to a raw material moulded into different forms and given different names accordingly, like the shaping of metal into multiple shapes and the separation of milk into different densities. Copper becomes a bangle, milk becomes curd, yet the same basic material persists throughout (e.g. 6.1.4–6). This modal view of materials was common, and it was widely assumed that objects are capable of both a 'subtle' (*sukṣma*) and a 'gross' (*sthūla*) form of existence.

## Sāṃkhya and the modal worldview

Classical Sāmkhya was one of the most prominent voices to promote doctrines of transformation. It played an important role in providing a coherent philosophical framework that united the intuitive understanding of natural processes with the idea of an underlying ground. The transformative capacities of reality had been a central theme of the long and diffuse movement that Gerald Larson (1969: 95–133) has termed 'Proto-Sāṃkhya', growing from approximately 400 BCE to 300 CE. But the idea of a substrate with the capacity for change into different forms became central to classical Sāṃkhya ideas about worldly reality, taking it to be the modifications of an underlying substrate. In *satkārya-vāda*, or the 'doctrine of the pre-existence of the effect [in the source]', the *Sāṃkhya Kārikā* argued that change is really the manifestation of the hidden forms that exist as a potential within each object. The argument differentiates between *avyakta* unmanifest states that cannot be seen because of their ontological subtlety and *vyakta* states of manifest visibility. But here there is a reversal of the West's common assumption that what is visible and concrete is the 'most real' level of things. In the *Sāṃkhya Kārikā*, what is visible and immediate to the senses is associated with impermanence, contingency and distinct individual identity. It is the unseen *unmanifest* level that is most stable and real:

> The manifest is caused, perishable, not all-pervading, active, plural, dependent, mergent, composite, and not self-governed. The unmanifest is the opposite of this.
>
> Of three qualities, indiscriminate from them, the object of perception, universal [or public], unconscious, and of a productive nature is the manifest, that is the material [of creation]. (10–11)

Such is the manifest world in which we habitually live and to which our senses are most directly attuned. But one can infer that another 'unmanifest' level must exist. In an early statement of the *satkārya-vāda* theory of causality, it is argued that contingent things must already have some form of latent existence in their prior sources because (a) nothing can simply come into being out of nothing, and (b) it can be seen that particular things have an innate tendency to produce particular sorts of new things rather than others (9). Thus what is newly 'created' must have some special relationship to what preceded it, and the text argued that this is best seen merely as the activation of what was already potential within the prior source. This insight is then applied to the whole of the manifest world. The Kārikā points out that the existence of an unmanifest reality can be determined from a number of factors that suggest a great deal about metaphysical assumptions in the classical period:

> It is from the distinction of changing things, from universality or inherence [in all things], from the source of activity in a prior power, from the distinction between an effect and its cause, and from the undividedness of the world that the cause is the unmanifest (*avyaktam*). (15–16)

The argument given here assumes that when something undergoes change, but these contingent changes are overarched by a continuous identity, then it is merely demonstrating the prior possibilities that existed unmanifested within the underlying substrate. It seems clear that such Sāṃkhya prioritization of the fundamental continuity of any single multiform existence sought to counter Buddhist claims that there is no continuous substrate of reality, only individual phenomena in constant flux. Larson (1969: 167) glosses this idea as 'an undifferentiated plenitude of being' – bringing to the fore notions of plenitude and potentiality that were important to many subsequent Vedāntic (e.g. Bhedābheda Vedānta), tantric and other philosophies that were later influenced by Sāṃkhya and also by the *Chāndogya* and *Taittirīya Upaniṣads*' discussions of modal substantialism (Samuels 2008: 282–5). A view of things as full of potential and prone to manifest unseen latent forms acquired a firm place in Hindu assumptions about the nature of reality.

Where this theory is applied to the self, action can then be interpreted according to this modal conception of reality, with the agent providing the substrate for multiple actions that are seen less as *events* than as *modes* of being. Just as a sea remains the same despite the action of its waves, or a serpent is the continuous substrate for actions of coiling and uncoiling, so also an agent can provide the unchanging ground of actions that are less like discrete 'movements', in the English sense of the word, and more like shifts in state or modal transformations in its being. In this sense one can say that an acorn 'acts' in becoming a tree, and vice versa: that all action is a form of becoming something new.

In this context, the *satkārya-vāda* doctrine of Sāṃkhya thinkers serves not only as a theory of reality, but also as a theory of agency. In explaining the rationale behind this idea it outlines an argument that potentially applies to all cases of change in any being (including the intentional changes that we call 'actions'): change arises from a continuous substrate in which all potential effects already pre-exist before their coming-to-be in time (*Sāṃkhya Kārikā* 9), and are successively made manifest. All change and activity requires the latent pre-existence of the new states as a potential already intrinsic in the substrate, lying in wait:

> Since what is differentiated must be a modification [of a thing from one form to another], since there is a homogeneous nature [of a thing that is consistent throughout those differentiations] and since there is a functioning [of the thing] through [its] potency [for change], since there is a differentiation into cause and effect, [and yet] since there can be no differentiation of what has a universal nature [spanning those differentiations]; there exists a cause which is unmanifest [within a thing prior to its manifestation in an actual causal action]. (15)

This highly condensed passage focuses on the idea that a universal nature spanning different modes is actually the locus of both unmanifested possible forms and an innate potency for change. The argument is that in any being that undergoes change, one simply sees a shift in actualization of its multiple potential states. There is no one true mode (I am never essentially walking or sitting, young or old): there are only manifest and unmanifest states, but at the deeper level all of these exist *in potentio*. Knut Jacobsen (1999: 126) explains that in contrast to the contemporary Buddhists who saw movement as a 'staccato' succession of momentary acts, in this Sāṃkhya view, 'it is a legato movement, no distinct breaks, movement is compact, the momentary changes are the changes of a fluctuating substantial stuff with which they are identical'.

The idea sketched here was developed in many later literatures, and one particularly apt example of a modal theory of agency was provided by the science of grammar. The fifth-century grammarian and philosopher Bhartṛhari used the verb *vṛt*, signifying modification, change or growth (rather than the usual *kṛ*), to express this kind of agency. He employed it to describe action (here linked to linguistic differentiation) as the manifestation (*vivarta*) of various potential modes by an underlying inner controller. In doing this, he drew on prior linguistic analyses of being (*bhāva*) by early grammarians such as Yāska and Patañjali who described it as having different modes (*vikāra*) which could also be seen as actions, and which explained the development of tenses (see Ogawa (2005: 203–7) for a summary of these ideas). These came to acquire important ontological implications; the first verses of Bhartṛhari's *Vākyapadīya* work through the idea that something that appears to change and have separate parts may in fact be a case of different manifestations that cause it to seem 'as if' changefully differentiated by its capacities or actions. It is '*bhinna śakti-vyapāśrayāt*' – divided by virtue of its foundation of potentialities or capacities – and thus it remains without parts ('*apṛthaktve 'pi*') even though it manifests and transforms as if by the 'parts' that are its capacities ('*śaktibhya pṛthaktvena iva vartate*'). The resulting manifestations are the result of this power of change which is associated specifically with the 'power' of mutating existence through time (*kālaśakti*; see *Vākyapadīya* 1–3).

Bhartṛhari's language-based, temporal understanding of transformation was not the only 'modal' approach to change and activity. Others gave their own specific modal accounts of the body. The twelfth-century theologian Rāmānuja, whose main interest was the application of this model to divine agency, emphasized the way in which this view of action shifts the ontological status of the body by treating it as a constantly fluctuating expression of the different modes possessed by the underlying agent, the self or *ātman*. The body, he argues, is merely the tool of actualization of the self's innate potential, and as such is always supported by the more fundamental, permanent existence of the self as the 'support':

> This relationship between *ātman* [self] and body [comprises] the relation between support and thing supported such that the latter is incapable

> of being realised apart from the former, the relation between controller and thing controlled, and the relation between principal and accessory. The *ātman* – from *āpnoti* ['it obtains'] – is that which in every respect is the support, controller and principal of that which is the thing supported/controlled and the accessory, i.e. the body' or form which exists as a mode [of the mode-possessor, the *ātman*], incapable of being realised [apart from the latter]. Now this is the relation between the [finite] individual *ātman* and its own [material] body. (see Lipner 1986: 123–4)

In appropriating ideas of causality and manifestation derived from the tantric Pāñcarātra tradition, Rāmānuja offers a *satkārya-vāda*–style radical revisioning of agency as a succession of manifestations of one's potential, and of the world as something that consists not in discrete objects that 'do' things in time, but in pluripotent substrates each of which contains a plenitude of potential forms, manifesting at different times. The material world is not, thus, seen as still and inactive but as ripe with imminent changes, and persons are never intrinsically passive, but are always possessed of potential new acts and developments. Modal agency is not a doing, but a manifesting of potentialities: true action is not change to a new state, but the *catalysing* of imminent change.

Modal views alter a culture's vision of reality at the core: the identity of things, persons and places all become unstable yet full of potential to become something else. Western assumptions about the stable, material, mechanical nature of the world are misplaced in this much more dynamic view of materiality. But Hinduism's early awareness that substances have a 'modal' nature does have parallels in Western cultures: the anthropologist Peter Reynolds (1991: 129) has pointed out that Western science sees material reality both in terms of biological systems characterized as a 'soft, wet, interdependent web of organic processes', and also in terms of the abstract forces of physics that constitute a 'hard, dry, crystalline structure explicable by energy transactions'. Both exist as potential modal states of the material world, even according to the modern empirical schemes of contemporary science. The implicit worldview of Western natural sciences produces an attitude to environment that has some continuities with Hindu transformative worldviews, but these varying views of material selfhood are rarely taken on board as an intuitive factor in identity and agency. The world of the scientist and that of the non-specialist in his or her quotidian life are kept separate by the circumscribing of the scientific worldview as a specialist field, whereas Hindu transformative practices open up possibilities of material transformation across a range of subtle and gross realities. As the alchemist coaxes a transformation from the metal, and a chemist catalyzes change in a chemical, so we may coax the world and its inhabitants to bring forth their hidden aspects.

# 5

# Agency and the art of the self

We have seen that in these texts 'em-bodiment' as the West envisions it might equally be termed a process of 'en-worlding' that builds us from those very physical and mental materials of which the world is made. Karel Werner (1978) has argued that this vision of the self is already embedded in the earlier Vedic conception of personhood as a 'very coherent theory of human personality which, expressed in our contemporary idiom, sounds very modern'. But it has remained largely invisible to Western scholars because of their inclination to seek a soul on the one hand and a body on the other. Instead we see that

> Man, in the Vedic understanding, is a complex being. His personality is a structural unity of dynamic forces or elements which are themselves impersonal and universal by nature. But they are no blind mechanical or physical forces, rather they possess an inherent intelligence of different grades which leads them to the formation of functional units with inner hierarchical structures, on both cosmic and individual levels. Thus cosmos emerges out of chaos and individual beings out of the interplay of cosmic forces. (276)

Werner's reading of the Vedic self seems consonant with the elemental perspective that we have seen described in early and mid-period Upaniṣads, locating personhood not in a unique substance or particle within the body, but in the intelligent agency that underpins the structured 'formation' of individual beings out of their parts. His vision of agency prefigures more recent accounts of Indian classical selfhood as, for instance, a strikingly modern form of naturalism in which the self turns out to be an activity of appropriation (Ganeri [2007] 2012: 184–213), or the emergence of new qualities (e.g. of perception and will) from constituent parts (see Ganeri 2012a) or a 'dynamic constant' that anchors the play of changing embodiment as a 'process' (Watson 2014: 184). The modal perspective on materiality emphasizes the latent potentiality of embodiment: existence in any form is intrinsically unstable because it already *is* many other unseen forms, but this means that it is always also possessed of a hidden plenitude that enables things to become more than they currently seem to be. Each body appears as a 'snapshot' that reveals only one of its many possible forms. As we have seen, the two views together – structured elements and modal forms – provide an ontology of the body in some of the early to middle period Upaniṣads, and in many texts that draw on them.

## The fabric of embodiment

Two features are central to this conception of embodiment that clothes us in the volatile materials of the natural world:

1. First, it encompasses multiple components, both material and physical, that make up an embodiment which is always open to diffusion and change. There is no single body and thus no single identity to which the self is intrinsically attached – a fact that, as we will see, underpins the many cultures that seek to constrain identity through rituals of initiation, and constrain action through conceptions of right *dharma*, auspiciousness and purity, and also the cultures of self-creation seen in certain yogic and tantric contexts.
2. Second, the self is not only 'open' to the world, but is one instance of it – partaking of an embodiment that spans the five elements of nature, the sun and stars, language and thought itself. The Western tendency to see embodiment as a specifically *human* issue is, in many respects, tied up with its dualistic habit of opposing humans to nature as two separate spheres. In these Hindu classical worldviews the mind and body of the self are seen as continuous with the broader materials and ideas that make up the reality. Embodiment is simply what it means to instantiate one part of the world with its parts and processes, perceptions, feelings and ideas – it is our experience of having control over one shifting part of the world.

The narrative of complex and dynamic embodiment is explored in an early Sāṃkhya-influenced story told in the *Mahābhārata* about a teaching given by Sulabhā, a female yogi. Seeking to convince an arrogant king that the body does not determine one's true identity, Sulabhā describes the 'twenty-fold aggregation' (12.308.111) of elements that constitute the self. She then goes on immediately to describe the stages of change undergone in the process of being a physical body, from blood and semen, embryo and limbs developing in the womb, to gender designators, childhood, youth and old age. In a sense, she describes both the elemental body and the modal body before using them critically to ask what it is that constitutes any continuous self. This text is particularly sensitive to the distinction between natural movement and intentional action, asking just what role such processes play in the constitution of that 'higher' process of agency – also a movement of composite things, but one characterized by will.

> The constituent elements of the body undergo a transformation from moment to moment in all creatures that is not apparent due to its subtlety. The birth and death of particles in each successive condition cannot be marked, O king, even as one cannot mark the changes in the flame of a burning lamp ... such is the state of the bodies of all creatures, that is, when that which is called the body is changing incessantly like the fast movement of a fine horse. (12.308.121–5)

Here the embodied self is a quick-moving complex to which identity cannot easily be pinned. The challenge (which Sulabhā goes on to address) is to take control of that stream of change and direct it consciously towards desirable developments. Thus the momentum of embodiment raises underlying questions about agency: how is it that unifying direction can be applied to the chains of movement of which we always already consist? And who is it that would take on the role of such an agent, when thought itself is part of the stream of flux and flow? In this way, the body's plurality naturally raises questions about its unity; and it is the idea of a cohering agency of the self, integrating the whole into a single will – if only temporarily – that provides an answer.

Embodiment here functions as what Sarah Coakley (2000: 3) calls 'an Archimedean point' that provides a central locus of perception, thought and action. Here this Archimedean point is by definition a shifting one, triangulated according to a moving map of world, mind and desire so that the classical Hindu body naturally exceeds 'the limits of individual fleshliness' (4) due to its layered, energic, plastic and transactional character. Rather than possessing a single body with a fixed fabric, it is more appropriate to think of each person as a multibody containing within it different levels of self, nested within each other and bearing complex causal relations that change according to environment. Body is food, it is ideas, it is air, it is movement towards a goal. In this sense the classical Hindu body may best be seen as a moving set of vertices in the shifting fabric of the world, shaped through that curious process called 'agency' which is what unifies the self.

While textual contexts frequently sought methods of liberation from the body, they also sought methods for taking cognizance and control of this variable process of embodiment. This meant (a) transforming bodily materiality into an instrumental tool of action, a *karaṇa* or *prakāra*, and (b) constituting one's own agency within the materials of the self. That is, the skill of agency meant not only interacting and becoming, which are processes that happen automatically to all material realities, but doing so in a way that is directed by intelligence.

As we have seen, in texts such as the *Kena Upaniṣad* (which speaks of that 'by which' one thinks, but which cannot be thought) and in classical Sāṃkhya one finds the idea of a core self who is none of these embodiments and stands in relation to them either as a passive 'witness' (*draṣṭṛ*) or as an 'inner-controller' (*antaryāmin*). Werner (1978: 278–80) has traced this idea back to Ṛg and Atharva Vedic sources that describe the existence of a controller or 'herder' who directs the elements of which we are constituted, differentiating between the 'unborn' self and the phenomenal self or *tanu*. This idea of a core 'director' of embodiment served as a philosophical puzzle: it was necessary for an account of the specifically intelligent form of agency, over and above the automatic causality of the non-sentient natural world. But two millennia of subsequent theological attempts struggled to explain what such a 'discriminating self' could consist of if it was independent of its embodiment. What could such an agent do, think or enjoy when it had no body, no world and no mind in the normal sense?

Various answers were attempted, and this centrifugal counterpoint between the aspects of selfhood that serve as a central decision-maker and those that function as a responsive body remained a founding premise of much Indian classical thought, becoming intertwined with conceptions of rebirth and liberation: while liberation could mean freedom from rebirth and future lives in the world, it could also mean taking charge of the body and mind in order to steer them out of their habitual paths grounded in natural processes, towards higher possibilities that are rooted in discriminating reflection. Religious and ethical traditions that upheld the value of cultivating particular actions or ideas had to acknowledge that agency (even soteriological agency that seeks to escape its own nature as an agent) necessarily entailed embodiment of some kind. Freedom *of choice* was what mattered – a freedom derived from the way in which the different levels of embodied self could unhinge from each other causally, to influence and alter each other in deliberate and even creative ways. As a result, various techniques developed that served as the tools to achieve the 'art' of reconfiguring causal relations between different levels of selfhood, so that mind and body could be reshaped. Such techniques included yogic concentration, the physical rigours of ascetic discipline and the thought-exercises of visualization and narrative; these formed the basis of key traditions of Hindu practice, as we will see.

Thus where no purely witnessing disembodied 'core' of the self was acknowledged, projects of self-control and transformation had to be premised on the possibility of dislocating the different levels of embodiment, and establishing relations of creative influence *within* one's own self between mind and body, or judgement and desire, or discrimination and judgement. The self needed to be trained to be active in some parts, and passively receptive in others, leading to an 'ambiguity of passivity and activity in the South Asian context' and particularly in the far-reaching ascetic elements of the culture (Flood 2004: 64). Tales such as Arjuna's dilemma in the *Bhagavad Gītā*, in which a character is caught between the social causality of duty and his own discerning intelligence, dramatize the difficulties of this ambiguity. But it could also serve as a fruitful tension between the agent and its body: the material body could be approached not as a cage, but as a *medium of expression*.

## Hindu dualism: core and contingent selves

The curious duality of the self as an agent consisted not in *mind* and *matter* (since, as we have seen, on this account mind is *part* of materiality), but in *contingency* and *core*, the changing, automatically active and the abiding intelligently discriminative parts of the self. Classical Sāṃkhya had tried to put the psycho-physical body on one side and the pure disembodied awareness on the other, culminating in Sāṃkhya's ultimate goal of *kaivalya* or the total isolation of pure awareness, but this relegated the role of the core self to mere 'witnessing'. It could not think, assess and act because thought, desire and action were part of the fabric of embodied reality which the pure self had escaped. However other sources recognized that the separation of body and consciousness was wrongly conceived from the perspective of agency, because contingency and core are relative values able to establish a counterpoint at different levels. The physical body can influence the social self and its expressions, mind can alter and control the physical body and discriminating thought can alter and control the sensations, judgements and emotions that fill the mind. The hierarchical structure given to many of the lists of bodily constituents, then, also served to map out power relations of causal influence between different levels of the self.

The Upaniṣads dramatize the growth of this idea out of intuitive everyday situations: *Kauṣītaki Upaniṣad* 4-19-20, for instance, has a king point out a sleeping man to his befuddled Brahmin student and ask where the man's conscious faculties have gone to, and from whence they return on waking. The implied question is, 'What is it that directs the wakeful active self?' The *Kaṭha Upaniṣad* suggests an answer by advising that one 'look within' to discover both the level of contingent experience with its movement into and out of consciousness, and another level which spans both sleep and waking life. This level, in its immortality, does not provoke the grief that attends all temporary and changing aspects of the self:

> The Self-existent one pierced the apertures outward, therefore, one looks out, and not into oneself. A certain wise man in search of immortality, turned his sight inward and saw the self within ... appearance and taste, smells and sounds, touches and sexual acts – that by which one experiences these, by the same one understands – what then is here left behind?
>
> So indeed is that! That by which one perceives both the states of sleep and of being awake; knowing that it's th' immense, all-pervading self, a wise man does not grieve. (4.1–4)

Here the Kaṭha draws a distinction between sensations connected to the outer world, and the inner world of the experiencer–comprehender, and this is repeated frequently in different forms throughout the Upaniṣads. This distinction in levels marked out two different narratives of selfhood: on one hand, the idea of an unchanging self became the subject of an elaborate history of technologies of self-seeking and self-purification. The true self was positioned at the top of a hierarchy of perception and the surrounding embodiment:

> Higher than the senses is the mind;
> Higher than the mind is the essence;
> Higher than the essence is the immense self;
> Higher than the immense is the unmanifest.
> Higher than the unmanifest is the person,
> Pervading all and without any marks . . .
>
> His appearance is beyond the range of sight;
> No one can see him with his sight;
> With the heart, with insight, with thought,
> Has he been contemplated –
> Those who know this become immortal.
>
> (6.7–9)

Where the West tended to lump together the different features and functions of thought, this text makes an internal distinction between organs of perception, and the higher organs of discrimination (*hṛda maniṣa manasa*) which are able to judge the perceptions and control the body's response to the outer world. The *Kaṭha Upaniṣad* is itself much influenced by early forms of Sāṃkhya and Yoga. It advocates a state in which speech, mind, sight and desire are eschewed, and the 'knots that bind the heart on earth are cut' so that agency is eventually relinquished (6.12–15). But in many other texts the core retains more of its embodied character. The *Kena Upaniṣad*, for instance, retains the vital, active, unifying and impelling quality of the core:

> By whom impelled, by whom compelled, does the mind soar forth?
> By whom enjoined does the breath march on as the first?
> By whom is this speech impelled, with which people speak?
> And who is the god that joins the sight and the hearing? (1.1)

The stylistic technique used here, of establishing an interrogative discourse that addresses open questions to the listener, was one way in which the dual drama of agency and embodiment was brought home to the Upaniṣads' audience as a real and present problem in which they were already engaged. The literary device of 'questioning' functions in the Upaniṣads as a way of beckoning the listener (who would, in the original context, often have been a student) into a shared process of reflection about his or her own embodiment. The *Kena* ('By What') and *Praśna* ('Question') *Upaniṣads* are named for this style. The *Praśna Upaniṣad* purports to convey doctrines given by the sage Pippalāda through six questions asked by men who come seeking knowledge. As Brian Black (2007) has shown, such stories and the strategies they conveyed were part of the contemporary desire to cater to more empirical and individualistic modes of knowledge, as well as to use that knowledge to demonstrate one's own priority in a first millennium BCE North Indian culture in which Brahmins sought to negotiate the social hierarchy through their provision of education. These stylistic strategies of direct address must also have functioned to call attention to the fact that their object of discourse – the embodied self in its processes and internal relations – was necessarily present and active in each member of the dialogue. The questions gradually reveal a self which – for the listener – is at work in their very process of listening and comprehension grounding every perception:

> This intelligent self, namely the person – who is really the one who sees, feels, hears, smells, tastes, thinks, understands, and acts – rests on the highest, that is, the imperishable self … Whoever perceives that shining imperishable devoid of shadow, body, or blood – whoever so perceives my friend – knowing the whole, he becomes the whole world. (*Praśna Upaniṣad* 4.9–10)

We will look in greater detail at the idea that the self can 'become the whole world' in the second part of this book, but here we see that the two aspects of the dual self – that shining imperishable one, and the one of 'shadow, body, or blood' – are set out in contrast to each other. The *Bṛhad Araṇyaka Upaniṣad* also describes two different forms of self (one with a fixed shape, mortal and stationary, the other with no fixed shape, immortal and in motion) of *brahman*, the ultimate reality. It then goes on to describe a parallel structure of the body:

> The following is with reference to the body (*ātman*).
>
> The one with a fixed shape is this body itself insofar as it is distinct from breath and the space within the body; it is mortal and stationary; and it is 'Sat' [existing]. The eye is the essence of the one that has a fixed shape, that is mortal and stationary . . .
>
> The one without a fixed shape, on the other hand, consists of breath and the space within the body; it is immortal and in motion; and it is 'Tyam'. The person within the right eye is the essence of the one that is without a fixed shape, that is immortal and in motion . . .
>
> Now the visible appearance of this person is like a golden cloth, or white wool, or a red bug, or a flame, or a white lotus, or a sudden flash of lightning. And when a man knows this, his splendour unfolds like a sudden flash of lightning.
>
> Here, then, is the rule of substitution: 'not –, not –', for there is nothing beyond this 'not'. And this is the name – 'the real behind the real', for the real consists of the vital functions, and he is the real behind the vital functions. (2.3.3–6)

Here the fixed body and its mere sensation are relegated to a lower level, and it is the 'subtle body' that is the 'essence' of the self and provides motion (as well as an immortal root). This distinction is combined with a further contrast between the vital functions that underpin animate life and the more 'real' self 'behind' those functions. In a later passage, possibly composed by a different group of authors, the core self is again defined by its mobility across different locations and embodiments: it is not confined to the body but is able to travel across 'this world', 'the other world' and the 'place of dreams':

> It is this person, the one that consists of perception among the vital functions (prāṇa), the one that is the inner light within the heart. He travels across both worlds, being common to both. Sometimes he reflects, sometimes he flutters, for when he falls asleep he transcends this world,

these visible forms of death. When at birth this person takes on a body, he becomes united with bad things, and when at death he leaves it behind, he gets rid of those bad things.

Now this person has just two places – this world and the other world. And there is a third, the place of dream where the two meet ... Now that place serves as an entryway to the other world, and as he moves through that entryway he sees both the bad things and the joys. (4.3.7–10)[1]

This vivid, almost poetic depiction of the core self creates a narrative of embodiment with the body made of perception and inner light as its protagonist: it travels, reflects, is able to transcend this world and take on new bodies, passing on to other worlds. Here the core self is not a pure witness but an active traveller pursuing its own journey through the spheres of classical Hindu embodiment. Across these different sources one can see that the attribution of qualities to the core self vary – in some it is perception, vitality and motion (as in the *Bṛhad Āraṇyaka* passages), while elsewhere it is the perceiver, or the impeller of perceptions, or something that stands 'behind' the impeller.

Classical Sāṃkhya tried to formalize these sorts of ideas into a basic conceptualization of the core self, while heightening the counterpoint between the two levels of self. In doing so it highlighted certain important features of the concept of a 'core'. It drew both on the early speculations of the Vedic tradition (see, for instance, Larson 1969: 75–95) and probably also on the cultural traditions of neighbouring kingdom such as Magadha (see the discussion of cultural differences between these 'two opposite worlds' in Samuels (2008: 48–93) and also in Bronkhorst (2007)). The various elements of the observable world were placed in binary relation to an ideal of unchanging selfhood perceived through discriminating insight rather than merely empirical perception – a contrast figured as the difference between scriptural or empirical knowledge and *vijñāna*, 'insight' (*Sāṃkhya Kārikā* 2). While the majority of the text is centred on the material source of the world (*prakṛti*) and its forms of manifestation, the *puruṣa*, or underlying person, is defined as:

**a)** the binding force that unites diverse elements in a composite entity (*saṅghāta*), which is

**b)** not essentially tied to the changing properties of the self, and which

**c)** provides a foundation or locus (*adhiṣṭhana*) for those properties, and which

**d)** perceives, experiences or 'enjoys' them (is the *bhoktṛ* or 'enjoyer'),

**e)** underpinning the goal of movement towards a state of unqualifiedness or purity (*kaivalya*) of existence. (See *Sāṃkhya Kārikā* 17)

What we see here is a form of selfhood that facilitates embodied life, bringing together notions of coherence, locus, the substance in which properties inhere and the phenomenological subject (which may originally have been separate arguments used against the Buddhists and other sceptics). Sāṃkhya defined the 'core' as a foundational awareness that provides a locus for those thoughts.

By contrast, the Vaiśeṣika 'atomist' school of thought emphasized other ways of defining the 'core'. It tried to identify the specific qualities defining the distinctive entity we classify as a person, listing eight marks or *liṅga*s that designate an embodied entity as a specifically human self. These included life-breath (*prāṇa*), animation (*nimeṣa-unmeṣa*), vital energy (*jīvana*) and action (*kriya*), and it went on to depict selfhood as the efficient causality provided by self insofar as it was understood to be a source of agency and effort (*prayatna*), happiness and sadness (*sukhaduḥkha*), desire and aversion (*icchādveṣa*; see Kano (2010) for a discussion of the *liṅga*s). Within the framework of Vaiśeṣika's broader atomist metaphysics, the human person is defined as the locus of a special combination of 'raw' materials of the body and mind, which in turn generates higher personality-making materials such as animation, action and desire. These emergent characteristics allow Vaiśeṣika's atomistic approach to account for the unique and complex features that shape what is sometimes called the 'will'. As such, Vaiśeṣika's analysis hints at a way of replacing the idea of a 'core witness', so important in Sāṃkhya, with a very different composite conception of the 'core' of the self. But both highlight important features of what constitutes a 'core' self – that is, that it serves as a locus of unity, continuity, subjective experiencing and shared motivation in the *Sāṃkhya Kārikā*, and that it furnishes animation, action, effort and the motivating values of happiness, sadness, desire and aversion in the *Vaiśeṣika Sūtra*.

Where self was seen as the 'core' in terms of that which bestows will, unity and direction on embodiment, it was oversight and autonomy that defined the 'core' in relation to the contingencies of embodied existence: particular ideas, desires or bodily forms. The self needed to be a ruler who guides its constituent parts into cooperation, and this idea was expressed through various analogies with a king, chieftain or 'lord' (*īśvara*). Prefiguring an image used by Sulabhā in the *Mahābhārata* (12.308.138–40, and 12.308.153–7), here the unity of the self is said to be like that of a leader and his people who together assume a single identity and purpose

> as from a blazing fire sparks fly off in every direction, so from this self (*ātman*) the vital functions (*prāṇa*) fly off to their respective stations, and from the vital functions, the gods, and from the gods, the worlds . . .
>
> To this self (*ātman*) cling these other selves (*ātman*), as to a chieftain, his own people. It is like this – just as a chieftain makes use of his own people, and his own people make themselves useful to a chieftain, so this self consisting of intelligence makes use of these other selves. (*Kauṣītaki Upaniṣad* 4.20)

The idea here is that the chieftain commands obedience, leading the subsidiary parts into a single shared 'body' of action. Part of what is implied is that this 'chieftain' is able to divert the people from their own, possibly wayward, agendas and redirect them to a shared and proper function. In this sense the idea of the self-as-leader gives voice to the important principle of command as a redirection and focusing of subsidiary agencies that may exist within the complex body.

But what is it that makes possible this autonomy of the self from the causal momentum of its subsidiary parts? Selected texts developed a theory by which the agent and his or her embodiment could be disjoined from each other, freeing the agent from its determination by the causal processes embedded in the material or social body, and creating a degree of autonomy at the level of action itself. Yoga was one source for the careful analysis of autonomy-creating processes in the self. The *Yoga Sūtras* give explicit instructions for wresting control of the 'reins' of the self (the word 'yoga' derives from a Sanskrit root meaning a 'yoke'), and redirecting the mind through patient practice. In this sense they describe the creation of a hierarchy of control within the psycho-physical body that can be used by the agent to reshape itself. The first section outlines techniques of stilling (*nirodha, virāma*) or steadfastness (*sthita*) for reclaiming control (e.g. *vaśīkāra*) of the mind from its incessant and automatic flow (*vṛtti*), which is motivated by cravings (*tṛṣṇa*) that flow from one's natural constitution:

> [P]ractice is the effort to be fixed [or steadfast] in concentrating the mind. Practice becomes firmly established when it has been cultivated uninterruptedly and with devotion over a prolonged period of time. Dispassion is the controlled consciousness of one who is without craving for sense objects ... Higher than renunciation is indifference to the *guṇas* [dispositions of the natural elements].This stems from perception of the *puruṣa*, soul. *Samprajñāta* [*samādhi*] consists of [the consecutive] mental states of absorption with physical awareness, absorption with subtle

> awareness, absorption with bliss, and absorption with the sense of I-ness. The other *samādhi* is preceded by cultivating the determination to terminate [all thoughts]. (1.13–20)

The *Yoga Sūtras* thus set up two different innate orders – of the natural world and of consciousness's inclination to be free, pure and still. The drama of soteriology arises out of the way in which they are opposed to each other, with sentient beings situated between them and attributed the capacity to negotiate them both. A skillful agent who has cultivated the skills of self-control and self-creation can thus deconstruct one order (that of nature, i.e. *prakṛti*) in order to reorient towards another (i.e. *puruṣa*). This hints at an empowerment of all free-willed minds to choose the order to which they desire to align themselves, and to structure or de-structure themselves accordingly through patient practice.

The techniques of Yoga were influential on a wide range of textual traditions including the theological synthesis found in the *Mahābhārata*, and there its conception of inner control was applied to more concrete physical forms of action. Early discussions of the nature of ritual action sought to explain the injunctive, ritual-enjoining power of Vedic literature as a discourse praising the special effects that action can have on the world. In a more negative light, the doctrine of *karma*, which probably emerged in or after the latest periods of Upaniṣadic composition, also emphasized the efficacy of human action. The *Bhagavad Gītā*, in particular, constructed a theory of action that focuses on the decision-making agency behind the action, using the distinction between modes of affectively engaged and disengaged (or attached and detached) agency to develop the idea that it is possible to engage in two different forms of action by either following the prompts of the psycho-physical body, or altering one's intentionality through discrimination. As it viewed the situation, the embodied self was firmly embedded in the world as the protagonist of an ambivalent narrative of mercurial rebirth and change:

> The embodied one passes through
> Childhood, youth and then old age,
> Then attains another body . . .
>
> Someone who has abandoned worn-out garments
> Sets out to clothe himself in brand new raiment;
> Just so, when it has cast off worn out bodies, the
> embodied one will encounter others. (2.13, 18, 22)[2]

Chapter three of the *Gītā* interpreted this in terms of the idea that embodiment is essentially agency-embedded existence. Action is not, in fact, the occasional, isolated choice of an otherwise inactive mind; rather it is the continuous and inescapable state of any embodied being, necessarily bound up with what it means to be embedded in spatio-temporal reality. Even unconscious action is action, and so too, the decision not to act is a potentially powerful form of action, as is made clear with a teasingly paradoxical statement in the text telling us that it is impossible to '*do* non-doing' (*akarma-kṛt*) for it is always really a form of doing.

> A man does not attain freedom from the results of action by abstaining from actions, and he does not approach perfection simply by renunciation.
>
> For no-one ever, even for a moment, exists without acting; everyone, regardless of their will, is made to perform actions by the constituents which originate from material nature (i.e. *prakṛti* – the fundamental constituent of all material reality). (3.4–5)

Thus action is a state of being that pertains to all embodied objects, but discriminatory decision-making was counterposed to this as a special capability possessed by the reasoning consciousness, enabling it to shape its activity in a unique way. One kind of desire compels action blindly merely because it craves rewards. But a different kind of desire motivates discriminating actions, shaped by the inner resolve that is informed by balanced reflection. This motivates considered and meaningful actions of quite a different kind from the automatic impulses that the *Bhagavad Gītā* sees as determined by the 'blind' impulses of nature's innate dispositions.

Blind actions motivated by unreflective impulses are seen to have a different causal impact from reflective decisions that are 'detached' from such impulses: desire-motivated actions tie beings to the laws of '*karma*' that determine their future circumstances, whereas considered actions do not, because they are not motivated by the automatic compulsions of nature. It is this capacity to choose between two different kinds of agency that makes minds into 'ethical' entities that are subject to the possibilities and demands of *dharma*. This discipline of discriminating agency is thus the basis for the essential capacity of freewilled action that underpins ethics in the classical Hindu tradition.

> You have received this understanding (*buddhi*) according to Sāṃkhya theory, now hear it as it applies to practice. Disciplined with such understanding, Partha, you shall throw off the bondage of action . . .
>
> Son of the Kurus, in this the resolute understanding is one, the intellects of the irresolute are infinite and many-branched . . .

> You are qualified simply with regard to action, never with regard to its results. You must be neither motivated by the results of action nor attached to inaction.
>
> Grounded in yogic discipline [i.e. reflective control of thought and action] and having abandoned attachment, undertake actions, Dhanamjaya, evenly disposed as to their success or failure. Yoga is defined as the evenness of mind.
>
> For action in itself is inferior by far to the discipline of intelligence, Dhanamjaya. You must seek refuge in intelligence. Those motivated by results are wretched. (*Bhagavad Gītā* 2.39, 41, 47–49)[3]

Even-minded intelligence liberates one from the bondage of action and makes possible new, better uses of agency. Recalling yogic forms of discriminative control over the parts of thought, this yogic control over the levels of action allows one to shift from one causal framework to another, intelligently guiding one's own participation in the structures of the cosmos.

Thus the *Bhagavad Gītā* constructs a theory of action that focuses on the decision-making agency behind the action. Gavin Flood (2004) has explored the way in which the *Bhagavad Gītā* problematizes agency as both passive, in the sense that it is not automatically driven by the drives of nature and the body, and active, in the sense that it requires the unique intervention of the decision-making mind. Here the ascetic self is an illuminating example of the core self, in that it is able to interrupt and assert independence from the automatic forces that normally determine embodiment: it performs 'the absence of will through the assertion of will' (64). Discriminatory decision-making is a special capability that enables the reasoning consciousness to shape its active existence in a unique way. Intelligence, it is revealed, has power over action and can provide a refuge in which to escape from natural systems (e.g. of desire or karmic reward) that otherwise operate as automatic.

## Creative agency

In these texts, it is intelligence, then, that facilitated autonomy, and autonomy gave to the core self an independent, discriminating, *creative* relation to its embodiment. The *Bṛhad Āraṇyaka Upaniṣad* emphasizes the creative capacities of the core self as it passes through different bodies and worlds, explaining that the dream world is 'made' 'with his own radiance' by the self who travels in sleep and who is thus a god-like 'creator' (see 4.3). Here the negotiation of embodiment appears as an *art*, and the self as a *creator*. Many Indian contexts allow imagination to play an important role in the constructive capacities of the self, according it valid reality as a medium in its own right, a tendency that scholars have noted in different contexts (e.g. Shulman's 2012 investigation of the constructive imagination, and the study of the 'mentally constructed body' described in the *Netra Tantra* by scholars such as Timalsina (2012) and Flood (2006)). It is one of the key elements that make up the mental self in a number of early accounts, and the Brāhmaṇas and Upaniṣads, possibly reflecting on visualization practices used in Vedic ritual, explore the nature of the imagined body that lives and acts wholly within the world of ideas. The *Bṛhad Āraṇyaka Upaniṣad*'s conception of the inner person made of subtle materials entails a powerful creative ability to shape the materials of the imagination:

> This is how he dreams. He takes materials from the entire world and, taking them apart on his own and then on his own putting them back together, he dreams with his own radiance, with his own light. In that place the person becomes his own light. In that place there are no carriages, there are no tandems, and there are no roads, but he creates for himself carriages, tandems, and roads ... In that place there are no pools, ponds or rivers, but he creates for himself pools, ponds, and rivers – for he is a creator. (4.3.9–10)

The 'person' has autonomous power to 'take materials apart and put them back together', creating landscapes and filling them with objects. The creativity inherent in intelligence plays an important role in these early conceptions of a core self. Is often implicit, but underpins every account of discriminating agency as a way of shaping the world. Just as the gross body has a causal relationship with the world of elements, the subtle body has a causal relationship with the world of ideas, and the discriminating intelligence stands above through its causal relationship with the world of understanding and intention.

We will look further at ritual practices of 'shaping the world', but the first point of creative agency is the shaping of one's own embodied materiality into something new and better. Since there are multiple kinds of bodies and different ways of configuring one's mind, the building of a self involves making decisions about what kind of person to be, and for this reason the production and assessment of *narratives* – stories that allow us to see alternative possible paths of action – often accompanied the theorization of agency. Our capacity to shape the self is a central feature of the mainstream narratives of identity and purpose that Hinduism provides, from the identity assumed by the domestic householder and upholder of regularized ritual culture, to that of the ascetic renouncer, or the medium of divine possession, or the devotee who takes on a new name as an 'initiated' follower or any other role in Hindu life. In their own way, such roles are 'bodies' that arise from the choices or each person as an autonomous self-shaping agent. The major narratives came to be clearly signposted in Hindu culture through heroes and heroines, and in some cases standard templates came to be promoted, such as the four *purūṣārtha*s or goals of humanity cited in numerous Śāstras as pleasure (*kāma*), success (*artha*), ethics (*dharma*) and liberation (*mokṣa*).

Indeed, the literatures devoted to outlining standard *dharmic* roles could be said to be the core of a systematic approach to embodiment primarily in terms of social roles. The *Mānava Dharma Śāstra* describes the proper social being of the student, the domestic householder, the renouncer, the Brahmin, the king, wives and others, while the *Kāma Sūtra* elaborates on the roles even of single men, courtesans and ageing second wives. The expert traditions found in architectural *Vastuśāstra*, aesthetic *Natyaśāstra* and *Śilpaśāstra*, political *Nitiśāstra* and *Arthaśāstra*s, the lifestyle advice of *Kāmaśāstra*, and the social models of *Dharmaśāstra* all formed an authoritative genre, a 'sāstric codification of behavior ... across the entire cultural spectrum' (Pollock 1985: 499) that sought to control and channel the innate creativity of the self that had been inherited from earlier Vedic sources.

The great epic narrative of *dharma*, the *Mahābhārata*, dramatized some of the tensions raised by the competing drives towards creativity and constraint in the individual. The *Mahābhārata* theorizes this self insofar as it explores, critiques, discusses and generally follows but occasionally redefines its dharmic identity. Olivelle (2005: 23) has argued that the writers of the *Mahābhārata* drew on material from the *Mānava Dharma Sāstra* itself, and it is certainly the case that the epic exemplifies a tradition in which the specificity of social identity and personal stories stands in counterpoint with the idea that the individual may seek to escape his or her dharma in pursuit of an underlying self that has access to a broader range of possible identities. Thus one of the main themes of the epic as a whole is the process of deciding whether to pursue the *dharma* of a king or the role of a renouncer, and identity switches became a common trope in Hindu drama and myth. It may be the case that the conscientious and empathetic Pāndava princes who are the heroes of the *Mahābhārata* were designed as an explicit contrast to the unreflective repression of creative reflection attributed to the early rule of the Emperor Aśoka in Buddhist narratives (Fitzgerald 2001: 64–5). The dramatic conflicts in the *Mahābhārata* are grounded in a world in which social embodiment comes into conflict with the autonomy of the individual agent who must negotiate a compromise with the means of his or her reflective intelligence. Thus we see anxious kings, frustrated wives, earnest students, marginalized ascetics and yoginis, and well-meaning brothers and friends, all having cause to stop, reflect and reason their way through difficult situations. The *Mahābhārata*, arguably the most influential narrative in Indian culture, is fairly self-aware in doing this; James Hegarty (2012: 13) has argued that 'the *Mahābhārata* sought to constitute itself very self-consciously as *the* authoritative "reflective" or "theoretical" resource for early South Asian religious and social life . . . [it] was a text that intended to be *used* [emphases in the original]' and thus had to speak to real concerns. In this text individuals are more than merely mouthpieces for isolated ideologies; their situation and the subsequent unfolding of events are tied to our understanding of what it means to question, assess, reflect, decide and act. The teachings about the nature of the self and of the divine in the *Bhagavad Gītā* are framed as a manual for taking control of the self and its embodiment, and negotiating both within the constraints of the social 'body'. This is fully functioning narrative ethical theory – a distinctive 'form of "thinking" ', as Hegarty puts it.

While we have emphasized the culture of seeking to define the 'core' self, it is important to see that the principle of contingency is central to that self; it is the volatile complexity and dynamism of the enworlded material being that makes agency possible. The frequent observation in Sanskrit genres of story and theology that the individual is only contingently situated in a certain body, life and social situation is central to the value of narrative ethics in Hindu traditions. As the *Bhagavad Gītā* (2.22) points out, each body or identity is but a garment to be exchanged at some point in the future, and hopefully for a better one. This would later contribute a theoretical underpinning to the Hindu religious use of drama as a way of loosening one's ties on the present identity and 'universalizing' the self through the identity-dissolving function attributed to the narrative arts by aesthetic thinkers such as Bharata in the *Nāṭyaśāstra*. This could be instrumentalized as a way of intentionally 'becoming' someone else in religious practices such as *rāgānuga bhakti sādhana*, a process by which devotees imaginatively identify with the protagonists of a divine story that takes place in a heavenly realm, shifting their identity into an alternative 'subtle' body that lives a simultaneous (and more vivid) life in parallel with their mundane material body (see Haberman's ([1988] 2001) study of this practice, and also Donna M. Wulff's (1984: 30–2) discussion of its theological principles and relation to the example of God as an actor taking on different roles within the material world). In such adoption of new roles, a different set of life circumstances, principles, reasons and conclusions are admitted. Such beliefs may allow the individual to literally change the embodiment, life-narrative and even the personal and ethical *truths* to which he or she is attached: by understanding embodiment as narrative one can better see the way in which it impacts on questions of worldview, truth and ethics.

## Rethinking self and embodiment

We have argued here that an early notion of psycho-physical embodiment is represented in Upaniṣadic thought and underpins many other classical Hindu contexts in the same Brahminical tradition. This notion took embodiment to be:

**(a)** mutable through variable aggregation and modal change;

**(b)** unified by a locus, substrate or coherent directing force;

**(c)** divisible into hierarchically ordered relationships of control;

**(d)** able to thereby constitute within itself a 'core', defined by its discrimination and relative autonomy over the subsidiary parts of the 'body';

**(e)** able thus to become other 'bodies' and identities (an ability that some traditions sought to control with prescribed roles.

The very materiality of reality that underpins this Hindu worldview is understood in ways that reveal the body to be not one simple vessel for its pilot, the soul, but a complex, multifaceted, self-constituting instrument of worldly existence. It is filled with changes and transformations at every moment, and is naturally prone to shift from one state to another, teetering on the volatile boundary between different modes of existence, yet continuous with the cosmos. As McKim Marriott (1976: 109–10) notes, the Hindu self tends to be a 'dividual' rather than an individual – a locus in the matrix of world, in constant interchange with other minds and bodies; thus 'what goes on *between* [emphasis in the original] actors, are the same connected processes of mixing and separation that go on within actors', and on this basis Marriott rejected 'the assumption of the easy, proper separation of action from actor, of code from substance' (similar to the assumption of the separability of law from nature, norm from behaviour, mind from body, spirit or energy from matter) that is common in Western formal and informal reasoning. There is no boundary that defines the embodied self absolutely, and it is liable to accrete or shed materials of the body at any time.

One consequence of this is that we must rethink the way in which the *ātman* in Hinduism tends to be seen as a 'disembodied' being. The sources we have looked at are intended to show that the image of the self as something that is 'clothed' in the 'garment' of the body is a misleading analogy, for embodiment is better understood as the synonymous self-expression and self-making of the self in its physical being and social identity, its thoughts and preferences and its own identity and motivations. When those things are stripped away the self is no longer a thinker, feeler, desirer or doer – it is 'not a possible object of consciousness' (Ganeri [2007] 2012: 27).

It is helpful to take advantage of Sanskrit concepts that are not so readily available in English. One way of understanding the 'core' self is as a *sthāna* – a locus, abode, place or state – within which embodiment takes place as an artful process in which key features of intelligence, value and will impose a new causality on the available materials, interrupting the momentum of their subsidiary parts in favour of a unified, coherent motivation grounded in reflection. In this sense, the classical Hindu vision of the embodied self fits with Marshall McLuhan's (1994: 123) redefining of embodiment as something that extends into media of all kind, insofar as they are appropriated (in)to the agent. Those observations about the role of different media and technology in extending selfhood have been further generalized to include objects and even other persons by David Chalmers and Andy Clark (2010) in their theory of the 'Extended Mind'. In asking 'where does the mind stop', they have sought to depict personal selfhood as something that we acquire and ultimately become. They too raise questions about which are the contingent and which the core parts of the self, and highlight the way in which the 'sea of words' functions to bind things (in)to us cognitively (32) – an observation that reflects another theme of the Upaniṣads, holding language to be something by which one can acquire and become the external world – an idea that we will explore in the next chapters.

It is important, in the Hindu context, to let Western theoretical assumptions about identity and embodiment be interrogated by the radically complex– even chimerical – nature of embodiment. Beneath specific life-roles, or even the basic existential narrative of birth, life and death (see Flood 2004: 23), lies the open narrative of the Hindu body as something that can be – and in a sense already is – anything. Reflecting on the way in which Western conceptions of selfhood were dismayed to discover 'the existence of a perilous otherness within the body', Michel Foucault (1989: xxvi) wrote that he aimed at 'restoring to our silent and apparently immobile soil its rifts, its instability, its flaws . . . it is the same ground that is once more stirring under our feet'. The classical Indian context echoes this sense that the body is rooted in a ground that stirs beneath and within us. But as we will see, it also has the capacity to work as a poet with this 'vast syntax of the world' (20), using reason and ritual as its tools of art.

# PART TWO

# Becoming the world: The self made of thought

# 6

# Theories of reason in classical Hinduism

In this chapter we look at the extended embodiment of humans in a new direction: through *thought* and *knowledge*. If one axis of selfhood measures the counterpoint of creative agency and constituent embodiment, then another measures the scale and scope of the thinking self, inviting us to move from smaller to larger forms of awareness. The process of theoretical reflection allows us to shape ourselves into beings spanning not only the here and now, but also the whole universe of facts and ideas. Classical philosophical reflection in the Upaniṣads and Sūtras show a fascination with knowledge as a reality that exists in its own right – a fabric of the world that constitutes both ideas, and also *us* to the degree that we reflect upon them. This is thus a chapter that explores the self as a thing made of thought.

If the classical Hindu worldview envisions a cosmos of complex, mercurial, shapeable realities of which we are an equally complex, mercurial and shapeable part, then it is also the case that realities which are stable, pervasive and comprehensive found their place in that system; it is in the area of *ideas* that classical Hindu thinkers were able to discover larger, more stable truths. In this chapter, then, we turn to concepts of reason, and theories of theory itself. It is in this realm – of ideas – that early theorists discovered extraordinary truths grounded in the rational mechanism of *inference*. Through this discovery classical Hindu thinkers realized that they could transcend their constant becoming *in* the world, to *become the world* itself. As Pierre Hadot (1995: 211) has remarked of the Roman philosopher Seneca's goal of 'plunging oneself into the world' through a redirected attention to the cosmos, so here too we see processes at work whereby early thinkers aimed to 'accede to the universality of reason within the confines of space and time' and be transformed by it.

## Genealogies of reason

A wealth of theoretical material presents itself to scholars seeking to explore forms of reasoning in Hindu cultures: early texts present a dazzlingly diverse range of speculations on knowledge, and many of these established a template for thinking about the cosmos and the self that lasted over the subsequent centuries. The Upaniṣads' philosophical discourse is expressed through the interweaving of image, narrative, analogy and argument, while the terse treatises found in the Sūtra and Kārikā genre of texts captured diverse theories of metaphysics, epistemology and linguistics as they concretized into shared doctrines belonging to coherent schools, while the dialogues found in the *Mahābhārata* depicted characters actively reasoning through arguments and counterarguments in a way that reflected real scholarly practices of debate. Meanwhile the genre of Śāstras served as manuals for applied theories of ritual practice, statecraft, medical science, civic planning, good living, astronomy, law, artistic style and innumerable other fields of knowledge.

These sources continued to live vibrant afterlives over the centuries. Sophisticated traditions of scholastic philosophy and theoretical sciences flourished in the medium of later commentaries, interpretations, auto-commentaries and expansions of the classical canonical material. All the while, the rich arts of India, including epics and divine narratives, folk stories and courtly poetry, ritual liturgies and devotional songs, and even the visual arts of sculpture and later of painting and poster, have promulgated these theories in implicit form, for they are often woven into the stories and theologies that they depict. Reason, then, spanned diverse contexts.

Yet in the face of this wealth, Hinduism's early processes of theoretical reasoning have too often been overlooked by scholars. This is perhaps because 'stories' about the development of theoretical reasoning are rarely told as part of the historical narrative of Hindu cultural history. This stands in marked contrast to the drama of rational Enlightenment that Western culture habitually tells about its own identity. The European conception of 'reason' has grown largely out of the Pythagorean and Platonic traditions' apotheosis of logic as a form of conceptual or *eidetic* being that is outside of time and does not decay. This idea, though tempered by the focus on kinetic transformation that characterized Aristotle's physics (in which he explored the tendency of natural objects to mutate and grow into new forms), nevertheless resulted in a preference for unchanging order over dynamic complexity. This preference would influence the subsequent 'taste' for unchanging truth in both the religions and philosophical traditions of the West.

Ancient Greece developed a well-stocked toolbox of different forms of reason, including technical knowledge (*techne*), mathematical comprehension (*arithmos*), the understanding of situations, ideals and goals in a practical form of wisdom (*phronesis*) and the creative formation of new ideas through a kind of productive theorizing (poeisis; see Aristotle's *Nichomachean Ethics* VI.5). Aided by this rich collection of reflective tools, reason became a tool of natural theology, and later of 'enlightenment', lauded as humanity's highest and most unique activity. With the development of classical humanism in the European Renaissance, and biblical hermeneutics in the Reformation, giving way later to republican sentiments in Europe and the Americas, reason also became the basis for claims to freedom from older authorities. For modern psychology it became the basis of a new stoicism that sought freedom from oneself: as Sigmund's Freud's account of the forces of the id, ego and super-ego celebrated reason's ability to counter the monsters that lurk within human nature and civilization.

But reasoning, as a distinctive part of the human project, also suffered a period of restriction with the rise of scepticism and the gradual acknowledgement of reason's limits. In many respects it was not understanding but certainty that formed a central theme for Western thought from the Renaissance onwards. The twentieth-century philosopher Edmund Husserl (1960) wrote of René Descartes that he initiated the 'complete reforming of philosophy into a science grounded on an absolute foundation', in the hope that philosophy would become a 'systematic unity' consisting of an 'all-inclusive science'. Philosophers following Descartes' example aimed at a 'transcendental turn': a 'radical rebuilding' based on 'insights behind which one cannot go back any further' (1–2), and for some this was the beginning of a new idea of truth in Western philosophy. But in the nineteenth century a further critical note brought into question the whole conception of reason in the West, with David Hume expressing doubts about the validity of induction – a central mechanism to all reasoning, and Friedrich Nietzsche (2008: 16) criticizing the way in which the realm of ideas was 'mummified'. This fraught Western history of debates about the proper place of reason has tended to influence scholars' study of Indian forms of theory – it too must stand up to the standards and goals set by the Western sceptics of each different age. In response scholars of Indian philosophy have often sought to assert that the science of discerning certainties thrived in India as well as in the West.

But genealogies of Indian reasoning can also be said to emphasize India's own distinctive historical conditions, assumptions, methods and desires, in contradistinction to the standard Western 'plot' in which naïve belief is characteristically defeated by conscientious scepticism. In his investigation of 'cross-cultural perspectives on human reasoning' The Classicist G.E.R. Lloyd (2015: 1) tried to recall his readers to other forms that the search for truth can take in cultures which – each in their own way – have developed 'amazingly powerful tools of investigation, aimed at discovering the truth, delivering explanations, verifying conjectures, showing that inferences are sound and proving results conclusively'. This drama of Reason, which Lloyd saw at work at the very origins of early Greek philosophy, is also one that strongly characterizes classical Hindu texts.

## The growth of metaphysics

For those interested in metaphysics, Hindu traditions of thought have presented a story of diverse, competing cosmologies that rival even the competing voices of the Pre-Socratics and the classical schools of Ancient Greece. According to this model, the story of the Hindu tradition of reasoning is one of increasingly complex growth from a few highly fertile questions that acted as seeds for the later tradition. Relatively few scholars have sought to trace the metaphysical speculations of Hindu India from the relatively objective standpoint of philosophical history, although Surendranath Dasgupta's comprehensive *History of Indian Philosophy* (1922) conveyed the coherent continuity of the tradition as it sought ever-new answers to classical questions.

Many late Vedic texts united religious, scientific and philosophical discourses in a manner that echoes the genre-crossing ancient writings of Greek or Chinese thinkers; as Francis Cornford (1912: i) remarked of Greek thought, here too religion and philosophy were not 'two distinct provinces of thought' separated by 'a sudden and complete breach'. Instead of a change from 'religious poetry' to 'secular philosophy', India developed a style of weaving metaphysical reflection into cosmological, mythological and other forms of discourse. This style would continue to shape forms of reflection on reality that are found in the epics, purāṇas, tantras and even in *kavya* poetry and the *gītās* or songs of the devotional saints.

Central philosophical problems about the nature of the cosmos were established in this period; the so-called cosmological hymns of the *Ṛg Veda* offered *genetic* accounts of the existence of the world, and the Upaniṣads sought *ontological* explanations of the material that constitutes the universe. Largely eschewing the possibility of creation *ex nihilo*, the challenge of early cosmological accounts was to provide an ontology that would explain the roots of reality in some self-existent ground that was not merely another entity within the universe (see Frazier 2013). This required that basic questions about the nature of arising, existence, contingency and identity be answered, and the concept of *ātman* (in its various meanings as self or body, and later essence or nature), became an important hook for inquiry into these thorny metaphysical issues. In this context, the doctrine of *ātman* quickly became much more than merely a treatment of the human body, mind or prospects for post-mortem existence:

> [I]nquiry into the true nature of the self serves as the organisational centre in the development of a broader range of philosophical conceptions and approaches. In metaphysics and epistemology, in the philosophy of language as well as the philosophy of mind, sustained reflection on the nature of self functions as a paradigm for conceptual elaborations whose application has a significantly wider reach. (Ganeri [2007] 2012: 214)

The concept of *ātman*, then, was the hinge for an array of wider philosophical problems about identity and permanence in Hindu thought, just as the doctrine of *an-ātman* ('no-self' or 'no-identity') became the basis of a general critique of permanent identities in Buddhist thought.

Such theoretical speculations in early Vedic texts set the agenda for much later metaphysical thought, but they also trained reason to see itself as a tool for explaining the cosmos, and situating humanity in relation to it. Erich Frauwallner (1973: 5–6) claimed to see 'a clear, uniform line of development' from the 'questions which an awakening philosophical thought formulated' in the Vedas, to the 'overpoweringly bold thoughts' of the classical and medieval periods that were systematized and could 'lay claim to giving a full, all-embracing world-picture'. Frauwallner's analysis of the Vedic approach to explanation produced a list of themes that in due course formed the pillars of these systems: each scholastic school aspired to a theory of knowledge, enumeration of the prime constituents of existence, a cosmological world-picture and account of the construction of the 'world-edifice', and inferences regarding topics such as ethics and soteriology (6–7). The profound metaphysical questions that Brahmins embedded in early Vedic texts with increasing density in the period of the second urbanization of northern India created a philosophical canon that would shape the next two millennia.

The growth of speculation and theory was gradual and polycentric, however, unrestricted by any clear arbiter of orthodoxy. The flourishing of theoretical traditions concerning language and meaning, logic and aesthetics, psychology and social sciences, which took place on the heels of the period of Vedic composition, was so rich in the millennium from 500 BCE to 500 CE that Frits Staal (1995: 112) once suggested that 'India experienced at an early date a scientific revolution in the *human* sciences' (emphasis added). Staal envisions this not as the ancient revolution in mathematical understanding that took place in Greece and later propelled Europe towards a scientific revolution, but rather as a revolution in the understanding of *linguistic* meanings that took place on the Gangetic Plain in the classical period, flourishing through the grammatical traditions of Mīmāṃsā and Vyākaraṇa. The intelligentsia of classical Brahminical culture thus followed a template based on semantics and grammar for centuries to come. Staal's view is important in that it emphasizes the early flourishing and subsequent growth from which Hindu thought benefitted; but it also emphasizes the distinctiveness of Indian thought, developing not out of an apotheosis of mathematics like the post-Platonic traditions of the West, but out of an apotheosis of language.

One effect of this linguistic bedrock was that it was able to support a striking range and multiplicity of interpretations: a mathematical problem can have only one solution, but a word can have many. The commentarial tradition that became the most popular genre of theological and philosophical reflection ensured a continuing awareness of the way in which texts allowed for a plurality of interpretations, and much innovation took place through the meticulous hermeneutic unpacking of the meanings imminent in the source texts. This in turn encouraged Hindu reasoning to engage with ambiguity and complexity: theories developed that could allow for hierarchies of conventional and absolute truths, or even encompass dialectically opposed ideas. The Hindu notion of *acintya* (unthinkable) or *anirvacanīya* (inexpressible) truths and the Jain doctrine of *anekānta-vāda*, the doctrine of 'many-sided' truth, were demonstrations of the Indian understanding that there may be many sides to a single issue and many aspects of a single truth (see Chakravarthi 2007).

The commentarial style of writing also contributed to the diversification of Hindu philosophies by securing the individual's ability to implicitly challenge a canonical text's conclusions and recast it in a new way, without undermining its value and authority. The contrast with Jewish, Christian and Muslim structures of doctrinal orthodoxy is striking; the comparative social history of Indian reasoning gives the impression that, as Sheldon Pollock (2001: 30) has put it, 'the only censorship in India is failure of imagination'. This tendency has contributed to Amartya Sen's (2006) depiction of Indian traditions as deeply liberal in their allowance of multiple voices within arenas of rational discourse and debate. Here again, the result was a proliferation and growth of metaphysical speculation that is evident in any reading of the Upaniṣads and the various positions represented in the Sūtras. To those who have studied classical Hindu thought as a multivocal discussion (rather than assuming it to be a confused expression of a single doctrine, as the interpretation of well-meaning Western scholars such as Paul Deussen have done; see Deussen 1908), the culture represents a strikingly rich interweaving of not one but many traditions, suggesting that 'many possible alternative histories' of classical traditions such as Vedānta can be written (Nicholson 2010: 25). The different views that can be expressed within a single text disagree with, but never silence, each other, and the result has been a many-limbed mass of speculations that has evolved through the rigorous systems of Hindu theology into a complex theoretical culture.

## The challenge of scepticism

The multiplicity-based model of Hindu reasoning has been influential as a corrective to tendencies to assume that the same search for absolute truths holds everywhere in all cultures, or that Hinduism had only one (monistic) philosophy to offer. But many scholars sought to put limits on the diversity of the traditions by emphasizing the great importance of validity and authority in actual practices of theorizing. In this respect, as in so many others, the dialogue of Hindu thinkers with Buddhist thought was influential. In the arena of meta-theory (reasoning about the nature of reasoning), Hindu thinkers were forced to defend the validity not only of their notions of entities, causes, selfhood, identity and meaning, but even of inference itself, the very basis of theoretical speculation. In later centuries these debates would prompt still more sophisticated theories about 'the nature of rationality, the metaphysics of epistemology, and the relevance of philosophy to the practice of religion' (Patil 2009: 4). The scepticism displayed by Buddhist 'gate-keepers' of good reasoning would prove to be a powerful inspiration for Hindu optimism about epistemological and metaphysical questions, and the resulting tradition of logic and epistemology has been a favoured theme of scholars (see, for instance, Bronkhorst 2011; Matilal 1971, 1986; Patil 2009; Ganeri 2001, 2011; Phillips and Tatacharya 2004; Arnold 2005).

One of the key complaints of sceptics was that reason could be an artificial phenomenon, imposing a false order onto reality. Hinduism itself was divided on this point, with some Advaitic traditions following the lead of Buddhist, Jain and Cārvāka critics and relegating conventional experiences to the status of *māya*, 'illusion', which functioned as a category of subjectively cognized false perceptions. But contrary to the later Western fascination with such 'illusionist' views (an interest cultivated by Arthur Schopenhauer's ([1969] 1818) promotion of Buddhist and Upaniṣadic texts as precursors of his own view that the world is merely a 'representation' – see the preface to *World as Will and Representation*), a majority of Hindu schools of thought affirmed the reality of perception and humanity's inferential reasoning on the basis of empirical truths or textual testimonies. The result was a sort of epistemological optimism that nevertheless frequently had to defend itself against the most radical forms of scepticism. One can organize Hindu views about reason and its truths according to a basic divide promoted by Bimal Krishna Matilal (1971: 14) among others, between Buddhistic sceptics, and those holding to the 'philosophic thesis which tries to show that reality is knowable and hence expressible in language'. Among Hindu optimists, theories developed about the way in which reason accesses the real 'essence' of things – their *svabhāva, ātman, sat* and so on.

Above all, it was the traditions of logical analysis that sought to provide regular methods of reasoning, and it was these that gained the attention of Western philosophers eager to defend the rigour of Indian thought. Bimal Krishna Matilal (1998) attributed the logical tradition to early practices of debate and the development of manuals in *vāda-vidya* or the 'sciences of speech' needed to cope with the vicissitudes of actual rhetorical discussions. Staal (1995: 79–87) has noted that the very structure of Sanskrit lends itself well to exploration of logical issues due to its case-based grammar, ease of nominalization of words into abstract nouns and tendency towards structures that approximate algebraic formulas.

The genres of treatise that developed – *sūtra*s and *śāstra*s that tried to capture key doctrinal views once and for all – can also be seen as part of the desire to establish knowledge as a fixed compass for human life. But this positivism never escaped a cautionary relationship with more sceptical voices: doubts about the existence of linguistic and ontological essences prompted the development of widely influential theories about the provisionality of reason. The recognition that reason can be put to the purposes of lying and persuasion meant that coherence with Vedic texts – generally seen to present access to truths themselves – remained indispensable even for many Nyāya logicians. Indeed, Halbfass (1991: 28–9) notes that the idea of the 'Veda' eventually extended beyond the original texts to function as the 'center and prototype' of a 'timeless framework of traditional knowledge' that is eternal (*nitya*) and a guarantee of the coherence of theories and their correspondence with reality. The Vedas, then, remained both the fertile source for Vedāntic metaphysical speculation and the touchstone for a vigorous skeptical tradition.

## The search for transcendental foundations

Another form of epistemological optimism about the possibility of authentic and certain knowledge existed in the traditions of introspection associated with Yoga and Sāṃkhya, and this has formed the backbone of a reasoning-oriented approach to those schools. Where earlier commentators on Yoga, such as Mircea Eliade ([1958] 2009), had emphasized the soteriological goals of the school and correlated it with the Stoic traditions of Greece as a practical means of liberation from suffering, Jitendranath Mohanty (1991) was one of the first to approach the analysis of consciousness found in Yoga, Sāṃkhya, Vedānta, and other Hindu traditions, in terms of a rational and rigorous epistemology. He departed radically from the approach taken by Matilal by asserting that it was not access to truth through logic that formed the root of reasoning in Indian thought. Instead, his genealogy of Indian reasoning asserted that

> [f]or almost all Indian philosophers, the ultimate ground for all evidence, the source for all 'establishment' (*siddhi*), is consciousness (*cit*), without which no 'being' or 'non-being' could be asserted or denied, and there would be 'universal darkness' (*jagadāndhyaprasaṅga*). (10)

A scholar of Husserlian phenomenology in the Western tradition, who had been inspired by a prior grounding in the Vedāntic tradition at the University of Calcutta (12), Mohanty thereby repositioned Indian thought beyond problems of truthfulness and accuracy (which he saw as a subfield), in relation to the broader idea that experience forms a framing medium for all phenomena. In Mohanty's view, much of the apparent metaphysics of the tradition consisted in attempts to produce 'a descriptive phenomenology of consciousness' (13), and debates about language, perception, and logic, as well as the different schools of metaphysics, all grew out of this project.

Mohanty (1991: 18) saw this foundationalism as informal and roughly conceived in outline only; he doubted that it rose to any systematically meta-theoretical attempt to ground rationality in transcendental argument, that is, in any argument for some self-evident certainty that is presupposed by reasoning and can provide its legitimating ground. Others, however, have seen both a 'metaphysics of experience' and something approximating to a Kantian form of transcendental argument in the Sāṃkhya-Yoga tradition, implying that the search for certainty found its true culmination not in inference about the structures of the universe, nor in logic, but in the transcendental conditionality of experience itself as the 'field or domain within which empirical reality exists' (Burley 2007: 13). Still others, such as David Lawrence and Sthaneshwar Timalsina, have explored the ways in which this consciousness-based orientation of Western thought led to distinctive arguments for the existence of the self and its universal nature as a ground of reality.

This narrative interprets the Indian history of philosophy in terms of a defining methodological approach that yielded insights into the experiential conditions of reason itself at certain historical points. It also provided a philosophical point of reference that could be used to compare Indian and Western approaches to reason, allowing cross-cultural observers to map Indian ideas in relation to the phenomenologically grounded philosophies of thinkers such as Kant (Burley 2007), Husserl (Mohanty 1991), Heidegger (Isayeva 1993; Grimes 2008) and Gadamer (Frazier 2008).

## Power and normative theory

While many have been excited to explore the *content* of the Indian intellectual traditions, others have noted that the *social history* of Indian philosophy could easily be seen as one of elite prestige and power. Specifically philosophical forms of theorizing were largely limited to Brahmins, whose training, production of texts and forums of exchange remained far removed from the experience of the vast majority of Hindus. For most, their output only became accessible through their popular incorporation into narratives, visuals and dramatic depictions or through the interpretations taught by gurus. More pertinent to the everyday life of the masses were the immensely prolific knowledge-traditions or 'sciences' of India, captured in the 'śāstra' genre and in other manuals. One might see the real conveyors of Indian theory, as an applied science, here. Over the course of a period of composition that stretched from the last centuries BCE through to the first millennium CE manuals composed by the Sanskrit-speaking elite were the medium by which were spread skills concerned with medicine (*āyurveda*), linguistics and grammar (*vyākaraṇa* etc.), aesthetics (*nāṭya-śāstra, alaṃkāra-śāstra*) and plastic arts (*śilpa-śāstra*), mathematics and astronomy (*jyotiṣa*), architecture and city-planning (*vāstu-śāstra*), good living (*kāma-śāstra*), politics and economics (*nīti-śāstra* and *artha-śāstra*) and other areas. This consolidation of a culture of 'sciences' has fascinated scholars seeking to liberate Hindu culture from the 'orientalist' assumption that it is fundamentally religious in its concerns.

These relatively secular fields of knowledge accorded well with the Marxist and post-Marxist critiques of ideology as a sociopolitical tool, due to the way in which they became important pillars of cosmopolitan civilization, rebranding reasoning as part of a new India in the key period of growth between the empires of the Mauryas (322–185 BCE) and the Guptas (c. 320–550 CE). Largely composed in the scholarly language of Sanskrit, they also served the specific interests of the Brahminical community by marking those sciences as a product springing from Vedic cultural sources. Thus significant sociopolitical authority-claims were implicit in such sciences. Sheldon Pollock (2006) has noted that language itself functioned as a sort of meta-theoretical medium for concretizing theoretical traditions in a single fixed text, and claiming them for a particular community. In Sanskrit textual sciences, theory was largely shorn of aesthetic creativity and subjective interpretation in favour of what Nietzsche termed the 'unity, identity, permanence, substance' to which reason may aspire (cited in Pollock 2006: 4–5). Reason was recast as a matter of patronage and power, rather than one of open speculation on metaphysical underpinnings or spiritual goals.

Here reason is 'revealed' as a normative tool by which individuals are assimilated into controlled forms of life that constitute society itself. Some genealogies of the Indian sciences see an 'Enlightenment'-like turn in history, in which the power of tradition was challenged by the gradual individualization of intellectual voices in Early Modern Indian culture. The intertextual complexity of later commentarial traditions allowed space for individual innovation, while the matrices of 'discipline, sect, lineage, community' together disrupted the unilateral force of authority in such a way as to empower individual authors to express their own innovative ideas (Minkowski et al. 2015: 2). In such narratives society and the individual are opposed to each other, and theory can serve both as a tool of power and also, eventually, as a medium of innovative dissent.

These and other genealogies of Indian theory have been told by scholars in India and in the West over the course of the past half-century or more. Hindu reasoning is interpreted as the expression of a primal curiosity to explain the universe that is native to human nature. But in its unfolding through discussion, speculation, teaching and text, the curiosity of reason becomes a rich generator of cosmologies and metaphysical visions that have continued to grow to the present day. Classical Hindu reasoning, then, can be seen as a culture seeking accounts of reality, the certainties of logic, or the different kind of certainties afforded by phenomenological self-reflection. It can also be seen as a self-creating tradition of theoretical 'truths', operating for the benefit of a particular community.

But in each of these cases, a particular idea of *what reason is* and *what theorizing seeks to achieve* is present. Thus a fundamental analysis of the *kinds* of reason is possible, assessing them into terms of the values that they exemplify in themselves. This results in an 'aesthetics of reason' that understands different cultural contexts in terms of the values, moods and hopes that each model encapsulates. Michel Foucault (1989: xix) offers an example of an aesthetics of reason when he notes that Western thought is fascinated with ordered theoretical schemes that create a 'utopia', 'a fantastic, untroubled region' of our thoughts, filled with the mental equivalents of 'vast avenues, superbly planted gardens, countries where life is easy'. So too, each of the narratives of Hindu reasoning in this chapter points to a different aesthetic of reasoning (as well as a different method, community and function). They include (in metaphysical traditions) the hunger for a sublime view of the universe, a cosmological account that underpins soteriology by sublimating the individual into something larger. In scepticism's straining of philosophers to arbitrate between different positions we see a combative desire to secure an unassailable truth. In the examination of consciousness one can see a desire for the visceral satisfaction of self-evident knowledge secured through meditative reflection.

These and other 'aesthetics of reasoning' exist within philosophical and theoretical traditions, lending them their standards and goals, and in exploring classical views we will hear the voice of cultures that were hungry to understand the world, and undergo the changes such understanding can work upon the human mind.

# 7

# Becoming the world through reason

The Brahmin authors of the *Aitareya Upaniṣad* assured their audience that

> [k]nowledge (*prajnāna*) is the eye of all that, and on knowledge it is founded. Knowledge is the eye of the world, and knowledge, the foundation. (3.1.4)

This strong valuation of knowledge sees it as something generated not merely by the effort of human minds, but as something which exists in its own right embedded at the core of the world itself. It reflected the way in which the late Vedic classical view tended to see the world of ideas, taking it to be possessed its own autonomous being as one of the many materials of reality. This attitude was motivated in part by a Brahminical sense of identity; they promoted themselves as the bearers of knowledge – ritual, scientific and metaphysical – in a broader range of communities where they needed to justify their value. Where others could peddle practical skills or trade resources in the marketplaces of first millennium Northern India, Brahmins provided unique access to a realm of 'immortal' resources: ideas, understandings and explanations. Knowledge, in the Upaniṣads, is something that subsists at the centre of the cosmos, accessible to humans – but not dependent on them.

This way of understanding reason strikes a very different tone from later debates that brought human knowledge into question. In this early period in the history of Hindu reasoning, the epistemological worries about validity that characterized later debates between Buddhist, Nyāya and subsequent *māya-vāda* or 'illusory' approaches, were preceded by a view that saw reasoning as a visionary faculty, manifesting real structures immanent in ourselves and in the cosmos. The texts that we will look at in this chapter approach knowledge with a striking optimism about its special status in reality. It appears as a valuable resource embedded beneath the visible appearances of conventional life, waiting to be excavated by sentient creatures. Johannes Bronkhorst (2011: 3–4) has spoken of early Vedic belief in a 'correspondence principle' linking language directly with the reality it seeks to capture by recourse to the 'original unity of names and forms' (citing, e.g. *Bṛhad Āraṇyaka Upaniṣad* 1.4.7). Here we investigate the development of this idea to explore the discovery of inference (*anumāṇa*), and its implication: that reason itself, and the theories it constructs, can be construed as a direct grasp on the widest truths of the cosmos. Ideas then become a sort of embodiment for the self as reasoner.

While the development of logic and formal epistemology in Indian thought has rightly received much attention from scholars, it is also important to recognize the ideals of reasoning that governed the Vedāntic tradition and many of the cultures that were influenced by it. Understanding the way a society reasons, imagines, creates new ideas and bestows its belief on particular theories is a cornerstone for understanding its picture of the world, and we will see that understanding of the cosmologies, metaphysics and 'theories of everything' that emerged from the Vedic tradition is ill served by an overemphasis on scepticism in India. The hymns and ritual material in the Vedas have received much attention, but the Upaniṣads, Sūtras and the nature of their diverse philosophical and doctrinal claims have earned only occasional critical attention from scholars, although Paul Deussen (1908) sought to construct an overall 'philosophy of the Upaniṣads', and Wilhelm Halbfass (1991) more cautiously explored elements of Upaniṣadic thought in the wider perspective of the Vedic tradition, while more recently Jonardon Ganeri ([2007] 2012) has tried to unravel questions about the self that were developed in dialogue with Buddhist thought, and Brian Black (2007: 170) has explored Upaniṣadic doctrines as means of 'establishing oneself as a successful Brahmin' among students, competitors, patrons and wives.

One recurrent theme in the Upaniṣads is the capacity of the mind to perceive causes and connections, to speculate and generalize. Yet this is a theme that has received little attention. In these texts, we see theorizing depicted *positively*, as a way of eliciting the essence of things and capturing the world in a thought. The mirror of Greek classical studies can be held up here: Pierre Hadot's (1995: 60) work on the roots of early Greek *philosophia* highlighted the practical spiritual goals of '*forming*' rather than '*informing*' the individual that lay behind the schools of Plato and Aristotle, Epicurus and Zeno, the Cynics and the Skeptics. Like Hadot's early Greek stoic and epicurean philosophies, the philosophers of the Vedas and early Sūtras used their rational practice both to shape the self and also to access realities they believed objectively to exist in the cosmos around them. The broader underlying realities they 'discovered' through their visionary capacity of philosophical analysis formed the basis of much philosophical material in the Upaniṣads, Sūtras, *Mahābhārata* and later philosophical literature. Reason is repeatedly taken as the point of access to a reality that elevates the human individual beyond his merely local concerns. As such, in the following chapters we explore a doctrine that speaks to the self-understanding of all theorizing, ancient and modern.

## The importance of knowledge

In these early Hindu contexts, one can trace a process of assessing the value of knowledge itself. The pedagogical traditions entrenched in Brahminical communities – many of which had become professionally reliant on esoteric knowledge as their trade in a complex and competitive culture (see Black 2007) – cultivated considerable reflection on the nature and uses of knowledge. In part, this was a result of the accumulated information amassed and passed down in Vedic ritual culture: the *Chāndogya Upaniṣad* lists a range of fields of knowledge including the four vedas and the *Smṛti* texts (narrative histories), grammar, mathematics, fortune-telling, treasure-finding, debate, astrology and the knowledge specifically associated with Gods, Brahmins, ancestors, spirits, kings and others (7.1.2–3). This body of wisdom, so voluminous and comprehensive, is nevertheless contrasted rather unfavourably with the conceptual understanding of the *ātman* which, as we have seen, can signify 'self', 'body' or 'essence'. A number of characters in the *Chāndogya* hope to acquire this knowledge of the true 'self' of things, and the text as a whole repeatedly tries to convey it using diverse analogies, thought-exercises and arguments.

The desire for this more abstract kind of knowledge is different from that which seeks the accumulated practical learning of the Vedic culture, and it may have seen itself as a counterpoint to thinkers who doubted the value of conventional concepts, and early radical sceptics such as the Cārvākas who questioned any but the most immediate of perceptions. Even if our everyday perceptions are wrong, then abstract ideas – the concepts themselves, in Plato's terms – seem to transcend the vagaries of life. In contrast to those early practical and sceptical approaches to knowledge, the Upaniṣads display a fascination with the positive ability of reason to reach beyond the empirical world that is immediately present to the senses, and grasp a larger – even universal – portion of reality. The *Aitareya Upaniṣad* contains a list of the cognitive faculties of the mind. The detailed taxonomy hints at the various modalities of thought that were of interest at the time, but all are said to be mere products of the 'self' which is here seen as an underlying power or source of knowledge, that *by which* one sees and which is also the foundation (*brahman*) of cognition for all living beings:

> 'Who is this self (ātman)?' – that is how we venerate.
>
> Which of these is the self? Is it that by which one sees? Or hears? Or smells odours? Or utters speech? Or distinguishes between what is tasty and what is not? Is it in the heart and the mind? Is it awareness? Perception? Discernment? Cognition? Wisdom? Insight? Steadfastness?, Thought? Reflection? Drive? Memory? Intention? Purpose? Will? Love? Desire? But these are various forms of cognition. ..
>
> It is *brahman* . . . It is everything that has life – those that move, those that fly, and those that are stationary.
>
> Knowledge is the eye of all that, and on knowledge it is founded. Knowledge is the eye of the world, and knowledge, the foundation. Brahman is knowing.
>
> It is with this self consisting of knowledge that he went up from this world and, having obtained all his desire in the heavenly world up there, became immortal. (3.1–4)

Various forms of reflection are subtly differentiated, and the way in which the terminology employs marginally different variations on the same roots (e.g. *saṃjñānam ājñānaṃ vijñānaṃ prajñānaṃ*) heightens the sense that a single unity must underlie the wide-ranging variation in thought-forms. Great claims are made for this knowledge of the foundation of knowledge, in relation not only to the knower for whom it provides a 'self', but to the world.

Already in this early Upaniṣad, we see a culture that is self-reflexively seeking to understand the nature of thought and the realities with which it deals. The scholarly explanation for placing such high value on knowledge is usually that knowledge of the true nature of the self provided the requisite basis for theories of the immortality of the (essential part of) the self in one of a range of forms 'including being preserved in the social memory, becoming one with the essential being of the universe, and surviving death in the heavenly world' (Black 2007: 10–11). But this answer seems inadequate to the conception of immortality that is at work here. The doctrine of liberation from rebirth does not seem to have been fully formed in the early Upaniṣads, and the idea of *mokṣa* or liberation as some form of union, return, reassimilation or identification with the underlying reality of things is not defined with any philosophical clarity. It seems that, if we do not read later versions of the doctrine from the Vedāntic theologians backwards into the Upaniṣads, then the process by which knowledge leads to immortality remains something of a puzzle.

But the answer may lie in the special relation between a thinking being and the ideas that it thinks. The version of self here is a complex mental being embodied in a wide range of mental processes including synthetic awareness (*saṃjñāna*), noticing (*ājñāna*), discriminative analysis or understanding (*vijñāna*), cognitive perception (*prajñāna*), mental 'seeing' (*dṛṣṭi*), reflective activity (*mati*), idea or judgement (*manīṣā*) and mental power or wisdom (*medhā*), as well as qualitative differentiations of steadfastness (*dhṛti*), resolution (*saṇkalpa*), desire (*kāma*) or will (*vasa*). The distinctions that are made in this passage testify to the subtle complexity embedded in Sanskrit concepts of what in English might simply be called 'thought'. This text treats thought as a complex reality of different modes.

But this passage goes beyond the simple cataloguing and celebration of thought to consider the way in which it can serve as an 'eye' or 'foundation' of the world, extending the individual's reach beyond what is merely present in one's current perceptions to embrace unseen realities. This is quite a distinctive goal, and marks out one trend within the Upaniṣads, somewhat different in nature to the goals of other taxonomies of cognition that are aimed at a gradual *pratyāhāra* or withdrawal of the self into a still state of non-cognition (as, for instance, in the *asparśa-yoga* of the *Muṇḍaka, Taittirīya,* or *Maitrāyaṇīya Upaniṣad*s; King 1995: 141–5). Rather, the Aitareya's list looks beneath those states to an underlying capacity for knowledge that is accorded a unique and exalted position in the cosmos as a whole.

In order to understand this we must again interrogate the assumption that the 'self' here necessarily signifies the human person or soul. We have seen that *ātman* as it was used in the Upaniṣads encompassed meanings ranging from the concrete idea of the body to more abstract ideas of the essence or vital principle of a thing; in one portion of the earlier *Aitareya Āraṇyaka*, the *ātman* is identified with the living essence of things – consciousness in humans, sap in plants (2.3.2). Here the use seems to highlight a distinction between the *apparent* identity of a thing and the idea of its 'essence' in the technical philosophical sense of that to which a thing's *true* identity is anchored. Olivelle (1996b: 363–4) notes that the word 'venerate', used in this passage (from the Sanskrit verbal root *upa-ās*), is often used to signify recognition of one thing as something else, or of the true identity of something, from which some ritual or spiritual benefit results. In earlier Vedic usage this reflected the idea that the efficacy of symbolic elements in ritual depends upon knowing their implied meaning. But in statements such as this in the *Aitareya Upaniṣad* passage 'veneration' is applied not to a specific item but to *all* things. Here, the text suggests that correct knowledge of the true identity of things produces a kind of essential knowledge that is the 'eye of the world', bringing all things within the purview of the knower.

A similar account of knowledge is given in the *Praśna Upaniṣad*, in which six men seek knowledge and are rewarded with a teaching about the 'highest' self, a self understood as that which grounds perception and by which one can 'become' or 'enter' the world:

> This intelligent self, namely the person – who is really the one who sees, feels, hears, smells, tastes, thinks, understands, and acts – rests on the highest, that is, the imperishable self ... Whoever perceives that shining imperishable devoid of shadow, body, or blood – whoever so perceives my friend – knowing the whole, he becomes the whole world. On this there is the verse:
>
> That on which the breaths and beings,
> And, with all the deities, the intelligent self;
> Whoever knows that, my friend, as the imperishable;
> He, knowing the whole world,
> Has entered the whole world indeed. (4.9–11)

Here the notion of perceiving the imperishable self is used synonymously with knowing the whole, and becoming the whole world. The phrase 'knowing the whole, he becomes the whole world' has an ambiguous meaning, but it appears to imply that knowledge is itself a kind of assimilation to that which is known. As we will see, it is tempting to interpret this in terms of later ideas in the Nyāya realist school which held that perception consists in a sort of extramission or contact between the mind's perceptual faculty and its objects; White (2009b: 71) argues that this externalization of the self through perception is part of a wider model of mind as something naturally prone to exceed its boundaries and interact with the world via physical contact and entry. It is difficult to determine what precise epistemology underlay this text, but we will see that conceptions of perception as kind of extended extramission – an installing of oneself into that which is perceived *and comprehended* – present one way of understanding this claim.

The growing fascination with language in post-Vedic literature offers another way of understanding the idea that knowledge of something allows us to *become* it. This interest in the capacity of language to capture abstract ideas prefigured the grammatical tradition's development of a 'metalanguage' designed to reflect the very structures of meaning. Sanskrit conceptual forms were invested with a kind of 'creative and infinite *energeia*' according to which they were able to expand and encompass ever-new contents and ever-new meta-levels of abstract thought (103). This idea voiced an increasing confidence about the capacities of language to capture the hidden abstract realities that stand alongside the concrete objects of everyday perception. According to this model, the knowledge that is of such importance in these early texts pertains to that metaphysical, abstract realm that the Vedic community began to explore around the middle of the first millennium BCE, and that was also central to their livelihoods and cultural identity.

These passages, then, suggest four important beliefs about knowledge that existed in that period:

1. That knowledge is not merely a tool of the mind, but exists in its own right, with its own autonomous reality
2. That it gives access to the world as a whole, allowing the reasoner to see with the all-encompassing 'eye' of knowledge itself
3. That the self is not a thing that possesses or contains such knowledge, but that it *consists* of it, being constituted from its ideas
4. That it exists at a 'pervasive' level that is not subject to the same conditions of finitude and change as physically embodied entities; its materiality is of a different, 'imperishable' kind

The final point is important for linking the new knowledge economy to the new goals of immortality: it suggests a 'Plato-like' belief that generalized knowledge enables the mind to move beyond the particulars of the world towards wider and more stable conceptual or 'eidetic' realities. As a result, the universality of ideas became a reference point for conceptions of eternal being.

## Language, liberation and the world of ideas

One key tenet of this view was the idea that knowledge does indeed correspond to reality – a position that was coming to be vigorously attacked by the Cārvākas and Buddhists. Reason is not arbitrary, but a reflection of 'the close connection between words and things' (see Bronkhorst (2011: 4–5) on the *Bṛhad Āraṇyaka Upanīṣad*, the *Taittirīya Brāhmaṇa*, the *Śatapatha Brāhmaṇa* and the significance of *nāma-rūpa* (name and form) in Vedic cosmogonic thought). For those who assumed a connection between the name and actual form of a thing, language – or at least Sanskrit – could be approached as an index of truth, rather than as a mere convention. As Jonardon Ganeri (2006: 1) remarks, in this worldview:

> Words have powers, as do the people who understand them. A word has the power to stand in for or take the place of a thing. Vibrations in the air, or ink marks on paper, manage somehow to act as substitutes for people and places, planets and atoms, thoughts and feelings. It is to this extraordinary function that the Sanskrit term for 'meaning' calls attention: śakti – the power or capacity of a word to stand for an object.

This fits with a theme in earlier Vedic literature that Laurie Patton (2005: 142–51) terms 'the quest for mental [and verbal] power'. If sacrifices tried to capture the gifts of the gods for human benefit, language could be used to capture higher realities. Recalling the poetic self-understanding of the original Vedic hymns and the tradition of Vedic writing that they establish, Patton shows that this quest for mental power underlies the intense energy that was devoted to speech (*vāc*) and mantras. The *Taittirīya Upaniṣad* highlights the phonetic context of unwritten oral discussion, and the text marvels at the way in which simple sounds produced with the help of the mouth enable the mind to capture meaning, and thereby the vast forces of the cosmos itself:

> In this space here within the heart lies the immortal and golden person consisting of the mind (*puruṣa manomāyaḥ*). And this thing that hangs like a nipple between the two palates, it is Indra's passage. Bursting through the two halves of the skull at the point where the hairs part, he establishes himself in the fire by making the call *bhur*, in the wind by making the call *bhuvas*, in the sun by making the call *suvar*, and in brahman by making the call *mahas*. He obtains sovereignty and becomes the lord of the mind, the lord of speech, the lord of sight, the lord of hearing, and the lord of perception. (2.6)

Here speech is depicted as the explosion of the mental self out of the heart, and the words thus produced are effective in establishing the speaker 'in' (*pratitiṣṭhati* – literally, 'placing to stand within') that which he names, including the natural forces of the cosmos – fire, wind, sun, *brahman*. The result of this speaking of concepts is that the mental self becomes 'lord' of the faculties of knowledge (mind, speech, sight, hearing, perception). Black (2007: 50–2) has interpreted the *Taittirīya Upaniṣad* as a celebration of its Brahmin authors, and in order to achieve this the text highlights the importance of the word as a device by which the mind becomes that which it knows; the elements of nature and also the far-subtler object that is the ground of reality (*brahman*).

It is important to note that it is not union with *brahman* that stands at the culmination of this passage, but rather the activities of thought – mind, speech, sight, hearing, perception – which establish the speaker *in* the world not as a mere part, but as a sovereign. This is a form of liberation that consists not merely in assimilation to a wider reality, but in this case at least, to a degree of mastery. The word-borne launching of the self into reality and with it the acquisition of a position of sovereignty over nature and thought indicate a special form of embodiment in the cosmos. One is not merely participating in the world here: the self has become the world in its generality. The text continues to confirm that the ultimate goal, as envisioned in this passage at least, is to unite with a form of foundation that has existence in truth, breath and mind:

> And thereafter, this is what he becomes – the *brahman* whose body is space (*akāśaśarīraṃ*), whose self is truth (*satyātma*), whose pleasure ground is the lifebreath (*prāṇarāmaṃ*), and whose joy is the mind (*manānandam*); the *brahman* who is completely tranquil and immortal. (*Taittirīya Upanīṣad* 1.6.2)

This passage is part of a 'general preoccupation with the transmission of knowledge' as explicitly linked to the importance of Vedic education (Black 2007: 46–52), but it also makes the point that aided by the tool of language, thought could be expanded to cosmic scale, establishing the self as a new being with a new sphere of sovereignty.

This faculty of self-expansion stands alongside the faculties of self-control and self-creation seen in the previous section's views about agency and the body, and it provided part of the intellectual capital that the class of Brahminical scholars carried into the well-appointed courts of new kingdoms. These technologies of the self replaced the old goods of *ritual knowledge* that possessed a diminished value in unorthodox '*nāstika*' non-Vedic cultures. Witzel (1997) described the shift in Brahminical status and rhetoric, as certain lineages colonized the 'new world' of the eastern Videha region. This knowledge had, of course, to be guarded as a matter of socio-economic necessity; the Upaniṣads are full of stories that dramatize education as a process of gatekeeping in which teachers such as the Brahmin Uddālaka Āruṇi and King Janaka or deities such as Yama (*death*), or even the ultimate reality itself (*brahman*), gradually reveal knowledge to their pupils in such a way as to display the power that it bestows. Brian Black (2007: 39) has illustrated these concerns by reference to the depiction of relations among Brahmins and their pupils as the 'primary means of controlling and delimiting knowledge'. Knowledge is power, prestige and commodity in these contexts.

Nevertheless, it would stray far from the self-understanding of these texts to assume that sociopolitical power was the whole story behind the idea that knowledge is the 'eye of the world'. One sign of this is that the style of knowledge transmission seems to have shifted from rote learning in the earlier stages of the Vedas, to shared explanatory reasoning, or in other words, *understanding* by the time of the Upaniṣads. The discussions depicted in the Upaniṣads show that – in an ideal situation at least – the onus, whether from father to son, husband to wife, Brahmin to Brahmin, teacher to pupil or king to courtier, was on explanation as a gradual process of working through steps of reasoning that together lead one to *understand* something better through the discovery of an underlying theoretical level. Deussen ([1906] 2000) interpreted the culture of knowledge that both generated the Upaniṣads, and was self-consciously depicted within them, as a culture primarily aimed at knowledge of the self. But these discussions seem equally concerned with knowledge in its own right as a form of reality that overarches and contains wholes that ordinarily would far surpass the bounds of the individual mind. The un-knowing mind might see and identify each tree before it, but the knowing mind comprehends the whole forest, and in doing so is itself expanded.

Knowledge implies possession, but understanding is quite a different process that entails the transformation of self and of one's relationship with the object of thought. The didactic cultures depicted in these texts dramatize this procession of reasoned understanding towards a conceptual broadening of the scope of thought. More than being merely a currency able to procure immortality, knowledge, then, was able to connect self with world – to *transform* self into world. This idea may sound familiar; many scholars have interpreted the Upaniṣads in terms of a central idea that *ātman* is *brahman*, self is world. This, however, is quite a different kind of identification and unity from that assumed by later Vedāntins and read back through time into the text. It is not simply an identification of the microcosm (*ātman*) with the macrocosm (*brahman*) as Brian Smith (1994: 12) suggested on the basis of earlier Vedic ritual ideas, for the *ātman* must achieve identification with *brahman* through knowledge that specifically 'places it within' that which is known. Nor does this seem to signify a merging into *brahman* through dissolution of one's substance or mind, for the state acquired is characterized by sovereignty rather than loss of self. By contrast with other forms of union more widely associated with Vedānta, this suggests a distinctive conception of the unity of self with whatever is known – fire, wind, sun and *brahman* – through words and the conceptual grasp that they impart.

This particular idea of knowledge as a medium 'in' which things are able to subsist occurs repeatedly. *Praśna Upaniṣad* 4.11 uses the verb *viś*, 'to enter' (often associated with possession), to speak of the process by which 'knowing the whole world', one 'has entered the whole world indeed', and in an earlier passage in *Praśna Upaniṣad* 4 this idea is given greater definition: the *mental* person within the self perceives everything by day, sending out rays that grasp the world and retract in dream so that it can relive it all by night, containing within itself the world:

> [W]hich are the ones that go to sleep within a person here? Which are the ones that keep awake in him? Which of these deities sees dreams? Who experiences this bliss? And which is the one in which all these are established?' He told Sauryāyaṇī: 'As, when the sun is setting, all the rays of light gather together within that glowing orb and shoot out again every time it rises, so, Gārgya, all of them gather together within the highest deity – the mind ...'

> There, in sleep, this deity experiences his greatness. He sees again whatever he had seen before; he hears again the very things he has heard before; and he experiences over again what he has experienced before in various places and in remote regions. Being himself the whole world, he sees the whole world – things he has seen and things he has not seen, things he has heard and things he has not heard, things he has experienced and things he has not experienced, the real and the unreal. (4.1–2, 5)

It is this person who knows and 'enters' the whole world, both identifying with it and transcending its particularities. Again, there is a striking difference from the self-as-consciousness conceived in later Vedānta as a non-dual reality without content, divorced from perceptions and thoughts. This is a self that unifies with the world precisely insofar as it *imagines and understands it.* This is an idea echoed in the *Chāndogya Upaniṣad,* which also takes language as its medium for thinking about the extension of self into the world:

> Now, then, man is undoubtedly made of resolve. What a man becomes on departing from here after death is in accordance with his resolve in this world. So he should make this resolve: 'This self (ātman) of mine that lies deep within my heart – it is made of mind; the vital functions (prāṇa) are its physical form; luminous is its appearance; the real is its intention; space is its essence (ātman); it contains all actions, all desires, all smells, and all tastes; it has captured this whole world; it neither speaks nor pays any heed . . .
>
> 'This self (ātman) of mine that lies deep within my heart – it contains all actions, all desires, all smells, and all tastes; it has captured this whole world.' (3.14.1–4)

This seems to be one of the original senses in which the *ātman* is able to unite with the world; it is precisely through its capacities of perception, imagination and 'knowledge' – here defined as a capacity of comprehending – that it is able to achieve a union and self-transformation into something that transcends its infinite locus. The more yogically inclined Upaniṣads emphasize the idea of a withdrawal of the mental capacities into a 'pure' self; this model is described in the *Muṇḍaka Upaniṣad,* a later and somewhat anti-Vedic text that seeks to establish a new identity for the independent tradition of 'Vedānta' (literally, the end or fulfilment of the Veda). It speaks of a self that 'cannot be grasped, by teachings or by intelligence, or even by great learning', sought by ascetics 'purified by the discipline of renunciation', to become fully liberated' and 'freed from name and appearance' (3.2.3, 6–7). That conception may represent a later (or concurrent alternative) understanding of liberation influenced by the 'pure-consciousness' idea of the self that had been advocated by classical

Sāṃkhya. But in the strand of texts concerned with knowledge, conceptual knowledge is seen not as extraneous to the 'mental self' of the Upaniṣads, but as a part of it, and it has the quality of being self-transformative because to know a thing entails incorporating it into the self; world-*knowing* is world-*becoming*. A similar view of knowledge was proposed in the twentieth century by the hermeneutic philosopher Hans-Georg Gadamer (2004, 1981, etc.): he highlighted the transformative nature of understanding, developing this insight out of his phenomenological analysis of the way in which we experience knowledge. Where Gadamer drew on a meticulous European genealogy of concepts of truth that reached from Plato and Aristotle to Renaissance Humanism, Enlightenment philosophy and the modern natural sciences, here we see the classical stages of a genealogy of Hindu conceptions of truth as conceived from the perspective of human processes of understanding – it is a practice with important implications for who we are.

## Anumāṇa and the inductive power of the mind

But how is it that the mind, using the tool of language, is able to capture complex relations within a single generalizing concept? A move towards deeper analysis of what it is that allows us to abstract and assimilate the 'essence' of things came with more far-reaching inquiry into precisely what it is that concepts do. In *Muṇḍaka Upaniṣad* 1.3–7 a wealthy layperson called Śaunaka asks, 'What is it, my lord, by knowing which a man comes to know this whole world?' The answer he is given lists lower knowledge which consists in a range of different 'sciences' then recognized as fields of knowledge, including the four divisions of the Vedic texts, phonetics, ritual instructions, grammar, etymology, metrics and astronomy. But highest knowledge, by which one grasps the all-pervading reality from which all things spring, lies at an explanatory 'invisible' layer of reality:

> Two types of knowledge a man should learn … the higher is that by which one grasps the imperishable. What cannot be seen, what cannot be grasped, without color, without sight or hearing, without hands or feet; What is eternal and all-pervading, extremely minute, present everywhere – That is the immutable, which the wise fully perceive. (1.4–6)

This might be taken to indicate a non-conceptual reality that cannot be seen or grasped, but it also reflects claims that were made in the *Sāṃkhya Kārikā* about a special kind of knowledge of subtle realities. Gerald Larson ([1987] 2014: 5), citing Franklin Edgerton, has suggested that Sāṃkhya originally referred to any 'way of salvation by knowledge', but that it was devoid of 'any system of metaphysical truth whatever'. Yet a more specific meaning can be discerned in the epistemologically systematic reflections found in the Upaniṣads and in the classical Sāṃkhya of the *Kārikā*. This kind of knowledge was specifically concerned with finding pervasive qualities that combined diverse phenomena into a larger, shared reality. *Taittirīya Upaniṣad* 1.3 categorizes knowledge as one of the 'large-scale combinations' that shape the world around us:

> [W]e will explain the hidden connection (*upaniṣad*) of combination with reference to five topics – the worlds, the lights, knowledge (*vidyam*), progeny, and the self (*ātman*).[1] They call these the 'large-scale combinations'.
>
> ... With reference to knowledge – the preceding word is the teacher, the following word is the pupil, their union is knowledge, and their link is instruction. So it is with reference to knowledge. (1.3.1–3)

This text seems again to be concerned with the value of knowledge of particular words, but here it is their ability to identify *connections and relations* ('*sandhi*' – a word also used to denote linguistic combinations) that is placed under the lens. As is often the case, the identity of the 'they' to whom the text refers is unclear, but the idea of a large-scale combination (*mahā-saṃdhā*) here reflects the way in which particular elements or ideas are able to combine in relationships that create new, broader concepts. 'Combining' is glossed as gathering into a succinct and possess-able form, and words here act as a 'handle' or 'support' (*ārambhaṇa*) for larger things so that they may be 'carried' mentally, as they do in the well-known passage in *Chāndogya Upaniṣad* 6.1.4–6 to which we will return. After an interlude in which the *Taittirīya*'s Brahmin author calls for more students and the fame that they bring, the text carries on its train of thought by hailing those words and ideas that form a 'body' by uniting other ideas that are their 'limbs'. The same idea is found in *Chāndogya Upaniṣad* 3.18, and in each case the image of a body serves as a metaphor for the concept-uniting connections that link things into a single new 'self' or conceptual identity.

Staal (1995) notes an apparent tension within the *Taittirīya Upaniṣad* between such passages and the more well-known verse at 2.4 which declares a contrasting scepticism about any language that attempts to describe *brahman:* it argues that 'before they reach it, words turn back, together with the mind'. This is an attitude that he aligns with Buddhist culture (123) and it is possible that this section derives from a different source and possibly a different period from other parts of the Upaniṣad. But on Staal's reading the tension between the earlier affirmation of the combinatory power of language, and later doubts that *brahman* can be captured in words, dissolves if one takes it to be *ordinary* language that is turned back, rather than abstract thinking about associative relations and underlying foundations – theoretical language, in essence – which is what had emerged among the Brahmin intelligentsia.

Explicit awareness of the nature of generalized abstract reasoning seems to have developed 'through a detour' via reflection on ritual language as an exercise that had been passed down to priests and their pupils (Frauwallner 1973: 27). The appropriation of the idea of *bandhu*s, connections thought to link symbols with their signified objects, often by virtue of an innate formal similarity rather than merely conventional agreement, was central in spurring analysis of *analogy* as a mechanism that aids our understanding of the underlying qualities of things. When we are told that reality is 'like' clay moulded into different shapes, we learn from the juxtaposition of the two ideas about an underlying shared quality of mutability. The origins of this idea most likely lay in the development of Vedic conceptions of analogical or symbolic links. At the beginning of the *Bṛhad Āraṇyaka Upaniṣad*, a text with strong continuities with the earlier Vedic ritual culture, a *bandhu* is simply asserted as a symbolic equivalence between the horse used in the Aśvameda ritual and the sea (1.1.2). But in 4.1.2 *bandhu*s are rationalized in terms of language's ability to convey knowledge of distant things. Here the Brahmin Yajñavalkya explains the 'abode and foundation' of *brahman* in terms of a number of key cosmic constituents, beginning with speech:

> 'Speech itself is [*brahman*'s] abode, and space is its foundation. One should venerate it as knowledge.'
>
> 'What constitutes knowledge, Yājñavalkya?'
>
> 'Speech itself, Your Majesty', he replied. 'For surely, Your Majesty, it is through speech that we come to know a counterpart [*bandhu*]. Ṛgveda, Yajurveda, Sāmaveda, the Atharva-Āṅgiras, histories, ancient tales, sciences, hidden teachings (upaniṣad), verses, aphorisms, explanations, and glosses; offerings and oblations; food and drink; this world and the next world; and all beings – it is through speech, Your Majesty, that we come to know all these. So clearly, Your Majesty, the highest *brahman* is speech. When a man knows and venerates it as such, speech never abandons him, and all beings flock to him; he becomes a god and joins the company of gods.' (4.1.2)

Much of the Vedic Āraṇyaka literature seeks to establish *bandhu*s by reference to similarities in sound, function and appearance between different things. In doing so they presume that analogical likeness – between the way things appear – is not merely an imagined relation but in fact indicates a genuine shared quality that is embedded in the essence or nature of those things. The perception of such a correspondence, then, was essentially the subtle mental intuition of a structure, thread or connection that genuinely linked entities which were otherwise distant in time and space, and causally unrelated. The consequent theory that the universe is woven with hidden networks of properties provided the basis for the 'analogy form of magic' (Frauwallner

1973: 29) used to explain Vedic ritual. But as philosophical reflection advanced, it also became aware of the mechanism of conceptual abstraction that allows us to identify these underlying structures: inductive reasoning.

The discovery of induction – the process of acquiring a new knowledge by generalizing from particular items of knowledge – played an indispensable role in satisfying the classical desire for a coherent form of theorizing that would deliver the world in a comprehensible, thought-shaped form. Most scholarship on *anumāna*, 'inference', traces its use in the Nyāya school of reasoning as a general epistemological tool for testing and amassing 'true' statements (see, for instance, Chakrabarti 2007). As a procedural rule for identifying common connections in certain phenomena, and generalizing them for use in explaining other phenomena, inference mirrors the concerns of those Western epistemological sciences that have sought, since Plato, to teach tools for finding concrete certainties in the shifting world. But the early emergence of Indian inferential traditions out of earlier processes of generalization has been little considered: Upaniṣadic ideas and the strategies of reasoning that are central to classical Sāṃkhya are generally seen merely as relatively primitive precursors to later, more concise sciences of knowledge.

Yet these earlier texts pay special attention to inference. The *Chāndogya Upaniṣad* records key realizations in the development of inductive reasoning as a way not of confirming specific items of knowledge, but of discovering illuminating generalities. In perhaps the most influential section of that compendious text, composed by priests specializing in the chanting of the hymns that accompany the rituals, the first principle of study is said to be 'the rule of substitution'. This initially signified a symbolic substitution of one thing for another in ritual practice – the establishment or use of a *bandhu* – possibly with particular reference to the way in which a single word (e.g. 'Auṃ') can stand for all other words (see Olivelle 1996a: 215). In this sense substitution remained alive as a key component in modern as in ancient Hindu ritual practice (see Michaels (2016: 74–111) on the continuity of classical ritual grammar in modern practice). In the later theories of the grammarians, substitution acquired still another meaning, coming to refer to the idea that one linguistic unit can serve as a placeholder for another.

In the *Chāndogya Upaniṣad*'s chapter six, however, it seems to designate the leap of understanding by which broader truths can be recognized – specifically through knowledge of the underlying material or essential character of a thing, such that its continuity through changes, other instances and analogous cases can be recognized:

> 'You must have surely asked about the rule of substitution' by which one hears what has not been heard before, thinks of what has not been thought of before, and perceives what has not been perceived before?'

> 'How indeed does that rule of substitution work, sir?'
>
> 'it is like this, son. By means of just one lump of clay one would perceive everything made of clay – the transformation is a verbal handle, a name [*vācārambhaṇaṃ vikāro nāmadheyaṃ*] – while the reality is just this: it's clay.'
>
> 'That, son, is how this rule of substitution works.' (6.1.3–6)

This notion of understanding the pervasive reality (here the material of clay) underlying diverse forms, in relation to which words are seen merely as items we use to get a handle on a temporary modification, provides impetus for the notion of *brahman* as an underlying material of all things by which everything is known despite flux and diversity. Here we have a core statement of the importance of induction. It goes beyond the signification of something by virtue of some *shared* feature (as in the earlier explanations of *bandhus*), to the *explanation* of something by reference to a *constitutive* feature that both defines it essentially and links it with other things. Where phonetic connections linked things by reference to non-essential characteristics such as the chance inclusion of certain sounds, these new substitutions tried to point to those qualities which are pervasive and essential in a thing insofar as they persist despite variations in the contingent name and form. This is the use of an analogy (i.e. between a lump of clay and a pot) as the basis of an inference that identifies the continuous level of truth that underlies both: clay. Uddālaka Āruṇi, the Brahmin teacher in this passage, thus advocates the analysis of objects through the following processes:

**a)** Associating such objects with different things that share some continuous feature of identity (the objects here are referred to not as autonomous 'things', but merely as temporary identities using the phrase *nāma-rūpa*, 'name-and-form'; here these would be pots, sculptures and other clay things).

**b)** Identifying the common feature that is pervasive across those cases, a constant that functions as a kind of underlying essential identity (here this would be the clay). This is done via the discriminative power to identify the essence of a thing by sifting its properties into contingent and core categories so that those features which outlive change can be identified. The terminology used to express this is the contrast between that which is merely a *vācārambhaṇa* or 'word-handle' and that which is *satya* or 'real'.

**c)** This is the quality that is then inductively generalized as present in other, as yet unforeseen, cases, providing a wider picture that allows one to perceive 'what has not been perceived before'.

**d)** Note that the point of interest in this passage is less the way in which generalization allows us to understand other pots, but the way in which it helps us to understand clay and its forms in general, that is, the result is a general ontological picture, not only an individualized specific one.

As we will see, later a form of 'epistemological induction' was developed as a way to gain valid information about particular facts. In the classic form of epistemological induction that was popularized by the Nyāya school of logic, one learns to identify the presence of fire as something that is always present when there is smoke – thereafter a specific phenomenon can be discovered from a different one. But the fire has no power to explain the underlying nature of the smoke: they are not part of the same thing, and fire does not necessarily explain smoke in terms of a more permanent and defining essence. By contrast, this deeper explanation is what Uddālaka Āruṇi seeks to give in identifying clay as the truth underlying pots of different shapes. One should not focus only on the pots where one sees clay; one should understand pots *in terms of* clay. Thus this is an induction that links things into broader realities that one can now know in advance and from afar. What the *Chāndogya Upaniṣad* introduced is a form of '*metaphysical* induction' in which the property of a thing that is generalized to secure new knowledge actually reveals an underlying level of the identity of the thing and a wider reality of which it is a part.

Not every Upaniṣadic account of the 'rule of substitution' is of this kind, but many accounts in the Upaniṣads and beyond hint at it. Earlier the *Chāndogya* (3.1–5) describes the rule of substitution in terms of the image of the sun as a repository of 'honey' made from the 'lustre, splendour, power, strength and foodstuff': in 3.5.1 the rules of substitution are said to be the 'bees' that extract the 'honey' of *brahman* from the specific teachings of those texts. In 3.18.1–2 the substitution reveals the true identity of other things with *brahman*, and this idea is further expressed through the analogy of *brahman* as a body that connects many limbs. In the subsequent passage the idea of a pervasive underlying reality is itself explained in terms of material causality, by casting *brahman* as a 'hatchling', emerged from a primeval egg, which gave rise to the universe:

> 'Brahman is the sun' – that is the rule of substitution. Here is a further explanation of it. In the beginning this world was simply what is nonexisting; and what is existing was that. It then developed and formed into an egg. It lay there for a full year and then it hatched, splitting in two ... The outer membrane is the mountains; the inner membrane, the clouds and the mist; the veins, the rivers; and the amniotic fluid, the ocean.

> Now, the hatchling that was born was the sun up there. And as it was being born, cries of joy and loud cheers rose up in celebration, as did all beings and all desires. Therefore, every time the sun rises and every time it returns, cries of joy and loud cheers rise up in celebration, as do all beings and all their hopes.
>
> When someone knows this and venerates brahman as the sun, he can certainly expect that the pleasing sound of cheering will reach his ears and delight him. (3.19)

This text is distinctive in connecting the cosmogonic stories with which the Vedas are filled with the later semantic idea of substitution. In doing so it indicates the ultimate goal of this metaphysical induction: to produce an idea that explains the changing phenomena of the whole world. *Chāndogya* 7.256 explains to its readers the way in which certain concepts can be identified with a much wider range of cosmological instances. Thus 'I', 'plenitude' and 'self' are said to be phenomena that 'extend over the whole world' and are described as words that can be 'substituted' in all places (below, above, west, east, south, and north) and in each they remain pervasively true. The author was eager to highlight the immediate benefit of this way of thinking, telling us that a man who sees in this way 'becomes completely his own master' and 'obtains complete freedom of movement in all the worlds'. In the *Kena Upaniṣad*, probably a later text, the 'rule of substitution' is similarly illustrated by an account of how *brahman* inspires a 'lightning flash' realization that he is the source of the elements' power (3–4.4), a realization that induces knowledge 'when something here comes to the mind somehow and through it the imagination suddenly recollects something' (4.5), that is, when present perceptions prompt the imagination's memory of past instances to produce a generalized conclusion rooted in the underlying common ground of those instances.

This notion that is being developed in these Upaniṣads is employed more systematically in classical uses of the idea of inference or *anumāṇa*. The *Sāṃkhya Kārikā* demonstrates a stage at which the processes that were part of the rule of substitution in Upaniṣadic thought, had come to be seen as part of the activity of 'inference', here functioning as a tool for deriving subtle (*sukṣma*) and unseen realities from observed ones. As Parrott (1985: 239) puts it, 'One could say that inferences extend the capacity of the senses into greater realms; they are the radar, microscope, and radio of the senses'. It lists three sources of valid knowledge (the mark of a thing, the precedent with which it is continuous and that which it signifies), and explains that they are able to provide knowledge of realities that are unseen:

> Inference is divided into three sources that are the sign, the possessor of that sign, and the precedent (*liṅga-liṅgi-pūrvakam*) ... The knowledge

> of non-sensory things is obtained through inference obtained from the perception of generalisation (*sāmānyataḥ*). Things that are beyond the sensory (*parokṣaṃ*) that are not established in that way can be established through scripture (*āgamāt siddham*). [The non-apprehension even of existing things can occur] from great distance, proximity, impairment of the senses, absent-mindedness, subtlety, intervention, suppression (e.g. being hidden by another thing), and mixture with another thing. [A thing's] not being perceived is due to its subtlety, not to its non-existence. It is apprehended through its effects [which are] the *mahat* (substance of material reality) and the rest. Some have the form of *prakṛti* and some have different forms. (*Sāṃkhya Kārikā* 6–8)[2]

Some of the key apparatus of what would become the later doctrine of inductive inference are in evidence here, such as the idea that certain phenomena can act as a 'sign' for others, when one is able to generalize based on preceding observations. The usefulness of this is made more explicit by offering a detailed list of the categories that can lead to a thing being as-yet-unknown.

But alongside its concerns to formalize inferential reasoning, this later text also brings into the foreground the importance of deriving broader general explanations of reality. In this case, the metaphysical form of inductive reason in the *Sāṃkhya Kārikā* leads the reader towards the concept of *prakṛti* as a procreative material underlying *all* observable phenomena. Reason is able to elicit things which are beyond the senses (*atīndriyānāṃ*) as a result of being too far (*atidūrāt*), or hidden (*abhibhavāt*) from our perceptions. But reason can also reveal those things which are *innately* imperceptible by the senses because they are of a subtle (*sukṣma*) non-sensory nature – and here the context tells that this refers to things which are of a metaphysical rather than a physical nature.

The argument here is the prelude to a presentation of the distinctive Sāṃkhya theory of *satkārya-vāda*, the doctrine that effects pre-exist in their cause, as trees (in some sense) exist *in potentio* in seeds and curd (to follow the typical Indian example) exists latently in milk. It is very possible that texts such as this one were developed in dialogue with the belief of non-Hindu Cārvāka thinkers that no unobserved realities exist (Chakrabarti 2007: 2–9). Here the whole purpose of such reasoning is to identify the unperceived (and by definition unperceivable) realities that can broaden our knowledge and provide a 'theory of everything'. The *Sāṃkhya Kārikā* identifies only part of the self (the embodied part consisting of thought and the physical body) with the underlying reality of *prakṛti* that it takes to be revealed through inference; like some portions of Upaniṣads such as the *Māṇḍūkya Upaniṣad* and some forms of Advaita Vedānta, it also posits a disembodied self. But the strain of Upaniṣadic thought that sought ways to 'become the world' through knowledge used inference as a practice for acquiring a new 'body' of pervasive and persistent ideas. Here, far from the assumption that religious liberation and discursive philosophy stand opposed in Hindu thought, reason functioned as an important tool for religious self-transformation.

Texts such as the *Chāndogya Upaniṣad* and *Sāṃkhya Kārikā* are relatively unconcerned with the derivation of certain knowledge. They celebrated induction as a powerful and exciting form of theory, yielding explanatory power rather than certainty. Unlike deduction, which involves entailment and therefore is essentially an analysis which unpacks what is already assumed to be true for a particular belief, induction is often intrinsically open-ended. Indeed, two millennia later in Europe, David Hume (1711–76) made this point in his *Enquiry Concerning Human Understanding*: while we can be sure that all sons come from women who were not barren (to borrow an old Indian example of a deduction), we can never be sure that the sun will always rise or that all daffodils will be yellow. John Stuart Mill (1806–73) believed that inductions should dispense with the middle 'generalizing' step in the process because it is too approximate and speculative. Indian thinkers were similarly uncomfortable about the existence of a 'middle term', a thing that grounds the link between one phenomenon and another, but which – if found – would require us to reason to a further ground for its link with the phenomena (for which ground a further ground would be required, leading to an infinite regress of explanation; see Matilal's (1986: 257–61) summary of this problem in Indian debates). Both Indian and European philosophers came to realize that applying inductions would always turn out to be an enterprise that is subject to various contingent conditions of probability.

But this was irrelevant to the aims of these texts: the *Chāndogya Upaniṣad*'s main goal is to make the metaphysical leap to determine what wider underlying substrate might underpin the generality of a phenomenon. In some cases the underlying cause of generality is easily observed, as in the examples of the nectar in different flowers (6.9) or the water in different rivers (6.10) or the sap that runs throughout a tree (6.11). In other cases the underlying cause is less easily seen, as in the energy that animates a fire (6.7) or the consciousness hidden within a sleeping man (6.8) or the invisible vital energy that links a seed to the banyan tree it will later become (6.12). But metaphysical induction in the Upaniṣads primarily seeks *abductive* (best fit) explanations, rather than *certainty*; it is satisfied by the way in which the new theory enables the mind to travel further, and perhaps even to the furthest reaches of our reasoning about existence itself.[3]

The fact that such inductive approaches are *ampliative* – that they involve creating predictions that reach beyond what is known with certainty, and thus involve the constructive formation of speculative theories – was not a problem for these Hindu metaphysicians who, in any case, associated such thinking with the poetic insight of seers, rather than the unassailable arguments later sought by classical and early-modern Naiyāyika logicians, or the practical predictions made by today's scientists. Indeed it was this strong thread of inductive reasoning towards 'knowledge of the world' that provided a foundation for the immensely prolific metaphysical traditions of Vedānta.

# 8

# Theories of everything

The authors of classical texts recognized that ideas of certain kinds possess the power to extend our knowledge out beyond the self, across the world, and into the deeper levels of things. But these early thinkers were not content to marvel at this capacity of reason; they aimed to construct concrete theories that would actually capture the world in an idea. For this reason, many passages in the Upaniṣads (as well as the *Ṛg* and *Atharva Vedas*) attempt not only to laud knowledge of the world, but to formulate it through some conceptualization of the whole of things. A wide range of such theories populate the Upaniṣads in the form of short metaphysical formulations or brief philosophical disquisitions, and often they are condensed into terse images and analogies. In the millennia to come they would provide the platform for the growth of many different cosmologies within the Hindu tradition of Vedāntic metaphysics. *Dṛṣṭānta* analogies developed, likening creation to the formation or division of substances, the emanation of spiderwebs, the spreading out of sparks or the transition of milk into curds. The Epics, Purāṇas and Tantras sometimes expressed these ideas in narrative form or lifted analogies directly from the Upaniṣads to be used as the basis of theological commentary and elaboration. Where Buddhism encompassed a range of distinctive concerns with epistemology but struggled with metaphysics' tendency to reify things into a single coherent picture of things, one of the Vedāntic tradition's characteristic interests would be in cosmological and metaphysical theorizing. This was the most ambitious of all purposes to which the extraordinary powers of thought could be put: the discovery of ideas able to encompass the world as a whole, and thus assimilate the self to it, assuming world as a kind of vast embodiment.

## Cosmological theories of everything

At least two different approaches were taken in the attempt to develop theories of everything. One 'naturalistic' approach either predates or parallels the philosophical thinking that came to dominate Vedānta, and it sought a single universal element of the natural world, a material or energy, for instance, to serve as the basic force animating the cosmos. Various lists of principles of reality are found in the *Atharva Veda*, Upaniṣads and in texts influenced by early Sāṃkhya, and they suggest a scramble among contemporary thinkers to identify the one thing that could explain all. The *Śvetāśvatara Upaniṣad*, for instance, begins with a list of questions that were current in its surrounding milieu, and canvases a number of possible solutions:

> What is the cause of *brahman*? Why were we born? By what do we live? On what were we established? Governed by whom, O you who know brahman, do we live in pleasure and pain, each in our own respective situation?
>
> Should we regard it as time (*kāla*), as inherent nature (*svabhāva*), as necessity (*niyati*), as chance (*yadṛccha*), as the elements (*bhūtani*), as the source of birth (*yoni*), or as the Person (*puruṣa*)? Or is it a combination (*saṃyoga*) of these? (1.1–2)

A late Upaniṣad, the *Śvetāśvatara* particularly explores theories related to Sāṃkhya, Yoga and theism, suggesting a list of components (time, essence, necessity, etc.) that also appear in other classical sources, hinting that each had its advocates in current metaphysical debate. As we have seen, early Sāṃkhya-Yoga is generally thought to have explored a wide range of possible 'primary materials' of the universe, making some of Hinduism's 'first and groping attempts at systematic thinking, which proceeded by determining and enumerating the components of anything' (Larson 1999: 4). This early Sāṃkhya approach may in turn have been part of a wider '*svabhāva-vāda*' discussion among Sāṃkhya, Cārvāka and Vedāntic thinkers seeking to account for the nature of things (see Bhattacharya (2012) on sources that oppose *yadṛccha* or 'chance' to the idea that the world unfolds according to a determining essence or *svabhāva*). A passage in the *Mahābhārata* that claims to represent the teachings of the proto-Sāṃkhya thinker Pañcaśikha gives a more extensive list that hints at an even wider range of basic cosmic constituents that later circulated among Sāṃkhya thinkers, including opposites (*dvandva-yoga*, 'linked pairs'), time (*kāla*), the five great primal elements (presumably of earth, air, fire, water and ether), existence and non-existence (*sadasad*), destiny or conduct (*vidhi*), light or brightness (*śukra*) and force or power to act (*bala*), as well as the assemblage (*sāmagrī*) of parts as a binding principle of the universe (12.308.103–111). Eventually *prakṛti* – literally, 'procreation' – was finally settled on and formalized with the help of contemporary epistemological practices, but in texts such as the *Upaniṣads* and *Mahābhārata* one sees older enumerations still being weighed and evaluated as viable metaphysical systems.

But the *Śvetāśvatara Upaniṣad* goes on to reject most of the theories it lists, and the *Bṛhad Āraṇyaka Upaniṣad* lampoons this very tendency to propose diverse models that all fall short of the mark; in 2.1 a learned Brahmin priest variously proposes that it is the deities in the sun, moon, lightning, space, wind, fire, water, mirror-image, echo, cardinal directions, shadow and body that should be considered as the universal foundation of things, *brahman*. But eventually this plethora of different answers is found wanting, and at the end the Brahmin must submit to the greater knowledge of a king who shows him a sleeping man and takes him through a series of reasoned arguments for why it must be the central vital energy of life (*prāṇa*) that lies behind all beings. Similarly, the *Kena Upaniṣad* presents a short, somewhat satirical narrative explaining the inadequacy of such natural forces to serve as the ultimate explanation of things: the powers possessed by fire (*Agni*), wind (*Vāyu*) and the powerful deity Indra are all shown to be derivative of the more abstract but universal power of *brahman* on which they all rely (3–4).

Such attempts to identify an encompassing physical substrate were positioned as an alternative to the atomistic metaphysics proposed by thinkers such as the early Buddhists, Jains, Cārvākas and also the Vaiśeṣikas, all of whom believed that no single reality could underpin all things. These groups have been collectively termed a 'first episteme' of early Indian systematic thought by Johannes Bronkhorst (2006). Opposition to the possibility of a single explanatory substance or force can be seen in both the Buddhist account of things as *skandhas* ('aggregations') of components (*dharmas*) that themselves have no inherent existence and the Vaiśeṣika philosophy that everything is made of different types of atoms: both reject the possibility of any single fundamental ontology of existence itself per se. Ultimately, theories that vital breath, wind, sun, food or any other element could explain the whole of the natural world seem to have fallen prey to their scepticism, and the Upaniṣads frequently portray such attempts as short-sighted – despite their continuing importance in the development of 'sciences' of biological and chemical theory. Such explanations were limited in that they aspired only to the level of a mechanics, and did not rise to the more fundamental analysis of the origin and nature, dynamics and disposition, structures and characteristic forces that define a thing at its most basic level.

Scepticism about naturalistic cosmologies of the kind that we explored in Part I cleared the space for more explicit philosophical thinking. The *Nāsadīya Sukta* (*Ṛg Veda* 10.129) is one of the most well-known and influential early examples of Vedic cosmological reflection that sought an all-encompassing explanation of the universe not in the form of a simple creator or material cause to account for the physical cosmos, but rather in the sense of a single principle that could explain the whole of things – including both being and non-being – and thus existence in the most fundamental sense:

> Then even nothingness was not, nor existence, There was no air then, nor the heavens beyond it. What covered it? Where was it? In whose keeping? . . .
>
> The gods came afterwards, with the creation of this universe. Who then knows whence it has arisen? Whence all creation had its origin? (10.129.1, 6–7)

This text hints at a philosophically astute approach to the paradox embedded in its questions, by pointing out that any source that one might propose as the origin of the world would necessarily be included in '*sat*' or what exists. It is because it masquerades as a myth about the origin of the cosmos but ultimately poses a profound critique of the very concept of a cosmic origin that Brereton (1999: 249) called this text an 'anticosmogony'. It takes a step towards metaphysical thinking in its desire to raise issues about the nature of that which frames the very *possibility of* existence. In this sense, the *Nāsadīya Sukta* asked sophisticated meta-theoretical questions about the nature of any possible explanation of existence as a whole: he who seeks to explain the world cannot make use of anything that might be found *in* the world. Indeed, Brereton's (1999) stylistic reading of this text as a thematic and syntactic riddle has led to the claim that it locates the solution to the question not in the sphere of physical beings or elements, but in the sphere of *thought*. On this reading, the poets or bards (*kavi*) in the poem parallel the readers of the text: 'their response, their active mental engagement, mirrors the original power of creation' so that their act of poetic composition appears as a *mental* cosmogony, enacting the 'discovery that thought is the first creative activity' (255).

The *Bṛhad Āraṇyaka Upaniṣad* was one of the earliest extant Indian texts to begin to develop a more explicit answer to the *Nāsadīya Sukta*'s question. Although it is far from doing any form of systematic philosophy (as Johannes Bronkhorst (2006: 288) has pointed out), it returns repeatedly to the theme of that by which the whole range of particular aspects of the world can be encompassed in a broader knowledge. A well-known sequence recounts the existence of the first being, its loneliness and its consequent procreation of itself into many beings. In this it echoes the earlier *Puruṣa Sukta* of *Ṛg Veda* 10.90. But the *Bṛhad Āraṇyaka Upaniṣad*'s version of the story develops a lesson about hidden realities and subtle identities, for it goes on in the following section to explain the way in which that person who provided the underlying material of the cosmos remains present within all beings, including the self, presenting a 'trail to the entire world':

> At that time this world was without real distinctions; it was distinguished simply in terms of name and visible appearance – 'He is so and so by name and has this sort of an appearance'. So even today this world is distinguished simply in terms of name and visible appearance, as when we say, 'He is so and so by name and has this sort of an appearance.'
>
> Penetrating this body up to the very nailtips, he remains there like a razor within a case or a termite within a termite hill. People do not see him for he is incomplete as he comes to be called breath when he is breathing, speech when he is speaking, sight when he is seeing . . . These are only the names of his various activities. A man who considers him to be any one of these does not understand him, for he is incomplete within any one of these. One should consider them simply as his self (*ātman*), for in it all these become one. This same self (*ātman*) is the trail to this entire world, for by following it one comes to know this entire world, just as by following their tracks one finds [the cattle]. (1.4.7)

Here, like in the *Nāsadīya Sukta*, the text alludes to an initial formless time, but highlights the way in which name and appearance (*nāma-rūpa*) create a basis for speaking of individual aspects while acknowledging the way in which the continuing substrate of those names and appearances pervades them and undercuts their merely contingent individuality. A person who understands the common efficient and material cause of all things goes beyond the 'incomplete' picture and gains a 'trail to this entire world'. The next section goes on to point out the value of the 'self', here defined as that which is necessary and non-contingent – standing in marked contrast to merely contingent, changing features:

> If a man claims that something other than his self is dear to him, and someone were to tell him that he will lose what he holds dear, that is liable to happen. So a man should regard only his self as dear to him. When a man regards only his self as dear to him, what he holds dear will never perish. (*Bṛhad Āraṇyaka Upaniṣad* 1.4.8)

What cannot be lost is what matters, and this applies to the contingent aspects of the self which are undercut by a more pervasive reality. We have seen that the significance of induction and inference was that they delivered these broader, non-contingent truths. Language played an important role in the development of such *abstractions* – the eidetic essences of broader systems and situations – and the mechanism by which abstract generalizations could be discovered was the phenomenon of *analogy*. These processes together facilitated a Hindu tradition that produced ever-new ideas of reality expounded in systematic theology, narrative, poetry and ritual genres.

## The new theories of everything

Paralleling and eventually replacing the old naturalistic accounts of reality, new 'theories of everything' were advanced, and these improved on the physicalist search for cosmic principles of nature such as *prakṛti, kāla, prāṇa, anna* and so on. The new theories tried to do this by shifting from the search for a *constitutive substance* to the search for a *pervasive structure* or property of things. The new theories of everything sought images of the universe that demonstrated an underlying structural property that unified the whole, such as a substance that takes different forms, or a medium that is divided into different parts, or a being that multiplies or can be seen in different ways. These images, often taking the form of analogies that liken the universe to some familiar case that aids comprehension, proliferated in the shape of *dṛṣṭānta*s, philosophically illuminating models that served literally as a *dṛṣṭa-anta* or 'observed-case' of a broader pattern. Simple analogies evolved into symbolic explanations in the later sections of the Vedic corpus, and became the basis for thoughtful reflections in the more philosophical late Vedic material and the literatures that it inspired.

This can be seen in the *Brahma Sūtra*'s attempt to systematize the accounts of *ātman, mokṣa* and *brahman* found in the Upaniṣads. It uses succinct images– of cloth folded (2.1.19), milk curdling (2.1.24), grass growing (2.2.5) or a magnet attracting (2.2.7) – to illustrate specific structures of constitutive material or developmental change or the emanation of new forms. The authors of the *Bhagavad Gītā* made particularly vivid use of *dṛṣṭānta*s as a form of explanation that would be accessible to its wider readership; thus the divine, now personified in the form of the deity Kṛṣṇa, explains its own pervasion of the universe through the analogies of a thread that runs through and unites diverse parts (7.1), a space in which things move (9.6) and the characteristic quality that defines each thing individually (7.8–11). Indeed, the *Bhagavad Gītā* is a particularly syncretic text, appropriating vastly different theories through casual allusions; Sāṃkhya theories that the world is a 'field' of phenomena united by a single 'knower' (in chapter 13) are juxtaposed with the Upaniṣads' idea that the uniting level of things is an all-pervasive vital energy (like the 'splendour of the sun which is shared by fire and the moon'; 15.12–14), and also with hints of the Vaiśeṣika suggestion that the world is an aggregation that coheres with the manifestation of the universe, and dissolves with its dissolution (9.18–22). As Lipner (1997: 69) has noted the text shows a preference for a rich profusion of explanations over any single systematic proposition, with the result that it is happy to 'incorporate an element of semantic fluidity'. The profusion of potentially contradictory theories in this piece of presystematic Hindu theology is not considered problematic; indeed, its redactors seem to have framed the theoretical discourses in the main body of the text within a Vedic framework (on this analysis of the *Gītā*'s structure, see Jeźic (2009: 628–38)) that explicitly refers to Upaniṣadic discourses on secret knowledge, and empowers the reader to reflect on its account according to his own reasoning:

> I have declared to you the most
> secret knowledge in all the world.
> Reflect upon all parts of it,
> And then do as you wish to do!
>
> Hear from me now, the supreme word,
> The greatest secret of them all . . .
> Be mindful of me and devoted,
> Make sacrifices and revere me,
> And you will surely go to me . . .
>
> (*Bhagavad Gītā* 18.63–65)

Here the *Gītā* casts its emerging devotional ideology in the older language of a special Upaniṣadic form of special knowledge that allows the reader to 'go to' that larger truth which it describes.

In these and other cases of expansion from an analogical theme the rule of inference was at work turning each rough idea into a more sophisticated theoretical concept able to express a much wider truth, serving in that way as an 'eye of the world'. But these analogies also provided evidence of the real status of ideas expressed through speech, knowledge and 'substitutions', because they pointed to the shared structural features that connect thought and reality together into a unity of meanings. The underlying structures of similarity to which the analogies point seemed to all intents and purposes to be real, and so they seemed to bring a *really existing* eidetic connection to light.

This 'realistic' dimension of reasoning with analogies has been discussed by cognitive linguists Georges Lakoff and Mark Johnson (1980), who note the way in which insights into the way metaphors function can question the assumed divide between thought and reality. Such assumptions have been common in the West since Immanuel Kant located the structures of cognition within the mind rather than the world. They argue that metaphor charts a route between mental subjectivism and worldly objectivism because it avoids the 'myth of objectivism' according to which thought and reality are divorced, with structural properties accorded either to objects with independent properties *or* to judgements that human minds make about those objects in the autonomous realm of thought (185–209). Their strategy is to propose a new 'experientialist myth' which emphasizes the way in which structural analogies intersect both the objects of perception and our own cognition of them, framing reason within 'the perspective of man as part of his environment, not as separate from it' (229).

They come close here to the Vedic view of reason's grasp on truth, which is grounded in the belief that the poet-seers or *ṛṣi*s who revealed the Vedas *perceived the nature of reality* in aural form and expressed it directly through structures of language. As the *Nāsadīya Sukta* (*Ṛg Veda* 10.129) says, poets could be imagined as having searched in their hearts for the existent's link to what is non-existent, in order to know what was above and what below: mental insight was accorded the power to reach across realities. This robust confidence in the validity of metaphysical theories ensured their continuance. The classical philosopher carried on the lineage of the Vedic authors insofar as he retained a lingering association with the original function of the *ṛṣi* or seer able to perceive inductive patterns and underlying identities, and of the *kavi* or poet able to develop linguistic expressions of the world itself.. Theory possessed the status of vision, and reason provided real revelation into the nature of things, pointing the way to a form of union with the world via the analytic imagination.

One passage in the Bṛhad Āraṇyaka Upaniṣad portrays Vedic seers as an example of those who are able to 'become' something by knowing it:

> Now, the question is raised: 'Since people think that they will become the Whole (literally "all", *sarva*) by knowing brahman, what did brahman know that enabled it to become the Whole?'
>
> In the beginning this world was only brahman, and it knew only itself (ātman), thinking: 'I am brahman' As a result, it became the Whole. Among the gods, likewise, whosoever realized this, only they became the Whole. It was the same also among the seers and among humans. Upon seeing this very point, the seer Vāmadeva proclaimed: 'I was Manu, and I was the sun.' This is true even now. (1.4.9–10)

This extraordinary passage conveys the thoughts of authors who saw knowledge as the means to a transformation into something broader and higher in scope – something to which the name '*brahman*' is given. What is more, this transformation through knowledge is one that can raise humans above the Vedic gods by accessing the world of ideas and becoming the reality that contains them: through ideas the human self can become the self of the gods – incurring their jealousy.

> If a man knows 'I am brahman' in this way, he becomes this whole world. Not even the gods are able to prevent it, for he becomes their very self (ātman).
>
> So when a man venerates another deity, thinking, 'He is one, and I am another', he does not understand. As livestock is for men, so is he for the gods. As having a lot of livestock is useful to a man, so each man proves useful to the gods. The loss of even a single head of livestock is painful; how much more if many are lost. The gods, therefore, are not pleased at the prospect of men coming to understand this. (1.4.9–10)

Humanity as *mind* is free, mutable and empowered by its theories of everything, for as a mental being it is able to transform itself into anything it comprehends, however vast and however abstract.

One sees hints of this idea in later portrayals of sages or *ṛṣi*s – figures who 'see' certain truths and are able to convey metaphysical, cosmological and ancient historical information to others. In the *Rāmāyaṇa*, the sage Narada's ability to view past, present and future history allows him to tell the story of Rāma and Sītā, and in the *Mahābhārata* the sage Vyāsa begins the whole tale with an extensive exposition of the scope of his own vision, which includes the origins of the universe, rituals, histories, different beliefs and practices, castes and lifestyles, as well as the dimensions of the heavenly bodies, the lengths of the ages of the world and the nature of the all-pervading spirit (see the first chapter of Book One). There may not be any philosophical dimension in the portrayal of such visions of the whole of reality, but in certain cases there is a sense that the sage not only *sees* particular truths, but also sees the whole – and occasionally even becomes it. The best example of this is the *Mahābhārata*'s story of Śuka, a rare narrative account of what liberation is like. The text is noticeably 'Vedāntic' in its orientation – Śuka is said to have been born with the Vedas within him, and he naturally gravitates towards a life of renunciation, narrated in stories that are peppered with adaptations of Upaniṣadic teachings and passages, particularly in chapter 313 in which the narrative even visits King Janaka's court where a number of Upaniṣadic tales were set. In *Mahābhārata* 12.312.16–18, Śuka, who has risen beyond the world on the wings of his father's teachings, travels into the sky like a bird, becomes the wind and enters into the sun (12.318.52), before finally casting off the three *guṇa*s and other trappings of the material world to dwell in *brahman* like a blazing fire.

Little has been said about the fact that this is a very different form of *mokṣa* than those envisioned in many later Vedāntic theologies: Śuka's story illustrates a form of liberation in which one becomes the features of the natural world, before becoming *brahman*. Andrew Fort (1994: 381) has written on the distinction between Upaniṣadic accounts of *mokṣa* as 'going' and as 'knowing', highlighting the tradition of texts which argued that 'one "goes to" immortality, but goes by knowing'. Śuka's story speaks to views about the liberation of learned sages who are rich in Upaniṣadic teachings, and whose understanding is able to transform them accordingly. The goal of union here involves an intimate experience of the world, and its liberating aspects entail a mental escape from the restrictive particularities of everyday thought into the realm of generalization that characterizes metaphysical reflection.

## Validity and logic: the systematization of thought

While the tradition growing out of the Vedas into Vedāntic metaphysics tended to use inductive reasoning to generate viable theories, another major tradition of strict inferential reasoning also developed that would eventually take precedence in the mind of modern scholars. This tradition (exemplified by the Nyāya school) was primarily *epistemological* rather than metaphysical, that is, it sought correct facts rather than general pictures. This regularization proceeded gradually; early expressions of wonder about inference's capacity to point to broad truths (seen in texts such as the *Sāṃkhya Kārikā*) gave way to a combative culture of attack and defence regarding specific positions.

The beginnings of this process were already in evidence in the *Sāṃkhya Kārikā*'s reference to inference as a 'three-fold knowledge' (see 5). This knowledge consisted originally in three key steps: the *liṅga* or observable sign of something, the *liṅgin* or thing that always possesses that sign and the *pūrvaka* or knowledge of the past precedent that these two always coincide and are never seen separately. It is this process that establishes facts that are empirically inaccessible to us (*atīṅdriyāṇāṃ pratītiḥ*) either contingently (because they are not before our senses) or in principle (because they are invisible or abstract truths).

The steps in the process are usually demonstrated by the standard example of the way in which we know that where we see smoke we can always infer that there is also fire, and the three early stages of inference are often set out as follows:

1. Phenomenon *x* is the case (e.g. one can see smoke) . . .
2. . . . and there has been seen to be a (so-far) unvarying relation to phenomenon *y* (e.g. we have always found that smoke goes along with the existence of a fire) . . .

3. … therefore phenomenon *y* is also the case (e.g. from the fact that there is smoke we can always infer that there is a fire).

For the *Sāṃkhya Kārikā* a key purpose of the process was that it could reveal metaphysical realities (such as *prakṛti*, the material that Sāṃkhya believed underlay the manifest natural cosmos).

But the Nyāya school of thought applied the same basic structure of syllogism to a different purpose that grew out of the courtly culture of debate. It saw inference as a way of verifying specific claims, that is, to epistemological questions about the derivation and validity of propositions, rather than metaphysical questions about the possible underpinnings of what one already knows. Thus Akṣapāda's model of the syllogism in the *Nyāya Sūtra* is adapted to take the form of a debate over whether something is the case or not. It incorporated the three steps familiar from the *Sāṃkhya Kārikā* into a five-step syllogistic process in which a third step or 'limb' was introduced, drawing on an example to illustrate a more general principle, and the fourth step established that the particular proposition in question was an instance of that general principle. The final step was then to restate that particular proposition as proven, bypassing any possible questions about the nature and implications of the more general principle in order to reground the inferential process as a foundation for the specific claim in question. The whole five-step process provided a 'fully fledged articulation of an inference schema' conceived as the validation of items of knowledge (Matilal 1998: 4). But it excised the metaphysical insights yielded by the process of generalization that lay at the heart of inference. Nevertheless this became the basis of the syllogistic reasoning used in a range of Indian schools of thought; indeed, it was rejected only by the Cārvākas who held on to a radical empiricist position. With this development, inferential reasoning became more narrowly applicable to specific cases of comparison and more broadly central to society as an arbiter of validity. At the same time its use as a tool for speculative metaphysical thinking waned, and with it, the use of 'theories of everything' as a practice of personal transformation also diminished: philosophers and theologians became associated with dialectical debate, rather than visionary contemplation of 'the whole'.

Later Buddhist thinkers around the fifth century CE queried the nature of the unvarying relation between the sign and the thing that it always accompanies, trying to clarify its nature by describing it merely as 'positive and negative concomitance' (*anvaya-vyatireka*) – the relation in which *x* happens always to be the case when *y* is, and never the case when *y* is not (see Dunne (2004) on early Buddhist use of *vyapti* from Dharmakīrti). This relation functioned as a way of avoiding the need to explain the cause of the inferential relation (i.e. what causes the concomitance? Does one phenomenon cause the other? Are they both caused by an underlying third phenomenon? Are they the manifestations of an underlying shared principle?). Positive and negative concomitance offered a way of avoiding awkward questions about the basis of inductive reasoning by tacitly accepting that strong precedent is enough for a pragmatic kind of certainty about future events in the world. The development of the doctrine was also, however, a way of refusing to ask questions of a metaphysical, explanatory kind.

Yet despite this development, early Nyāya had retained elements of the speculative, metaphysical dimension of inductive reasoning. The *Nyāya Sūtra* itself did not altogether forget the metaphysical implications of inference. It acknowledged both similarity to precedent cases *and generalization* as important steps in the generation of new knowledge:

> Inference (*anumāna*) is that threefold knowledge preceded by perception, which is generalisation seen on the basis of what is prior and posterior.
>
> Comparison (*upamāna*) is the knowledge of a thing through similarity (*sadharmya*) to what has already been established. (1.1.5–6)

This brief clarification makes an important distinction between comparison – the establishment of certain isolated truths by reference to others, and generalization – and the speculative establishment of general truths. The text later goes on to note that all perception could, in effect, be seen as inference from the fact that it grasps only a part of something but proceeds to broader knowledge about the object as a whole (2.1.92). It similarly goes on to emphasize the mereological basis of the inferential process, showing how the part that is known through perception relates to the underlying pervasive foundation (*avayavin*) that it indicates. It also defends the existence of pervasive levels that can be known through their parts (2.1.95–96). This is an important acknowledgement that the unseen pervasive truths that inference yields for Vedānta and Sāṃkhya were also important in this early stage of Nyāya. According to the *Nyāya Sūtra*'s definitions, the spheres of information that *anumāna* and *upamāna* give us are altogether different, and in many respects it is the object of the former category, the pervasive level of *anumāna* that explains and unites isolated observed phenomena within a whole, that contributed to the Nyāya and Vaiśeṣika schools' belief that specific cases must share in unseen eternal categories (*tattva-bhāktayaḥ*) which provide the fundamental structure of existence in which individual cases partake (*nānātva-vibhāgāt*; see 2.2.14–16). These eternal categories became the basis of Nyāya's own view of reality, and it thus applied inductive reasoning to its own creation of a metaphysics grounded in the need to assume pervasive unities underlying particular phenomena.

But it was the practical application of inference along with other *pramāṇa*s or knowledge-sources to the creation of shared rules of valid reasoning that motivated Nyāya's centrality for Indian theoretical traditions. The very first verse of the *Nyāya Sūtra* identifies sixteen categories as central to right knowledge:

> Supreme felicity is attained by the knowledge about the true nature of sixteen categories, viz., means of right knowledge (*pramaṇa*), object of right knowledge (*prameya*), doubt (*saṃśaya*), purpose (*prayojana*), familiar instance (*dṛṣṭānta*), established tenet (*siddhānta*), members (*avayava*), confutation (*tarka*), acertainment (*nirṇaya*), discussion (*vāda*), wrangling (*jalpa*), cavil (*vitaṇḍā*), fallacy (*hetvābhāsa*), quibble (*chala*), futility (*jāti*) and occasion for rebuke (*nigrahasthāna*). (1.1)

Such qualities set a standard for knowledge, and *ānvīkṣikī*, or inferential 'investigation' came to operate as a 'lamp of all sciences', 'establishing a procedural structure and firm rules and guidelines for the mutual scholarly controversies' that animated intellectual and religious culture (Preisendanz 2010: 28, 31). *Dṛṣṭānta*s, meanwhile, were also celebrated as practical tools with a concrete social application, explained as that meaning which allows the 'worldly' man and the philosophical 'reasoner' (*laukika-parikṣānāṃ*) to agree (*Nyāya Sūtra*s 1.1.25), a use that foregrounded the naturalness of such knowledge. The spread of such standards for formal debate attests to 'the obvious yearning of the Sanskrit world of letters to construct for itself a discursive universe that transcends the vicissitudes of history' (Minkowski 2001: 2).

One fictitious account of a good argument in which reasoning serves as a mediator in disputes between divided sectors of society occurs in a speech by the character of Sulabhā. Sulabhā is a female who uses her knowledge and lucid exposition (as well as her supernatural powers of possession) to shame the arrogant king Janaka. An educated single woman of an ascetic order, she prefaces the theory of identity that we looked at in Part I with an account of those qualities in which a good speech consists:

> [A] 'speech' has sophistication, careful discrimination, clear order, the presentation of a conclusion, and motivation – all five of these are aspects of the meaning to be conveyed.
>
> Listen to a careful description ... When there are several discrete things to be known, but the knowledge of them forms an undivided whole, the extraordinary understanding in that is 'subtlety'. When in regard to whatever subject he has in mind, one weighs the good and bad points according to the divisions of the subject matter, that is 'careful discrimination'. The experts on speech say that speech is 'clearly ordered' when one considers what one wants to say with 'This should be said earlier', and 'This should be said later.' There is a 'conclusion' when 'This is that' is said at the end

> of a speech, especially when some proposition pertaining to Merit, Riches, Pleasures, or Absolute Freedom has been stated. When a speaker arouses intense pangs of desire or aversion, that process is known as 'motivation', king. Watch and you will see that my speech will combine all five of these . . . to form a single meaning. (12.308.78–86)[1]

Her account of 'speech' (which here appears to signify something like lucid and valid courtly discourse) emphasizes the qualities of:

**a)** coherent synthesis into a single view (what she calls 'sophistication' or that which is *saukṣmya*),

**b)** discriminative analysis,

**c)** logical progression of the ideas from evidence to proof towards an established conclusion and

**d)** an affective, motivating response in the reader inspired by the conclusion.

These elements together embed inference within the broader qualities of coherence, systematic logical progression and results that are both lucid and significant. Sulabhā's account demonstrates the shared culture of 'good discourse' into which inference was inducted. The contemporary conceptions of valued discourse are put to a *critical theoretical* use: Sulabhā's assertion of the rational quality of her discourse is the means by which, as a single woman, she is able to claim an equal authority and voice to that of the king.[2] Ultimately she uses her theory to defend the validity of her lifestyle, and the king, impressed by her 'reasoned and significant statements', is silenced (see 12.308.191). The theoretical realm of essences and abstractions, generalized observations, valid and lucid reasons, and clear motivations is itself seen as the sphere in which persons of all backgrounds are able to gain a voice, win debates and claim authority with concrete societal results. In a sense, it is in the realm of ideas that all comers are able to speak with equal 'bodies', whether they are women or men, Brahmins, Kṣatriyas, or ascetics.

This is a pattern which is repeated elsewhere within the *Mahābhārata* (as, for instance, in the case of Draupadī, a female figure who also gives a compelling speech protesting the injustice of her apparent societal 'superiors' (see Brodbeck and Black 2009)) and has been explored more broadly in relation to notions of public reason.[3] Sulabhā's account of 'subtle speech' is a helpful window on a culture in which good reasoning had become a sign of autonomy and authority. But it should be noted that in her account, reason can be directed towards multiple goals (reputation, riches, pleasures, liberation) – all of them treating knowledge as instrumental to some beneficial result. The Vedic tradition had emphasized *coherence* of vision as the key marker of a valid theory, rather than valid precedent and its use for human agreement. But under the new dispensation theory became part of what Ganeri (2001) calls the 'proper work' of reason: a tool used for social purposes, but no longer sought and praised in its own right.

## Knowledge as embodiment: selves and truths made of thought

In the particular sources we have looked at here, we see a conception of the thinking human person as something vast and mutable, able to extend over the universe and assimilate it into himself or herself. With the mind as one's medium or 'body', humans are able to become sun, moon, fire and wind, to become as high as the gods; more than that, able to become 'all'. This is an important way in which thought provides a new medium of existence for humans, facilitating the transformation and extension of the self in a way that became central to certain conceptions of liberation or *mokṣa*.

It is important to note that there is an implicit realism in these Hindu conceptions of theory. The mind is believed to have access to *genuinely existing* levels of reality through the verbal power of language and our inductive capacity. This underlying structural reality was not merely assumed, but *demonstrated* for all to see by the existence of genuine analogies and generalities – shared eidetic structures – that can be immediately observed in the world. This epistemic optimism stands in contrast to both Buddhist and Western non-realist sceptical traditions that see concepts as mere conventions imposed on the world by the mind. In the sources we have looked at in this chapter, theory *is* revelation of reality, and thus philosophical theorizing retains its sense of sacred access to hidden truths of reality, for it is a process of discovery that transcends the modern distinctions between religious revelation and secular knowledge. In this sense, as we will see, the role played by the Vedic seer was in due course taken up by the modern philosopher–theologian who also saw hidden truths embedded in the cosmos. Early Hindu speculative thought was thus tied up with a wider cosmological project that transcended sacred–secular divides.

This suggests an important alternative to the common Western theoretical model of reason as a schematization imposed onto nature in order to 'domesticate' the world for human dwelling. The eighteenth-century philosopher David Hume dismissed induction as a fiction invented to comfort the human mind, but the Indian model reverts to the principle of analogy on which inductive generalizations are based as evidence that there really exist underlying *semantic* realities that are germane to cosmological reflection. Some Western thinkers took a similar path, treating the speculative dimension of thought as a creative project aimed at constructing meaningful orientations for our lives, rather than a search for certain knowledge; thus, for instance, the twentieth-century sociologist of knowledge Peter Berger (1967) highlighted ways in which humanity naturally creates pictures of the world as one of its first and most primitive activities. On the one hand, Berger's view recalls the Upaniṣadic attitude to knowledge-systems, for he sees religious theories as what he calls 'sacred canopies' that capture 'a meaningful order, or nomos', intended to shield us from the 'anomic terror' of an unliveably structureless world (19). He argues for a vision of human worldviews as instances of nomos – the nourishing conceptual spaces in which we must necessarily *live* as mental beings:

> Every nomos is an area of meaning carved out of a vast mass of meaninglessness, a small clearing of lucidity in a formless, dark, always ominous jungle. Seen in the perspective of the individual, every nomos represents the bright 'dayside' of life, tenuously held onto against the sinister shadows of the 'night' . . . the individual is provided by society with various methods to stave off the nightmare world of anomy and to stay safe within the safe boundaries of the established nomos. (23–4)

On the other hand, Berger's roots in the German theoretical tradition, with its Kantian underpinnings, lead to an axial difference from the Vedic view: in Berger's 'constructivist' view the order of mind is separate from the order of reality, so that such theories indicate nothing that is genuinely true about the world. The Upaniṣadic view of reason, by contrast, leads it to picture the mind as *part of* the world, and the structures of the mind as *continuous with* the structures of cosmos. Thus theory brings us *real* insight into reality through the genuine access afforded by mechanisms such as language and induction.

The materials of the self fully consist of both thought and matter, and so according to this model, the self is moved as much by mental hunger for the understanding that nourishes our minds as by the biological hunger for material nourishment that nourishes the body. Accordingly reason can be seen not only as instrumentally of value in terms of its uses, but also as intrinsically valuable by virtue of its ability to nourish and transform us. This distinction between instrumental and intrinsically valuable reason was addressed by the twentieth-century German philosopher Martin Heidegger (1978) in his critique of Western conceptions of truth; he pointed out that even in ancient Greece, the term *mathēmata* (now associated with mathematics) had originally signified a conception of truth as something truly basic that preceded even numbers. It indicated a digging deeper into the entailments of what one already knows, in order to discover the underlying foundations and presuppositions of knowledge. This was one expression of the old Greek notion of an inner dynamic energy (*dynamis*) governed by the inner direction or *telos* of minds and ideas; but this idea gradually changed into a Newtonian conception of mere regularity of movement in the natural world at large, something by which to measure practical facts (271–305). The sense of pursuing objects back into their own nature as objects, and towards the nature of knowledge itself – which is part of our own nature as always necessarily thinking beings – was lost.

But the classical Hindu view argues for recognition of the way in which metaphysical thinking reveals – and shapes – reality. It could be said that the material reality of thought means that, in some sense, all theories are 'true' – in Heidegger's sense of *aletheia*: whether or not they correspond to a particular set of relations among physical objects, they always reveal a particular set of relations among *ideas*. A genuine structure of thought, previously latent, becomes manifested in each theory. Naturally, no such theories could claim to be the sole ones, and none of the Upaniṣadic theories of *brahman* do so. As the field of language is complex and variable, so too theory must always admit that it captures only one facet of a wide range of possible interpretations.

This idea of the plurality of valid metaphysical models of reality was explored in the twentieth century by the French philosopher Gilles Deleuze. Deleuze (2001: 42–3) drew on David Hume's critique of inference to remind us that general theories about the world use 'principles of association' (of ideas) that combine 'fictive' ideas with associations seen in reality, to create larger theories that are in principle un-verifiable and un-falsifiable but which are essential to the human nature that creates them. In such cases:

> [T]he illegitimate exercise or belief is incorrigible, inseparable from legitimate beliefs, and indispensable to their organisation. In this case, the fanciful usage of the principles of human nature itself becomes a principle. Fiction and delirium shift over to the side of human nature ... [Hume shows] how the positing of the existence of distinct and continuous bodies, how the positing of an identity of the self, requires the intervention of all sorts of fictive uses of relations, and in particular of causality, in conditions where no fiction can be corrected but where each instead plunges us into other fictions, which all form part of human nature. (43)

Hume's rejection of the 'imaginative' basis of inferential reasoning, and the sceptical tradition that emerged from his legacy, continued to judge religious cosmologies, and eventually also metaphysical speculations, as invalid. This was a position that led eventually to the verificationist position which rejected any extrapolation that could not in principle be verified empirically, and thereby became sceptical about metaphysics and any field that concerned such elusive ideas such as aesthetics or values. It is to this tradition that the instrumental epistemology of Nyāya logicians has been best able to articulate itself. But the classical worldviews found within the Upaniṣads defended a creative, pluralistic practice of forming 'theories of the whole' and assimilating them into our own identities: this was part of the secret value of the Upaniṣadic tradition as a 'spiritual exercise' (in Pierre Hadot's (1995) sense), and a technique for shaping the self. As material reality can be manipulated to form a physical body for the self, so conceptual reality (with its unique structures of thought that span the whole universe), can also be manipulated to form a mental 'body' for the self. In such a worldview, validity and debate are secondary to the formation of powerful 'theories of everything' that can serve as 'idea-bodies' for the expanded self to which certain thinkers seem to have aspired. In texts such as the *Bṛhad Āraṇyaka*, *Chāndogya* and *Aitareya Upaniṣad*s, one sees remnants of the awe evinced by a culture that had found a way of grasping the underlying, unifying levels of reality, and transforming oneself into a creature embodied by that infinite materiality that consists of thought, and at best, of world-embracing ideas.

# PART THREE

# Shaping the world: Classical embodiment in practice

# 9

# Theories of ritual and practice in Hindu culture

The 'body' as we have seen it in Parts I and II is a mutable medium for our existence in the world: it is made of physical materials that we can restructure or catalyse into new modes, and it is also made of mental materials that we can refocus on or expand to encompass wider truths. In this section we will widen our scope beyond classical sources, and even beyond text per se, to explore the afterlives of these theories of self in later traditions of Hindu culture and in the world of practice. The views of materiality – mental and physical – that we have seen in classical texts represent only a few selected approaches within the ideologically diverse wider culture of ancient India. Yet they have had a lasting impact on subsequent Hindu practices. Indeed, they describe a pervasive 'order of reality' in the sense used by Clifford Geertz in his account of religion as a worldview, placing the body at the very heart of ritual actions, initiations and transmutations, ethical behaviour and interpersonal relationships. It is the conception of self as an agent embodied within the materials of the world that provides the basis for lifestyle practices; it is the foundation for religion's creative patterning of human life.

## The importance of practice

Scholars of Hinduism have long realized that practice is a powerful and pervasive indicator of the worldview shared by any particular religious community. While Western culture has tended to make a distinction between doctrine on one hand, and practice on the other, in Hindu culture actions are often the most earnest expression of a worldview and its theoretical underpinnings. Key beliefs may be encoded in the mental and emotional dispositions that accompany the prescribed actions found in practices such as life-stage rituals, temple *pūjā*, theological debate or pilgrimage to sacred spaces. Practices are rarely just thoughtless action: they are what the sociologist Pierre Bourdieu (1977) calls a *doxa*, an implicit yet instinctive set of values, taste and logic, all expressed through the actions of the body. While relatively few Hindus have read the Upaniṣads, and many have never heard of them, it is through practice that these theories shape the lives of individuals within Hindu traditions, connecting them with larger traditions that cross generations and connect regions, tying together 'Hindu' culture more effectively than any particular doctrine and giving 'shape and a degree of unity to Hindu traditions' (Flood 1996: 198). Practice is so pervasive in Hindu cultures that a number of scholars, following Staal, have claimed that 'Hinduism is orthoprax rather than orthodox: if one behaves correctly, it does not matter what one believes' (Doniger 1982: 7). In many respects the *lived* text of religious practice is a more robust manifestation of Hinduism than its written texts, for rituals are more reliably passed down through time, creating a point of reference across both cultural and theological shifts 'in contradistinction to a changing, and often politically unstable, political and economic history'; in some sense, Flood (1996: 198) suggests, 'ritual defies history'. But ritual is never merely a repetition of the past; each performance of a recitation or offering, interaction or social identity is a point at which the past intersects with the present in a fresh creation. Contemporary practice must be read in this way in order for it to retain its hermeneutic richness: it is in ritual life, influenced by classical sources, that one is able to see the effects of earlier theories.

In addition to the implicit level of practice in everyday lives, Hindu culture is also rich in explicit discussion and theorization of action, or 'karma' – it asks cosmological questions about the origins of action, ethical questions about right and wrong actions and metaphysical questions about the nature of action. Practice is how we express our freedom in the world, yet it is important to note that in Hinduism acts cannot be reduced into a simple system of 'right' and 'wrong'. Instead they are mapped onto *multiple* grids that may include merit and misdemeanour as described in the *māhātmya*s, prudent and foolish conduct in *nītiśāstra*, detached and attached action in the *Bhagavad Gītā* or *laukika* (worldly) and *alaukika* (otherworldly) actions in aesthetic theory. We have seen that in a cosmos as rich in binding threads of complex materiality as that of classical Hinduism, however fraught our range of options may turn out to be, there is no escaping the world of action. It is a metaphysical necessity, for even to restrain action is to act, as the *Bhagavad Gītā* points out. Thus what is to be sought is an understanding of the subtle *vṛddhis* or 'modalities' of action. Much of Hindu culture takes place in the medium not of words, but of movements, looks, murmurs, journeys, eating, breathing and other forms of action, and the worldviews we have seen recognize that such actions are more than fleeting forms of life – they are important entities that shape self, society and cosmos.

## Dharma and the structuring of society

One of the key influences on early theories of ritual and practice in Hinduism was the trend towards functionalism: sociological explanations of action in terms of its function in society. The French school of sociology initiated by Emile Durkheim and further developed by Durkheim's nephew Marcel Mauss (who studied Sanskrit and comparative religion), tended to see ritual as an instrument with the function of creating social cohesion, and this idea was applied to India primarily through the analysis of caste and the ideology of *dharma* that supported it. The *Sūtra*s and Śāstras related to *dharma* such as the famous *Mānava Dharma Sāstra*, or 'Laws of Manu', established an abiding orthodox idea of the person as it is and should be according to the different social roles allotted to it. It is this level of Hindu selfhood, specifically associated with the designations of caste and community, which has been the main focus of anthropologists and sociologists of Indian cultures. Thus Louis Dumont's 1966 study of the caste system, *Homo Hierarchicus*, contrasted the citizen-individual of European political philosophy with Hinduism's hierarchical organization of individuals into caste members and renouncers. His analysis suggested that the Vedic ideal of a categorically structured society ultimately contributed to a Hindu philosophy that regarded the destiny of the self as twofold, divided into the freedom of the individual reasoning self, and the constraint imposed on the self by ideological structures or social controls:

> One the one hand society, under the aegis of the brahmans, was to become more and more settled into the categories of strict interdependence, having the pure and the impure as their axis; on the other hand the individualistic philosopher of the previous age was to become the renouncer, Hindu or heterodox. (186)

It is by means of the caste system that Hindu society manages to achieve 'the encompassing of the contrary' (239), that is, the incorporation of positions of freedom within the limitations on individual autonomy that are instituted by the social Whole. Dumont's model suggests that Vedic culture developed into a twofold reality of Hindu understandings of the self as characterized either by traditions of identity, involvement and constraints, or by forms of willed, individualistic self-determination. The counterpoint of constrained and creative selves is expressed here from the perspective of the Brahmin caste that saw itself as a control-keeper: ensuring that order is preserved.

Other scholars have sought to refine Dumont's idea of Hindu hierarchy – as with Gloria Raheja's (1988) proposal that it is centred on a feudal centre–periphery structure prioritizing the landowner, or Sheldon Pollock's (2006) emphasis on the way in which Brahminical cultural tastes served the power-claims of the elite. Others argued that the key values of purity and pollution, or auspiciousness and inauspiciousness, served to embed *dharmic* ideology throughout life, body and action (see Raheja (1988); and also Carman and Marglin (1985)). Caroline Humphries and James Laidlaw (1994) have also sought to refine Dumont's theories about the way in which Indian renouncer traditions make space for the *individual* within a special category of formalized social (non-)participation. They critique the Maussian idea of ritual as a commercial exchange by counterposing to it the 'free' gifts given to Jain monks and nuns; As such, ritual can be the free expression of individual agency, not only a social duty imposed from above. But such contributions tended to remain within an essentially Durkheimian functionalist framework that interprets ritual as a prop for the cohesion of Hindu society, or a Marxist assumption that its ulterior motive is to arrogate power to a minority.

Anthropology's structuralist turn injected new life into contemporary approaches, often interpreting Hindu ritual in terms of the sciences of correct grammar that arose out of Vedic reflection on language. Much Hindu practice could be rendered as a precise language of appropriate action with a syntax all its own. Axel Michaels (2016: 312) has done much to demonstrate the way in which this structural obsession extends throughout many different periods and traditions of 'Brahminic–Sanskritic' ritual. On this reading much ritual remains premised on the extraordinary powers of language – its ability to create structures of communication that extend our cognitive world far beyond immediate perception, and its ability to produce infinitely creative structures of recursive syntax by which new meanings can be generated. Many scholars accepted this structuralist approach and took ritual to be a structuring mechanism for life and society, and Frits Staal's (1996; 2008: 227–31) well-known and controversial assertion of the 'meaninglessness' of Vedic ritual took this idea to an extreme, arguing that the distinctive feature of Vedic ritual was its fascination with *infinite* structures (particularly of recursiveness and self-embedding) lying at the heart of Hindu ritual syntax. Michaels seeks to augment Staal's reading by highlighting the way in which Hinduism's tradition of meticulously structured ritual creates 'constructions of a world' that partake in 'transcendence' while minimizing 'nature or mortality, or contingency and uncertainty'. For Michaels, Brahminical ritual structures do impose order on human action, but they do so with the goal of elevating that action to a higher sphere of influence, rather than curtailing it. In this light, such Hindu practices can be seen to remain part of a religious search for the sacred, rather than merely an attempt to impose existential or social meanings on life (see Michaels on Staal: 317).

## Ritual as the art of shaping reality

In contrast to theories that see ritual as a form of social constraint, some scholars have emphasized the elements of creativity and self-determination in Hindu religious life, identifying a participatory, innovative and expressive dimension in many practices. Rituals are passed down through the generations, yet new variations appear all the time, and practices often augment the mundane world by trans-substantiating materials and elevating participants into a heightened reality. Indeed, it is this potentially empowering quality to ritual life that may recommend ritual participation to individuals such as women, lower castes or regional communities, confirming Catherine Bell's (2007: 4) argument that ritual can be 'constructive and strategic', allowing ritual agents to 'appropriate or reshape values and ideals' (see Pintchman (2007) on women's rituals and the theories of Catherine Bell). While Western scholarship has emphasized the role of ritual in shaping society, Hindu perspectives take a cosmos-wide view, approaching it as a science that reshapes the unseen aspects and dimensions of the universe.

Thus ritual, in India, can be seen in terms of the plurality of different realities and worlds that are accessible to humans – what David Haberman ([1988] 2001) in his study of the role of imagination and theatre in Hindu devotion and pilgrimage calls 'world-openness', borrowing the term from Peter Berger and Thomas Luckmann:

> The contention that reality, for human beings, is neither fixed or singular is now commonly accepted in academic circles. Though we possess a similar biological body, multiple realities or worlds of meaning are available to us ... Our malleable nature enables us to experience a wide and seemingly endless range of possible realities. This facet of human experience, sometimes called 'world-openness', has been well noted by many working in the human sciences. (4)

Haberman reminds us that the creative dimension in ritual opens up new spheres of experience to human discovery. It also reminds us that there is an introducing an experiential dimension to practice. Vedic hymns are poetic tools that evoke key experiences of the world (Patton 2005), Tantric visualization causes the body to be 'envisaged and constructed as divine in the ritual imagination' so that it can serve as 'a technique of experiencing a higher reality for the practitioner beyond the imaginatively restricted world of sense experience' (Flood 2006: 172–3), devotional arts use the natural pull of empathy to provide us with other, improved personalities (see Haberman 1988) and the material cultures of worship in temple and home are the tools of 'a powerful act of the imagination' by which the 'invisible is made visible in stone, wood or clay' (Preston 1985: 30). In each such case ritual functions *phenomenologically* as a vehicle of experience, making multiple worlds that are imminent in the reality around us present for the individual.

Many scholars have taken ritual in Hinduism as a matter of accessing different, ostensibly higher, 'sacred' realms. The 'sacred' is a term that has been used in different ways by various thinkers: for Rudolf Otto it signified the holy space (interrupting normal place and time) in which humanity encounters what is irreducible to worldly things, while for Emile Durkheim it designated anything that functions as a 'totem' by evoking the precious emotions of social effervescence. Mircea Eliade ([1958] 2009) used the sacred specifically in contrast to the counter-value of the 'profane', to signify that which we place above quotidian life in a sphere outside of time and normal space. Eliade was one of the first to use this term in specific relation to Hindu religion: for him the soteriological traditions of India tend toward a 'desolidarization' of humanity with the cosmos, by which humans seek to cut their ties with the normal world or to master it by rising higher (10).

Eliade's usage reflects the wider range of theories of ritual that see it as a period of interruption of norms, and escape from established structures (rather than a reaffirmation of them as in Dumont's approach). Perhaps the most well-known such theory is that of Mikhail Bakhtin (1984b: 9) who argued that ritual performances create a 'carnivalesque' interruption in the usual order of things, allowing for a limited interstice of 'moments of death and revival, change and renewal', a kind of constructive disorder that disassembles and reforms whatever needs to be made new. This approach to ritual has been influential on theories of Hindu practice such as Diana Eck's (1985: 5) study of the worship rite of *darśaṇa* (which was explicitly influenced by Victor and Edith Turner's study of Christian pilgrimage for its interpretation of Hindu images as a point of access to the divine). Humphries and Laidlaw (1994: 211–4) write about Jain *pūjā* as at once meaningless in semantic terms, and simultaneously invested with meaning as a state of *bhav* or 'quality'. Pilgrimages and also temple architecture naturally tend to support such theories in the way that they marshal worshipers into discrete spaces of aesthetic or affective intensity, and often explicitly claim to be a *tīrtha*, a portal to a sacred level of reality. In such cases the constructive effect of human agency is put to use in securing access to that which is of value.

These various theories of ritual action thus reflect the open, malleable character of the Hindu cosmos: embodiment is naturally active, but this means that it is volatile, dynamic and must be constrained – nevertheless it can be controlled in order to reshape (both outer and inner) reality and gain the highest levels of the universe for the practitioner. The self that we have seen embodied in the physical and mental materials of the universe can be controlled through special practices, but it can also be trained to use its powers creatively, in order to become or interact with higher levels of the cosmos. In the following chapters we will explore four styles of practice that, each in their own way, have drawn on and developed the theories of embodiment first outlined in classical sources: (a) *structuring practices* that give structure to world, society and self and *transformative practices* that engage with the many modes – subtle and gross, material and conscious, worldly and divine, in which reality can appear; (b) *interactive practices* that enact an interpersonal relationship within our broader community of beings, human or otherwise; (c) *speculative practices* that seek to reorient the self in terms of a wider comprehension of the cosmos.

# 10

# Practices of materiality: Structuring and transformative rituals

Inspired by traditions of Hindu practice, Brian Smith (1998: 51) has written that 'ritual forms the naturally formless, it connects the inherently disconnected, and it heals the ontological disease of unreconstructed nature'. As we have seen, it may be said that the ritualist echoes the actions of the gods in shaping the cosmos: whether human or divine, the discerning agent acts in such a way as to structure the material chaos of elements and ideas into a meaningful, well-appointed order. According to the model established in Dharmaśāstra, Hindus who participate in social customs and ethical relationships also fit this model of the good practitioner, developing the order of elements into the functioning structures not only of the living body and the comprehending mind, but also of the flourishing society. Practitioners whose task is to alter and shape the material world may also want to destabilize its present order, altering that materiality through transformative practices that catalyse and call forth new modes of existence. But whether supporting or deconstructing the present order of things, such manipulators of reality must be sensitive to the hidden order waiting to be manifested. Events fitting the proper order of the cosmos do not just 'happen'; they can only be realized and made concrete by a proper human sensitivity to the latent order of things, and the possible modes of being that wait *in potentio* within them. In many ways, the cultures of Hindu ritual, yogic discipline and social custom are all about imbuing in individuals the 'ethos' of that awareness of imminent realities and empowering them to intervene in creative but responsible ways. In this light, many Hindu 'structuring practices' can be interpreted as formal procedures for using the creative influence over the world that is entailed in our embodied and en-worlded existence.

## Vedic and dharmic patterns of practice

Vedic culture placed great value on ritual action's capacity to bring order to the world. Some texts see the ritual itself as essentializing that structural order. One text in the Atharva Veda speaks of the *uchhiṣṭa*, or leftovers that remain after the burning of the sacrifice, as a repository of the conceptual order of things (literally the 'name and form'), as well as the abode of natural and heavenly bodies, being and non-being, strength or energy, and all creatures, leaders and gods:

> In the sacrificial leavings are deposited name and form, in it the world is deposited, within it Indra and Agni, and the all are deposited. In the sacrificial leavings heaven and earth, and all beings, are deposited; in it are deposited the waters, the ocean, the moon, and the wind.
>
> In the sacrificial leavings are both being and non-being, death, strength (food), and Prajāpati. The (creatures) of the world are founded upon it; (also) that which is confined and that which is free, and the grace in me. He who fastens what is firm, the strong, the leader, the brahma, the ten creators of the all, the divinities, are fixed on all sides to the sacrificial leavings as the (spokes of the) wheel to the nave . . .
>
> ... Order (*ṛta*), truth (*satya*), creative fervour (*tapas*), sovereignty, asceticism, law and works; past, future, strength, and prosperity, are in the sacrificial leavings – force in force. (11.7)

The *uchhiṣṭa* was the condensed order of the world itself, and it was the unique power of language that instilled the cosmos into it through the appropriate *mantra*s and other symbols. Frits Staal (1996) noted that new gestures, words, offerings and so on could be introduced or omitted in the sequence of ritual, but it is the implicit underlying order of different *kinds* of ritual element that determines the correctness of the ritual itself. This Vedic conception of ritual offered a way for humans to participate in the structures that shape the universe, although the ritual instruments of change tended to be highly restricted by traditions of learning and initiation. Nevertheless, in the Vedas and Upaniṣads we see a stage at which – in some texts at least – Brahmins seem to assume that man is able both to control his own embodied presence in the world, and also to 'create his own ideally ordered universe beyond death and destruction' (Heesterman 1978: 91).

This is dramatized in the cosmogonic hymn to Puruṣa in which the collective ritual action of the gods turns out to be the creative act par excellence:

> When the gods spread the sacrifice, using the Puruṣa as the offering, spring was the clarified butter, summer the fuel, autumn the oblation. They anointed the Puruṣa, the sacrifice, born at the beginning, upon the sacred grass. With him the gods, Sādhyas, and sages sacrificed. From that sacrifice in which everything was offered, the clarified butter was obtained, and they made it into those beasts who live in the air, in the forest, and in villages. From that sacrifice in which everything was offered, the verses and the chants were born, the metres were born, and the formulas were born. (From *Ṛg Veda* 10.90)

If the gods are read here not as inaccessible beings from a distant past, but as selves participating in the empowering art of ritual, this text dramatizes the art of shaping the material world and imbuing it with order through language and ritual, and it is this principle that is re-enacted in the human ritual tradition, as William Mahony (1997: 1–2) argues:

> Vedic religion in general revolved around the ideas that the wondrous marvels and powers of nature, the diverse personalities and behavior of the many gods and goddesses who gave form to and enlivened the world, the composition and dynamics of the human community, and the structure and destiny of the individual person are all somehow linked to one another through a transcendent universal order and harmony of being; that the power of this hidden principle could be harnessed and expressed in effective language; that, because of the interconnectedness of all being, actions performed in any one of such realms therefore affect the status of all others.

Mahony's analysis of the Vedic worldview leads him to the conclusion that the cosmic order should not be seen as a fixed structure that is imposed on a passive humanity, but rather as a creative medium conducive to what he terms an 'artful' human existence within it.

But as we have seen, the development of the concept of *dharma* provided the theoretical underpinnings for control of the human capacity for independent cosmic action. Patrick Olivelle (2005) has charted the development of the Brahminical concept of social order through the notion of *dharma*, exploring the way in which it was largely developed out of ideas linked to the sovereignty of the deity Varuṇa into a concept of good rule in the edicts of the Buddhist king Aśoka, and subsequently adopted as a Vedic concept of sovereign socio-moral order. Paul Horsch (2004: 423–48) also gives an account of the gradual progression of the meanings of *ṛta* and *dharma*, showing how the very polysemy of '*dharma*' contributed to the conception of a general and wide-ranging order of things that could apply to society, to rituals and to the foundations of the world and its parts in general. Just as the ritual was a form of 'supporting the world' (*jagataḥ pratiṣṭhāṃ*, *Kaṭha Upaniṣad* 2.11), so too practices in accordance with *dharma* were considered to be a way of maintaining the proper structure of the social and natural worlds defined in terms of their functional complementarity. Dharma ensures that the universe and society maintain a sustainable life-process. Barbara Holdrege (2004: 214) has tried to capture this complex holism of *dharma*, understood as a pervasive principle that shapes fundamental cosmic, semantic, social and ethical structures of the Hindu worldview:

> *Dharma* structures the universe as a vast cosmic ecosystem, an intricate network of symbiotic relations among interdependent parts, in which each part has a specific function to perform that contributes to the whole system . . . At each level an organic unity is structured in which the separation of functions among the various classes of beings is clearly defined, specific functions or modes of activity being assigned to each class of beings in accordance with its inherent nature . . . In its normative dimension, *dharma*, the cosmic ordering principle, finds expression on the human plane.

Holdrege's account of *dharma* brings out the interdependent holism that characterizes the 'structural' worldview in which every constitutive part of the cosmos or community has a significant role in maintaining the overall balance of things. The 'functional' conception of those parts plays an important role here; rather than discrete units with wholly separate natures and goals, individuals function as part of a symbiotic system, and consequently this view sees the understanding of broader effects as an important part of all ethical decision-making and action.

Throughout subsequent millennia, Hindu cultures continued to devote special attention to natural order through the mechanism of life-stage rituals and astrological festivals that marked out the natural progression of every life. Life-stage rituals or '*saṃskāra*s' could be performed to consecrate the order of human life through its acts of conception, pregnancy, the naming of a child, his or her first experience of going outdoors, the first solid food being eaten, the first cutting of the child's hair, the point at which a child begins to learn and starts to wear the sacred thread that signifies status as one of the 'twice-born' classes of society, as well as the first shaving of the face or first menstruation, and the commencement and end of studies, the later rituals of marriage and funeral rites. The connection of human patterns with natural rhythms is maintained through the astronomical calculation of the correct timing of such rituals and of other Hindu festivals. Astronomy was one of the *Veda-aṅga* disciplines associated with Vedic sacrifice, necessary for ensuring that the rites were in accord with the broader pattern of 'auspicious' times and spaces. For most contemporary Hindus the texts and rituals of the Vedic tradition are largely unknown, but the culture of structuring continues to connect communities to the order that is believed to underlie the visible universe. Such rituals do much to bring individual human experiences, the development of identity, attitudes to the body, memories, expectations and sense of time itself into alignment with dharmic structures. Indeed, they make good the original strategy of the *Mānava Dharma Śāstra* which, prefacing its social philosophy with an account of the creation of the universe, aimed to instill in each individual a sense of primeval order unfolding itself through the nature of the person, body and each phase of natural development.

Such structuring practices thus imbue human embodied existence on the broadest scale with a 'participatory' ethos, reminding humans of their continuity with the universe at large and even assuring them of their influence upon that universe. But they must also maintain a curious balance between the creative empowerment that this potentially bestows, and the responsible constraint of that power for the good of the existing order. Negative creativity is potentially like the dancing of Śiva, a frenzied and careless subjective activity by which the cosmos could be de-structured.

This counterpoint of positive and negative creativity – or structuring and de-structuring practices – also exists *within* the self. Where many tantric traditions sought to systematically dissolve the body and mind in order to rebuild it again in a new form, traditions such as classical Sāṃkhya and certain schools of non-dualist Advaita sought to de-structure the mind until no structure of embodiment is left at all. The tradition of mental structuring influenced by Yoga, with its sceptical attitude towards desire, was later paralleled by traditions of emotional structuring that emerged out of the development of Hindu devotionalism and its positive attitude to desire. As the trend towards emotion-oriented religious life (often designated as '*bhakti*') gained momentum from the early medieval period onwards, increasingly sophisticated aesthetic and visualization techniques were developed to structure one's emotional life and thereby acquire control over it. The 'new yoga' of emotion that became prevalent in much devotional practice was focused on techniques for the cultivation and intensification of affective states, but structuring was still required to avoid chaos and achieve a heightened and intensified new structure. June McDaniel's (2012) work on the excesses of *bhakti* devotional emotion highlights the importance of yogic techniques for gaining mastery over the emotional fabrics of the self even within traditions that 'idealize excess': yoga can cultivate emotion or control it, bringing 'runaway bhakti' under the aegis of a manageable habitus so that practitioners can 'modulate and fine-tune' emotional experience. Whether stillness or passion was the desired outcome, the inner sphere presented another materiality that could be shaped, presenting a space of self-creativity in which, one's commitment to dharmic action notwithstanding, and in which experiments in restructuring were possible.

## Structuring practices: celebrating the ordered cosmos

Like Geertz's model of a worldview, the various structuring practices of Hinduism thus have two dimensions in that they are both *descriptive*, highlighting the potential for order in the world, and also *prescriptive*, encouraging human beings to help create and sustain that order. As such the vision of an ordered cosmos that first takes form in the Vedas is an 'aesthetics of ritual and reality' that colours Hindu perceptions of the world and motivates action within it. It reflects the underlying Vedic ethos of mastery by which humans can influence the most fundamental structures of thought, society and nature. Structuring practices allow humans to participate in the cosmos and ultimately to 'own' their place within it.

In his anthropological study of ritual, exploring the way it creates both 'structure and anti-structure', Victor Turner (1969: 7) wrote about humans as being constantly engaged in a struggle against chaos: 'by verbal and non-verbal means of classification we impose upon ourselves innumerable constraints and boundaries to keep chaos at bay'.[1] Each structuring ritual relates to a *nomos*, to borrow a term from Peter Berger (1967), a meaningful order of reality that we celebrate, and in which we seek to embed ourselves. These approaches speak to the motivations behind many Hindu ritual traditions, seeking the establishment of structure itself, as a form of existence that is valued as sacred regardless of the particular context, place or time. Dissolution into non-embodiment may have its value in certain Hindu traditions that seek to help the self escape its embodiment and leave the world, but to be embodied is to seek the proper functioning of that body and the actualization of its potential.

This foregrounding of structure can be seen as a major feature of Hindu worldviews regarding the relationship of self and world: rather than merely 'training' ritual participants into following predetermined rules, it alerts them to their place as participants in the cosmic principle of structure, and emphasizes its importance as a prerequisite of all life. In many respects these sources invert the functionalist idea that religion's goal and origin lies in its fulfilment of practical functions; instead functionality itself – the proper operation of things – is elevated to a cosmological status. This inversion underpins the shift from the 'etic' to the 'emic' dimensions of understanding Hindu ritual: social functions are only one instance of the broader principles of structuredness that are celebrated in certain kinds of Hindu practice.

Importantly, while ritual has tended to be seen as a constrictive practice that favours tradition and the authority of precedent and top-down patterns of behaviour, this perspective reveals the creative dimension of ritual *ideology*. As we have seen, William Mahony and Brian Smith (1998: 53) emphasize this creative aspect of ritual: 'reality, according to the Vedic savants, is not given but made ... Sacrifice for them was not ... regarded as a symbolic representation of an already concretised reality ... the ritual was the workshop in which reality was forged'. The set order of actions followed in every ritual practice become *participatory patterns* through which the basic human capacity to create new actions, sounds, objects and images is elevated as a way of contributing to the broader structure of the universe. Practitioners are put in the role of an engineer or artist of the universe. In this respect, Hindu ritual engages humans in the artisanship of the world. Awareness of this participation may become highly sublimated for the practitioners, but it is embedded in the pressures that encourage ritual participation in the first place: ritual is done because it avoids the social and cosmic misfunction threatened by 'inauspicious' situations. One of the most celebrated examples of this willing decision to participate in the world-upholding structures of society is Arjuna's decision to maintain his caste dharma in the *Bhagavad Gītā*.

Thus one of the goals of structuring rituals is not only to use one's agency to explore the possibilities of embodiment, but also to cause one's own small part of history to follow a more perfect path. While in most rituals individuals do not have the right to spontaneously alter the structure of a collaborative public rite or a life-stage ritual, scholars such as Axel Michaels (2012: 17, 19), working on regional variations in ritual form, have shown that the syntactical order of common rituals does indeed provide a prescriptive 'grid' for correct action, 'but not at the price of neglecting local customs or ritual elements that might even come from a folk or tribal background'. Ritual 'grammar' 'in this sense means rules that can be followed, varied and extended by those who know them'. Certain Hindu contexts of practice, such as pilgrimages, more than others such as Brahminically directed Vedic rituals, extend creative participation in the cosmic order to a wider cross-section of society (including women, children and non-priestly castes), extending the opportunity for 'practical participation in divine truth' to the community at large (Michaels 2008: 227).

But creative freedom is at a premium in such traditions, partly by virtue of their very functionalist conception of order as a sustaining necessity. Creativity had to be private and undertaken within the parameters of a carefully limited scope for free action in the world. Laurie Patton's study of *viniyoga* has helped to highlight the precise mechanisms of poetic creativity within the performance of Vedic rituals, drawing on each specific real-life context, and the associations that participants bring to the constitution of ritual symbolism, to introduce an individual creative element. According to this model rituals that appear repetitive on the outside may actually incorporate an imaginative, poetic process (Patton 2005). It is the unique challenge of human life to find ways of collaborating constructively with the structures of reality through ritual, social custom and ethical choice, arts and other media. Humans enact their identity as free-willed, creative participants in broader cosmic structures through such practices, and for this reason Karl Potter ([1963] 1991) argued that Indian practice is deeply ethical, in the sense that it is premised on human free will and the striving for control and well-chosen goals. In classical Hindu culture, he argued, the primary concern

> is not morality but freedom, not rational self-control in the interests of the community's welfare but complete control over one's environment – something which includes self-control but also control over others and even control of the physical sources of power in the universe. (3)

Potter contrasts this Indian emphasis on freedom with the stoic ideal of self-limitation in Western thought. Indian detachment and dispassion are tools of a struggle for control (not primarily of others as in power relations, but of oneself and the embodied world at large), and he highlights the work of mastery or structuring around which so many narratives of Hindu religious life are built. As such, structuring practices summon distinctive emotions associated with the aesthetic of order – whether of gratitude for order, fear of disorder or the dogged determination to effect gradual change through a *yajña* ritual or *sādhana* discipline. This rich and dramatic complex of distinctive emotions accompany the human recognition that we live in a cosmos that depends in some measure upon us, and not a chaos over which we have no control. If the human body is 'open' to the world and participates widely within it, then the private human project of self-transformation should be seen as continuous with the global project of shaping the world.

## Transformative practices: the mutable cosmos

While the belief in an innate and imminent order in which we can participate provided an attractive narrative for Hindu practice, the modal view of reality outlined earlier became equally if not more central to Hindu ritual culture, due in part to the influence of Tantric traditions in which trans-substantiating practices, aimed at changing material realities into sacred ones, were common. To this purpose, certain kinds of ritual adopt a more destabilizing and radical aim than structuring practices – they transform the very substance of objects, places, the body or of consciousness. Such 'transformative' practices reflect a broader cosmological presupposition that the universe is susceptible to transubstantiation into materials with quite different qualities and values. We have seen that certain texts envisioned reality as capable of shifting between different modes, and one task of ritual is to act as a catalyst for that shift. Challenging modern Western assumptions about the material nature of the world, such practices deal in subtle bodies, energies and intensities, imagined, sonic and semantic entities, hidden potencies and spirit possessions. In such a multiverse of materials, techniques for effective human agency have an almost alchemical power to change the conditions in which we find ourselves. Far from reinforcing the pre-existing state, transformative practices allow practitioners to alter the world.

## Tantra, *mantra* and divinization

This conception of materiality was developed in a range of different Hindu traditions: the Sāṃkhya school's metaphysical scheme for explaining the transformation of a basic substance into the complex world we see around us had a long-standing impact on later philosophies. Yogic practices were also a tool for transformation, in some sources prescribing processes through which the mind can be 'smashed', 'melted' and 'liquified' (White 2009b: 72), and the energies of the body heightened and redirected. Tantric practices often included 'sacramental' techniques for turning material things into sacred realities, and such practices were prominent in initiation rituals (*dīkṣā*), and in the use of magical items such as *mantra*s (verbal formulas) and *maṇḍala*s (visual symbols), mental visualizations and sacred substances. Quotidian public practices such as festivals could also alter the nature of the world around the practitioner, transforming the mundane streets of a modern city into a *tīrtha* or sacred space that gives access to the divine realm (see Jacobsen 2008). Such religious practices presuppose that we live within a many-levelled reality, ripe for transformation. Even divinization is possible for those specialists – Brahmins, gurus, yogis, mediums and devotees – with the power to change old realities into new ones.

The transformation of substances was one goal of early medical schools of thought and of India's own traditions of what might be called 'alchemy' (see White 1998), and these ideas become particularly influential in Tantric genres; indeed, André Padoux (2011: 1) has written that 'since at least a thousand years, Hinduism has been very largely Tantric or "tantricized", not Vedic ... it is to be felt everywhere in Hinduism'.

Tantric rituals echo Vedic ones in their complexity and cosmological associations, but make greater use of substances and images meant to transform the materials of the ritual or of the ritualist. André Padoux (2011) has highlighted the special place of *mantras* – spoken ritual syllables – as a kind of entity that seems to exist across different modes of being. Sound is tangible through our sense-perception and can be 'captured' in symbols and integrated into coherent meanings. Yet it is non-material, and thus has the ability to bridge the worldly and supernatural realms:

> Mantras '... have a twofold nature: transcendent *and* empirical. On the one hand, they are conceived either as being in essence forms of *vāc*, the Word, the supreme unique cosmic power, or as being individualised powers, discrete supernatural entities, being in that case the highest aspect, the essence of deities or of specific aspects of deities ... But, on the other hand, mantras in so far as they are ritual formulas invoked, held in their minds or uttered by human beings, acting on (and through) their mind and body, exist mentally and phonetically on the level of the empirical world ... This, one could say contradictory, nature of Tantric mantras appears clearly in many of their ritual, meditative, mystical or magical uses. (6)

Padoux notes that this gives them the ability to transform other realities. *Mantras* used in ritual

> are supposed to be directly effective. They do what they say: they purify, they protect, they cut, they transform (water into *amṛta*, for instance, or the body of the performer into a divine one, or into one made a mantras, a *mantradeha*), they bring about the presence of a deity in an icon or on a maṇḍala, etc. (6)

Padoux's analysis demonstrates how important it is to take into account underlying assumptions about the nature of verbal utterances, before attempting to interpret their significance in ritual; in this case, *mantras* function not only semantically, but also instrumentally, as mediatory entities that span both the supernatural and empirical worlds, and also as objects of power that may have their own agency. They exemplify the way in which certain kinds of Hindu ritual are directly concerned with the capacity, open to initiated persons, to transform the immediate empirical reality around us. Here ritual appears less as a moral imperative or a social custom than as a technique for expanding the range of a person's interactions with the surrounding world.

A number of transformative rituals are aimed specifically at divinization of objects or the human body of the practitioner. In this context divinization was understood primarily as a transformation of the very substance of the body by mentally inscribing pre-existing sacred realities, such as texts, deities or a sacred cosmology onto the body. The mind itself had a powerful role to play here, able to transform materials through meticulous processes of visualization; indeed, this transformation of the body through rituals of recitation and visualization can be seen as a central 'root metaphor' in the tantric understanding of the cosmos (see Flood 2006).

*Dīkṣā* initiation could itself be seen as a symbolic act of burning away the old self and setting up a new one, a process that is sometimes linked to the accumulation of *tapas* or spiritual 'heat' acquired through personal sacrifices and envisioned as an energy that can be directed towards various ends. Charles Malamoud (1998: 44–8) interprets the ritual transformations of *dīkṣā* as a human version of the Vedic sacrificial offering; just as the fire of the sacrifice transforms mere food into a 'heavenly gift' to the gods through the process of burning, so the ritual transforms the merely material body into a new sacred form.

Śaiva tantras, in particular, emphasized the importance of swapping bodies for new divinized ones, both in the case of the deity and of the priest, as Karen Prentiss (1999: 122) describes:

> The Śaiva āgamas redefine embodiment as 'ritual transformation.' In the ritual context, both Śiva and the priests must take on appropriate 'bodies' . . . Both of these transformations are accomplished by the placing of mantras on the respective bodies. Prior to the invocation of Śiva, the priest begins his ritual sequence of self-purification (*ātmaśuddhi*) by imposing mantras on his hands (*karanyāsa*). This makes his hands 'Śiva-like' and fit for performing all subsequent rites . . . the priest then invokes Śiva to come down from the *dvādaśānta* (location of the undifferentiated Paramaśiva [highest Śiva] into the form of Sadāśiva, a 'differentiated divine body comprised of mantras, yet infused too with the presence of Paramaśiva'.

New bodily states are available at need (though considerable effort or sacrifice may be necessary). Where structuring practices allow material entities to be made and used in a positive, functional way, transformative practices ensure that one need not be stuck with any particular form of material embodiment.

One of the most striking examples of divinization is the elevation of pilgrimage sites – whole tracts of geographical space – into a sacred state with an almost sacramental power to purify pilgrims. Many Indian cities are built in the form of a vast *maṇḍala* in accordance with the designs set out in the Vastu-Śāstra literature on sacred architecture. Cities such as Jaipur in

Rajasthan, or Madurai at the other end of the subcontinent in Tamil Nadu, sought to situate the entire community within a geometrically reshaped space that bestows divine order on the chaos of urban living and sacralizes the city. Varanasi, also known as Kashi, the 'City of Light', is seen by many Hindus as one of the most important 'sacramental' spaces, purifying visitors by their very presence in it so that those who die there are said to be transported directly to heaven higher state.

The result of most initiations of a 'body', human or divine, is a transformation of the self either into a being possessed of special new powers, or into a being that exists on a higher soteriological level of reality, acquiring a *proximity to* or *identity with* the divine. Possession is often best understood in Indian contexts as a transformative event; it is less an interaction of separate 'self'-objects in which one displaces the other, than a kind of colouring, altering or pervasion of the self by new influences that transform it into something (or someone) else – Frederick Smith (2006), for instance, has noted that emotions are paradigmatic of many kinds of Indian possession in that they alter the character and disposition of the self rather than displacing it (see 345–62). Alongside the biochemical paradigm for understanding transformation that is prominent in Atharva Vedic, Upanisadic, Yoga and Sāṃkhya influenced literatures, possession then offers another way of understanding transformative practice as constantly introducing new qualities to the innately receptive canvas of material and mental realities. This is a particularly striking point of view in light of the fact that many possession practices are effectively divinizations of material reality: rather like the Holy Spirit in the biblical Book of Acts, deities can act as transformative forces that 'colour' the impressionable material reality into which they enter (see Frazier 2016). The human person then seems less like an autonomous monad with impermeable boundaries than a 'sponge' that soaks up influences; transformative religious practices such as *ḍīkṣā*, invocation of deities, and inversely, exorcism, all work to manage that sphere of influence.

In modern Hinduism, images of the divine – *mūrti*s – and the sacred spaces in which they are worshiped became the most commonly transformed religious media, revealing the power of *divinization* practices to establish centres of the sacred in the midst of the material world of the practitioner. This required initiatory installation rituals (*pratiṣṭhā*) that could both bring the divine into the material realm, and transform the material object into a suitable vessel. Understood to breathe life into the image that is used for temple worship, this ritual was sometimes called *prāṇa-pratiṣṭhā* – the 'installation of life-breath' – an image that symbolically draws it within the cycle of biochemical processes characteristic of the biological body and emphasizes the capacity of the rituals to instate life, and with it consciousness, into otherwise inert vessels of mere stone or metal. Substances could convey the qualities of the deity to the devotee – ash to convey the detachment of Śiva, *tulasī* (sweet basil) and sandalwood or turmeric to convey the sweetness and pleasantness of Viṣṇu and kumkum powder to convey the hot-blooded energy of the goddess. Offerings themselves become transformed into a subtle 'spiritual form' once they are offered to the deity: mere material food becomes *prasāda*, a sort of sacred substance, altered through its contact with the divine and now able to transform the worshiper who consumes it. Modal realities are pervasive and always ready to become something new.

## Theories of transformation: shaping the world

Vasudha Narayanan (2004) has interpreted transformative practices such as temple installation rituals as centred on 'the paradox of nonmatter'; she highlights the way in which an ignorance of the transformative science behind these religious practices led to confusion and horror among nineteenth-century Western missionaries. In order to comprehend the centrality of the *mūrti* image in Hindu practice, she argues that one must learn to see it as 'a bit of heaven on earth' (463). Thus one might say that trans-substantiation is as important in Hindu as in Catholic practice, but far more common. The manifold and volatile nature of reality is central to ideas of ritual and reality in both traditions.

William Sax (2009a: 80–1) has argued that trans-substantiation is paradigmatic of Hindu ritual, allowing the skilled practitioner to bring together seen and unseen worlds in a profound 'consubstantiation' of material: 'this is the pivotal moment of the rituals, when myth and iconography, context and social memory, power and morality, all come together. It is the moment when ritual fuses together 'the world as lived and the world as imagined'. The presence of transformation means that humans effectively live in a 'consubstantiate world' in which different levels are constantly present throughout one's self and environment. Hindu practices frequently maintain our contact with these points of fused reality, from divine images, to sacred places, to our own subtle bodies or transformed minds. Hindu ritual action thus reflects our place in what Victor Turner (1974: 24) would term a 'world in becoming, not a world in being'.

These practices invite us to alter conceptions of ritual itself. Arnold van Gennep argued that ritual creates a 'liminal' time and space outside of the normal processes of life, the purpose of which is to allow us to modify established structures before returning to a 'new' normality. For van Gennep, (1960) ritual creates a temporary period of instability in which other possibilities become available; but ultimately religion reinforces the existing order, restricting change as much as possible. However the Hindu view suggests a world which is permanently 'liminal', constantly verging on other natures that are possessed *in potentio*.

But the corresponding form of agency requires ritual specialists who not only *do* the practice, but can also *see* the possibilities that lie behind the apparently static material world that is empirically presented to them. Richard Davis (1997: 43) emphasizes the way in which transformative practices in devotional worship require a 'special' eye that can look beyond the limited data of the senses:

> The devotional eye takes the icon enshrined in the temple as the living presence of God, sees through its translucency brief glimpses into the fullness of his being, and then occasionally turns back on itself to observe the paradoxical quality of this transcendence within immanence.

The relativization of empirical reality, redetermined as a 'translucent' portal allowing us to perceive the greater 'fullness of being' that is believed to be present and real, is one of the key presuppositions for understanding this Hindu worldview (and, indeed, many others). Failure to grasp this is one reason why Hindu thought can remain so deeply opaque to interpreters who are shaped by the suppositions of the West's modern empirical sciences. By contrast the Hindu foregrounding of the problem of change, and its consequent view of reality as a multimodal plenitude, laid the foundation for quite different attitudes to mind and body, truth and falsity, the world and its immanent possibilities. As Wilhelm Halbfass (1993: 102) wrote of one Indian ontological concept:

> [P]roblems of translation should be taken as welcome opportunities to re-examine our own familiar apparatus of ontological terms and concepts, and to ask ourselves whether we really know what we mean by 'essence' and 'existence', 'being' and 'nothingness', 'possibility' and 'actuality', etc., and how binding this framework really is.

We are reminded that discussions of substance, causality, transformation, modes, essence and identity are not merely obscure philosophical topics divorced from any impact on lived and embodied forms of existence. Such ideas determine the way in which bodies exist, worlds make themselves available to our thoughts and actions. Here in marked contrast to the passive monotonal character attributed to matter in popular Western thought, Hindu materiality is understood as a phenomenon within which lay a 'latent, non-manifest, potential' dimension of reality that went unseen, but was existent nevertheless (43).

# 11

# Interactive practices: The community of selves

We have seen that the world, for classical Hindu culture, was something replete with hidden elements and orders, processes and potentialities. But one of the most important 'kinds' of reality to be found in the worldview of the Upaniṣads is the agents – the centres of higher reflective, decision-making and awareness – that people the material world. It is these beings that cluster together the elements of the cosmos, catalyse its changes and clothe themselves in thoughts of varying – and sometimes infinite – scope. These agencies are like us; they may be other human persons or beings in quite different types of bodies (animal, subtle or divine), who nevertheless dwell around humans – and even within them as the deities are sometimes said to do. Reality, then, is also composed as a collection of agencies, each of which controls a succession of 'bodies' that are themselves open to change and exchange. These many 'selves' form a far larger community than is normally taken into account by social theories of religion or ritual that focus on observable human society, but may be oblivious to the communities of hidden beings that are present in the indigenous worldview. Particularly important for Hindu ritual is the more-than-human community of gods and spirits, demons and ghosts, avatars and subtle bodies, all of whom provide the warp and weft of Hindu 'society' in its largest sense. Understanding of this trans-human community presents a necessary key for understanding the Hindu practice of interactions with such beings through worship, service or offerings. Hindu conceptions of community and communication must include neighbours who are considered no less real despite the subtle or transitory character of their embodiment.

## Divine agents and bodies

The definitions of 'agency' that we have seen are clearly not restricted to human beings: anything able to approach its embodiment with intelligent capacities of discriminating choice is an agent, and anything able to reflect and infer broad truths has the capacity to transcend the most immediate boundaries of its embodiment and become a 'larger' self. The implications of this account of the self is that each must mind be one of only many, and that this community of selves must extend beyond the human sphere to include divine and other bodies, forming a vast community that peoples classical worldviews and speaks to animist and theistic practice in all periods of Hindu culture. It also invites a fresh engagement with divine embodiment and materiality in Hinduism, a phenomenon which had previously been denigrated by Muslim and Christian thinkers alike as a form of idolatry:

> Only very recently have scholars of Hinduism begun to understand and 'to see' those fully embodied gods who inhabit small shrines and great temples or who walk as teacher and lord among their devotees; and, in whose living presence most Hindus, modern or traditional, orthodox or tribal, pass their lives. (Waghorne and Cutler 1985: 1)

Personal relationships of worship and reverence feature prominently in many aspects of Hindu culture, reflecting South Asia's history of animistic belief in local spirits, and its combination with the polytheism of the Vedic gods, tribal patron deities and the monotheism of later devotional traditions that were informed by evocative arts and exciting narratives. It is natural, then, that interpersonal practices have become a key element of Hindu activity, concerned as they are with creating, sustaining and deepening one's relationship with another being – a teacher, guru, spirit or deity. Some of the most popular practices, from the daily *pūjā* worship in the morning to *mūrti-bhoga* offerings to the image of the deity at mealtime, effectively allow humans to live alongside the divine, filling the daily routine with experiences of the sacred. The sociologist Emile Durkheim (2008) argued that religion derives from emotional 'effervescence' that arises when we feel part of a community; here we see a focus on the effervescence of communion not only with other humans, but also with divine beings.

If transformative rituals provide important support for interactive practices by providing concrete spatio-temporal 'bodies' that the gods can enter into, then interactive rituals cultivate our interaction with them on a mental and physical level. This allows for a particularly immediate and intimate kind of daily relationship. The meeting of the deity's eyes in the ritual of *darśana*, or 'seeing' the image of the deity, the performing of *seva* service to the physical image as if it were a living human body, the physical contact when anointing the deity in the *abhiṣeka* and the fully embodied interaction of speech and touch that are made possible by customs in which deities take possession of living humans, all create a form of interaction that is almost unique to Hinduism among the major world religions (although it shares common traits with the many animist traditions that still thrive on every continent except Europe).

In all of these practices an intensely *realistic* attitude to spiritual beings is in evidence: deities and spirits are seen to have their own autonomous presence, and we must develop relationships with them as we would with the neighbours, family members, friends, lovers, teachers or leaders in our human community. This realism is almost never made explicit in the Hindu world – there are relatively few theological or philosophical texts discussing the nature of the manifestation of the divine in natural objects. These spiritual presences are often primarily an *enacted* reality, all the more evident in the immediacy of religious experience.

The practice of interacting with spirits, ghosts, demons and deities is one that takes place across much of South, Southeast and East Asia and has probably done so from the earliest periods of religious practice. In the Vedas this is seen in the *yajña* rituals of sacrificial offering, which created a kind of formalized communication between earth and heaven. *Agni*, the fire, was seen as a messenger helping humans to communicate with the gods, while the altar acted as a place of gift-giving, and the ritual enclosure set the scene for eloquent hymns addressed to the deities directly.

In the *Ṛg Veda*, the importance of Agni, as a mediator between the worlds of gods and men, demonstrates the concerns of the early Brahminical community with access to divine persons. There is a clearly defined cosmology separating them, and this division reoccurs repeatedly in the early Vedic texts. This divide, which seems to have been mitigated in later Hinduism by the shift towards immanent deities present in *mūrti*s and within the self, distinguishes Ṛg Vedic thought from later traditions. In *Ṛg Veda* 1.1.1 Agni is asked to be present and easy to access, and familiar relationships are proposed as a model: he is asked to be like a father (*pita iva*). A certain anxiety about access to the divine is in evidence in the constant invocation of the gods, and the spread of theologies of embodied divinity, made present through natural and crafted images, helpsed to bring the unseen agencies into concrete relationship through material media. But the gods were not the only beings filling the space of the world; a wide range of kinds of person are described in the

*Atharva Veda*, from deities to sorcerers, demons and natural principles, and these show that from the earliest stages the community of beings who could be addressed for support or mercy was a wide one:

> We address Agni, the forest trees, the herbs and the plants, Indra, Bṛhaspati, the sun: let them free us from distress . . .
>
> We address the sky, the asterisms, the earth, the yakṣas, the mountains; the oceans, the rivers, the pools – let them free us from distress.
>
> The gods that are seated in the sky, and that are seated in the atmosphere, the mighty ones that are set on the earth – let them free us from distress . . .
>
> The niggards we address, the demons, the serpents, the pure-folk, the Ancestors; the hundred-and-one-deaths we address; let them free us from distress . . .
>
> All the Gods we now address, of true agreements, increasers of righteousness, together with all their spouses; let them free us from distress. (6.6.1, 10, 12, 16, 19)

These beings have each their own powers and spheres of activity, as a passage about the character Ajātaśatru reminds us in *Bṛhad Āraṇyaka Upaniṣad* 2.1.2 when he gives a long list of deities describing the virtues and blessings associated with each;

> the person in the moon sustains food,
> the person in lightning makes one radiant,
> the person in space brings children and livestock,
> the person in the wind makes one invincible,
> the person in fire makes one irresistible,
> the person in the waters will make one gain what resembles him,
> the person in the mirror will make one shine,
> the echo of a person will gain one a full life span,
> the person in the quarters gains one companions,
> the person consisting of shadow avoids death,
> and the person in the self (*ātman*) gains one a self.
> (Summarized from 2.1.2–13)

The acknowledgement of these 'persons' present throughout the cosmos, each with their own powers, reminds us that reality was seen as a pluralistic texture of many agencies, human and otherwise. Here 'agency' is located liberally throughout the universe, present wherever animation stirs materiality to movement and action.

## Worship as the communion of persons

The Vedic ritual style of offerings – which emphasized exchange and communication between the communities of humans and gods or spirits – was very different from the forms of worship that later developed in the context of temple shrines. A new style of Brahminical 'care' of the deities, and public visitation of them, developed, and one of the most striking aspects of this new form of interaction is that its instrumental purpose as a way of obtaining divine aid was sidelined behind the idea that the interaction itself has an intrinsic value. The *Agni Purāṇa* is a text that compiles together the rituals and accepted practice of a range of different deities and traditions, and it gives an account of the way in which the bodies (images, *mūrti*s) of the deities are to be treated. The priest should

> go to the shed where the image has been made ready accompanied by the sculptors and custodians of the image ... Having placed the image in the pavilion and having adored and worshiped the dressed image (one has to say) 'I bow to you the sovereign lady of celestials who has been made (ready) by Viśvakarman (the divine architect).' I make obeisance to you who is resplendent and is the sustainer of the entire universe ... Having submitted thus that idol should be carried to the bathing pavilion. The sculptor should be satisfied by offering articles (of present). A cow should be given as a gift to the priest. Then the eyes of the image should be made open with the syllable *citraṃ deva*. (58.1–7)

After this the deity is bathed, clothed, perfumed and given the appropriate objects for personal use – a parasol, mirror, fly whisk, ornaments, fan – and once it has been put to bed, clothing and food should be left by the bed, and household objects submitted to the deity (here, the Goddess) for her approval. As servants of the deity, the priests must involve her in the activities, addressing her and asking her approval. The true creator of the image is not the sculptor, but (through him) the divine craftsman of the gods, Viśvakarman. The deity is not simply for show and at the service of worshipers: objects are left for private use by the deity alone during the hours of the night.

Such practices continue little changed today, and a simpler but similar basic pattern forms the structure of interaction at many village and wayside shrines, where an image or a natural form such as a stone, tree or stream will mark the presence of a local deity or spirit for whom offerings of food, flowers, valued substances or other gifts will be left by its community. These offerings establish a relationship of benevolence – one might say an agreement – with the being who receives the gift, usually resulting in aid if it is a powerful being, or placation, if it is one that threatens harm. As with any sentient being, the relationship must be maintained over time, and a well-established set of conventions may well arise around long-standing relationships, such as that between a village and the ancestor of the community, or the spirits of nearby natural features such as mountains, rivers and trees. David Haberman (2013) has highlighted the presence of widespread but under-theorized worship of trees – treated as 'people' – throughout India.

Often this interaction with spirits and deities reflects the standard relationships (e.g. familial, feudal, friendship and love relationships) that are more familiar to humans within the community. The Goddess Saṣṭhi, for instance, is envisioned as a just arbitrator and supporter of women who are vulnerable because of misfortunes or the sometimes restrictive kinship structures of the community. She is an ally and defender who is brought into the community through the rituals that are done in her honour, including 'vows' or *vrata*s in which women will perform certain set actions, and will then listen to the narrative about Saṣṭhi to which those particular actions and images relate (see Sengupta 2010). Such stories confirm that Saṣṭhi possesses her own autonomous life and personality, telling of life as a woman dealing with the adventures of health and illness, relationship and reputation – issues that females typically face. In that community, the *vrata* ritual places the practitioner within that narrative world as one of the women who turn to Saṣṭhi for help. Similarly, rituals in Rajasthan may place local husbandry communities in a relationship of support and advocacy with the clever herder Pabujī (see Smith 1991). Such local rituals are effective in redrawing the circle of relationship around divine as well as human members of the community.

The ritual enactment of a profoundly interactive relationship with the divine is nowhere more explicit than in the practices of *darśana* by worshipers, and *mūrti-seva* by temple priests. In these cases, in addition to participating as a member of the divine community, a neighbour of the gods, as it were, one also undertakes direct personal bodily interaction with the physical form of the deity on earth. Diana Eck's (1985) study of *darśan*, the practice of ritually meeting the gaze of the divine in a consecrated statue or picture, emphasized its importance as one of the most widespread of all Hindu practices. She combined ethnographic work with an awareness of the relevant textual traditions to help interpret the practice:

> A common sight in India is a crowd of people gathered in the courtyard of a temple or at the doorway of a streetside shrine for the *darśan* of the deity. *Darśan* means 'seeing'. In the Hindu ritual tradition it refers especially to religious seeing, or the visual perception of the sacred. When Hindus go to a temple, they do not commonly say, 'I am going to worship', but

> rather, 'I am going for *darśan*'. They go to 'see' the image of the deity – be it Kṛṣṇa or Durgā, Śiva or Viṣṇu – present in the temple ... The central act of Hindu worship, from the point of view of the layperson, is to stand in the presence of the deity and to behold the image with one's own eyes, to see and be seen by the deity. (3)

Eck aims to go the heart of this common practice by focusing on the specific interaction that makes the experience significant to worshipers. The experience of looking into someone's eyes is common in everyday life as a mark of recognition, of understanding and, when prolonged, of intimacy. Here Eck shows how the embodiment of the deity in visual forms enables Hindu culture to harness that powerful human experience of intersubjective recognition, understanding and intimacy using it as a core feature of Hindu relationships with the divine.

This sense of direct encounter within the deity's own home can be difficult to convey for those used to seeing Hindu images in galleries or as a symbolic depiction. Richard H. Davis (1997: 23) contrasts the purely visual encounter with Hindu statuary in an art gallery with the highly tangible, imaginative and sense-rich way in which practitioners would have interacted with the same deity-images in their original temple setting:

> As a result of Śiva's theophany in physical icons, human worshipers considered it incumbent upon them to treat his physical embodiment as a divine person. The primary liturgical practices of medieval Śaiva temples, accordingly, involved the same kinds of respectful services a diligent host might offer an honored human guest or an attendant at court might offer his mortal lord, but presented in this case directly to God, personalised within an icon. So worshipers before Śiva received the deity graciously, offered him water to sip and rinse his feet, bathed and dressed him, adorned him with ornaments, fed him, gave him after-dinner condiments, entertained him with music and dance, bowed humbly before him, and petitioned him to grant them his all-powerful grace.

Davis highlights the way in which the Hindu theology of divine embodiment facilitates a particularly intense form of personal theism in which practitioners not only think of the divine as analogous to a person, but are able to appropriate the full interactive relationship between persons, including physical care, sensory entertainments and arts, and physical modes of expressing reverence, and apply them to God. Davis highlights the idea that the Hindu divine image is almost never just 'a visual object only to be savoured objectively', but instead is the object of 'much more physical' interaction (17). Like a living human, each image also has its own 'life', sometimes shifting residence, owning property, receiving patronage from different rulers or groups and taking on new connotations and identities over time. Here a bridge is built between different agents, allowing them to interact directly, person to person through special forms of embodiment that span the worldly-supernatural divide.

The image may be a statue as in many temples, a picture as in many people's domestic rituals of worship, an iconic object or a visualization as used by many devotees in their private religious practices. Often in performing the offering ritual of *pūjā* one's body will be washed, shoes will be removed, the image or *mūrti* of the deity will be approached, the priest will anoint each person's forehead with a sacred substance and offer the light and fumes of the lamp so that the worshiper can gather some of its scent and light over his or her head. An offering is likely to be left on the tray that the priest carries as a gift to the deity, and in this sense the Vedic idea that the priest, like Agni, is necessary as a mediator remains. But outside of temples, in the domestic appropriation of the *pūjā* tradition into shrines at home, in the workplace or even in one's vehicle, an unmediated relationship prevails, and a silent prayer may be said with palms together while offering the 'subtle' substance of incense and meeting the gaze of the deity. In this way the act of offering culminates in a concrete personal encounter of the most direct kind: just as the meeting of someone's eyes creates a psychologically powerful interaction, so the meeting of the deity's gaze – directed outwards through the eyes of the image – also creates a unique moment of interpersonal relationship that is intimate in a more intense, immediate and embodied way than is found in many other traditions.

Such practices remind us that the theories of embodiment we have explored focus on the relation between agents and their bodies. But what happens when an agency encounters another agency? Practices such as *darśana* answer that question by suggesting that an unusual kind of perception and encounter takes place. Temple priests claim a particularly intense embodied relationship with the divine. Acting as the personal 'manservant' of the deity, typically the *pūjāri* will symbolically wake the ritually consecrated image of the deity in the morning and bathe it in various auspicious substances such as milk in the ritual of *abhiṣeka*. The deity will be dressed and taken through the day's routine of activities – giving audience to worshipers, listening to their petitions for help or blessing and enjoying the performance of devotional singing. Finally, deities will be ritually prepared for sleep and put to bed – either alone or, if the temple houses two deities who are consorts, together. Further, eating the consecrated offerings, or *prasad*, that have been made to the deity's image establish what McKim Marriott (1976) would call a 'transactional' relationship with the deity so that even at the physical level there is a mingling of bodies.

This is a transformative ritual meant to bestow grace and purification on the worshiper, but it is also an interactive ritual that creates the easy, social sense of community that comes from a meal 'shared' with the divine. This form of ritual interaction between humans and deities allows the relationship to approximate to embodied human interactions, placing the devotee and the deity on the same physical plane and using materiality as the basis of a shared and intimate life.

Many pilgrimages are locations that draw their significance from the actions of the gods, and at the forests of Vraja, the Śakti Pīṭhas or Mount Kailash devotees can feel themselves to be part of the *active* lives of the deities Krishna, Satī and Śiva, respectively. Indeed, the location of temples, the performance of communal singing and storytelling, and the imaginative life that the practices accompanying pilgrimage evoke, all work to recreate a sense of being within the spatio-temporal proximity of the deity, a participant in divine proceedings. David Haberman (1994) has used the pilgrimage to the deity Krishna's childhood landscape of Vraja, in Uttar Pradesh, to illustrate the way in which such pilgrimages allow practitioners to physically inhabit the world of divine dramas and passions. Festivals perform the same function, with special *times* replacing special *places*, as gateways into the divine story. In Bengal at Navratri the whole community enters into the emotions experienced by the parents of the goddess Parvatī as she weds the tempestuous deity Śiva; in a sense they become part of her extended family. Here it is not merely bodily materiality that serves to connect selves, but narratives of agency.

## Possession, gaze and intimate subjectivity

Cases where the divine and the human interact on a physical level are nowhere so immediately evident as in the many forms of possession that take place in Hindu cultures. Practices in which designated persons become ritually 'possessed' by the deity have a long history across cultures. In some traditions of possession, the goal is for the human person to become transformed into a being of higher awareness and supernatural capacities, but in many cases the main reason is to serve as a medium, a vehicle through which the surrounding community can interact with the deity. Worshipers come ready to 'meet' the deity.

Patricia Dold (2011: 55) has described the ritual of possession in which the goddess Kāmākhyā, in her ten different forms possesses male mediums known as Deodhas so that others in the community can have direct access to her:

> The Deodhas, each wielding the weapon(s) and wearing the color favoured by their god or goddess, move along the line of musicians ... Some Deodhas are more theatrical than others: Kālī's Deodha sticks out his (her?) tongue and triumphantly lifts Kālī's curved sword to the sky. All are received as deities by the assembled crowd. One by one, people approach different Deodhas with cautious reverence, giving them money, wrapping them in clothes and piling garlands so high around their necks that soon only their eyes are visible. They look like moving, living *mūrtis* (icons of deities). Within this intense atmosphere, I marvel at the sweetness of some of the exchanges between devotee and Deodha. I see great reverence and tenderness as I watch a woman and her son attempt to gain the attention of the goddess Calantā's Deodha. She holds up a garland, following the Calantā's dance back and forth. Finally the Calantā bows his head slightly to accept her garland, listens to her plea, and gently places his hands on the son's head and caresses the boy's cheek ... Such interactions, easily seen as a *pūjā* (worship) to the Deodha's deity, are constant.

Dold's account illustrates the human detail involved in ritual possessions by the divine: the standard iconography found on statues of the deity is present, but each Deodha is also able to express the deity's personality in different ways, offering a full personal expression of such divine attitudes as comfort and blessing. In the Himalayan rituals in which the deity Bhairav manifests in a human form through voluntary mediums – in a special form as Kachiya – the anthropologist William Sax (2009b: 45) notes that the community's potential doubt about the real presence of the gods, or their beneficial character, is dispelled when they encounter Kachiya as a bodily reality:

> This is the most persuasive and powerful appearance of the god, more compelling than any iconographic description and more immediate than any story ... This is a physical embodiment of Bhairav and devotees see it often enough to persuade them that he is quite real. Indeed, when I asked my friends if they 'really believed' in Kachiya, their most common response was, 'Of course I do. How could I not believe in him? He comes and dances, and you can see him right there in front of you!'

Such immediate and concrete interactions with the divine hint at the broader implications for Hindu attitudes to doubt and belief. Some possession rituals incorporate elements meant to demonstrate the presence of the deity in a human body, such as feats of unusual strength or the endurance of pain. The divine can be understood not only as an invisible, incorporeal reality, but also as a body with a uniquely powerful influence over its environment.

Drawing on Geertz's notion that ritual enables worldviews to become concrete realities for believers, William Sax interprets the divine manifestation in Hindu possession practice as an event in which everyday reality and the sacred and powerful 'otherworld' of the deities are able to unite in a coherent single experience. Possession rituals thus break down the boundaries between the different 'worlds' and forms of embodiment within the Hindu worldview, consubstantiating them as bodily, psychological, communal presences. Hindu practitioners are regularly incorporated into a broader community of sacred and supernatural beings in this way, staying intensely aware of this 'larger' community and factoring it into their schedules and plans: allocating parts of their work or income for support of the deity, cooking for the deity, communicating with it and sharing the ongoing narrative of their lives. Deities, in turn, had legal status in some regions where they were able to own land, and many festivals that celebrate events in the life of a given deity are meant to draw the community into the drama of the deity's own story.

Such interactive practices as these are rooted in an epistemology that looked beyond the merely empirical data of the senses to explore and describe 'other' realities believed to lie, latent, under the surface. Davis (1997: 41) has hinted at an epistemology of 'translucency and paradox' that underpins modal realities, and the *darśana* relationship focuses not only on bodily coexistence, but also on the experience of an eye-to-eye, mind-to-mind, subject-to-subject relationship that is renewed daily at the individual level. Bodies are translucent: with proper attention one can directly see that self embodied in them. Hindu interactive rituals thus demand a theory of the perception and assumed presence of minds, and as such they pose a fundamental challenge to the Cartesian phenomenology which presumed that the five senses and immediate self-perception are the sole criteria for perception. They highlight a blind spot in the way Western thought has catalogued the kinds of 'things' that we perceive and encounter, pointing instead to forms of perception and encounter that are embedded in everyday communication: this kind of transpersonal empiricism acknowledges that other minds are some of the most important of all the 'objects' that we find in the world around us, despite their apparent invisibility.

This points towards the broader presence of 'other' ways of seeing in Hindu epistemic practice. In his study of the worship of trees as persons, David Haberman (2013) draws on E.B. Tylor's original definition of 'animism' as a rational observation of person-like features in natural entities, and looks at Lynn White's (1967, 1205–206) argument that the West typically assimilates 'personhood' to humanness. Haberman calls for a greater awareness of those widespread cultures that perceive the world as a community of subjects rather than a collection of objects, and in doing so he evokes the work of Graham Harvey (2015) on animism, and Bruno Latour (2005) on actor-network theory.

But the extension of community in this way has significant implications. Emile Durkheim, Marcel Mauss and Max Weber have variously interpreted ritual as symbolically engaging communal relationships of commonality and comfort, or feudal and economic power. Such theories have had numerous proponents in the study of Hindu ritual contexts and have often borne much fruit, but these interpretations are not necessarily in line with emic accounts that express a powerful, direct and deep encounter with another 'person'; such relations sometimes stand within established communal roles, but at other times they may overarch standard human relationship structures, making ephemeral but deep bonds between travellers and the inhabitants of wayside shrines, or deities whose amorphous character transcends ties to any particular community. This autonomy from the social structure on-the-ground is sometimes ring-fenced through the pan-Indian dimension of such practices; they disrupt the local arrangement with a broader framework. Relationships that take place at the level of 'subtle' bodily interaction may involve the building of an imaginally constructed devotional self with a different identity, profession, status and even gender from one's acknowledged social role. In many cases interactive practices also undercut the existing social structure through the notion that deities 'see the true self' and not merely the present embodiment.

Within Vedic studies, the emphasis on the structure of the ritual and the caste-coding of its participants has dominated the field, highlighting its structuring function. But others have sought to think more deeply about the relationships with the deities that are expressed in the rich, evocative, sometimes emotional and deeply direct body of Vedic hymns; Jan Gonda (1989: 1–2), for instance, noted that the Vedic noun *āśis*, signifying prayer and propitiation, calls for a more serious hermeneutic study of what is entailed in that relationship. He points out that the Hindu practice of 'prayer' has hitherto received 'scant attention' by scholars who appear disinterested in 'terminology designating acts of human–spiritual communication', perhaps because the Abrahamic paradigm of prayer is uncritically assumed to extend to the Indian case. But implicit in this inattention is a reluctance to analyse 'realistically' the attitude of addressing and communicating with another subjectivity that happens to be divine.

*Darśana*, described so evocatively by scholars such as Eck, contributes a central yet distinctive Hindu paradigm for understanding ritual practice as the locus of a direct and intimate relationship with the divine. In contrast to Mauss and Hubert's (1964: 2) account of sacrifice as 'a gift made by the primitive to supernatural beings with whom he needed to ingratiate himself', the ritual of *darśana* prioritizes the striking unmediated directness of reciprocally meeting another's eyes. The study of 'intimacy' as a category of relation has made a start in the social sciences, spearheaded by the work of Anthony

Giddens (1992). But these accounts, so deeply rooted in post-Enlightenment Western sensibilities, have inspired debate on what intimacy might look like apart from the Western Cartesian assumption of the atomistic and autonomous individual. Lynn Jamieson (1998; 1999) has worked to question the universality of Western scholarly definitions of 'intimacy' as a 'closeness' achieved through discussion, self-disclosure and the mutual revealing and shaping of the personality. This kind of intimacy implicitly assumes that verbal communication is an essential medium, thereby rejecting the possibility of intimacy with non-verbal beings such as animals, objects and anyone who may simply withhold him or herself from this form of disclosure. Hinduism, by contrast, allows for more direct intimacy through its 'open' bodies and minds, with their capacity for assimilation and exchange. Drawing on the varying forms that 'families' can take across contexts and cultures (not necessarily rooted in biological 'kinship'), David Morgan (1996) has also helped to look more widely at practices that create intimacy, emphasizing mutual knowing and recognition of a 'deeper' self.

Useful insights have arisen through scholarly theorization on the specific phenomenon of 'gaze' within *darśana*. Maussian exchange-based accounts were challenged by scholars such as Diana Eck (1985) who emphasized the defining importance of the mutual gaze in the experience of *pūjā*. Subsequent scholars have sought to give a more detailed hermeneutic unpacking of the phenomenon of seeing in Hindu culture. Christoph Wulf (2013: 268) has tried to bring the phenomenological perspective of continental thought into dialogue with anthropology on this point, interpretively unpacking the experience of gaze:

> But what does to gaze mean? ... Gazes are linked closely with the history of the subject and of subjectivity, as well as with the history of knowledge. Power, control and self-control find expression in them. They are evidence of our relationship to the world, to other people, and to the self. The gazes of other people constitute the social sphere, and within this category, we may distinguish intimate from public gazes ... the gaze is active as well as passive; it turns outward to the world and at the same time receives it.

Gaze, which appears so informal and intangible an aspect of ritual action, thus takes on a central significance as the glue of relationships: it is a very special kind of embodiment that provides a medium for the central agency of the self. Further, it has a special intellectual background as a distinctively Hindu practice of intimacy. Looking to the detailed lexicon of kinds of gaze that function as dramatic gestures in Sanskrit court poetry, Jan Gonda (1969: 4) notes that 'in ancient India "the language of the eyes" must have been more advanced than it is with us', and also that the eye is an essentially important organ of action that is equal or superior to hands or speech through 'the coercive, defensive, influential, "contagious" and propitious look'. Gaze thus can function as a tool of relationship-building and community-shaping, creating or preventing bonds, adding the colour of dominance or service to relationships, and establishing empathetic and sympathetic dispositions in others.

This is not only a psychological effect, but also an ontological one that alters one's actual nature. David Gordon White (1998, 2009a) and Frederick Smith's (2006) works on possession have noted the special significance of the eyes as a gateway for both exiting one's own body and entering into that of others, and Tantric texts such as the *Netra Tantra* (the 'Tantra of the Eye') depict the eyes as an organ of power – a vehicle of an intense mental and creative agency that far exceeds the limited possibilities of the physical body. Knut Axel Jacobsen (2012: 471–2) has pointed out contemporary cases that preserve this notion of the eyes as a channel for a variety of powers – including the sharing, altering or improving of another person's mind, and process of depositing a bit of oneself permanently within the subjectivity of another. It has also become clear that the Nyāya epistemological school's account of perception contains a theory of *extramission* – the externalization of the mind through the eyes in such a way as to 'touch' the world with its perceptual organs and retract information about – or even an essence of – that world back into the self. White (2009b: 71) backs this up with yogic examples that describe the ability of a skilled yogi 'to enter into another person's body and come into direct contact with that person's self' (see also Smith 2006). In this sense, the touch of the eyes is a more personal touch than that of the body; it conveys authenticity, non-mediated directness, the 'touch' of subjectivities and possibly mutual 'knowing,' a feature that David Morgan (2009) emphasizes in his work on acquaintance and intimacy.

Greater understanding of the Indian trope of gaze can help to correct Western theories of intimacy. The *darśana* context is non-discursive, creating intimacy by revealing the self directly through the portal of the eyes. And because of this presumed directness, this is not a verbally or socially specific self: instead it is an open undetermined self. Thus the 'vertical' ritual relation between human and deity seems not to concretize the socially constructed self into a definite character, but rather to encourage the 'mutable, multi-dimensional, non-linear' nature of the self (Smith 2006: xvi). To borrow a distinction from Friedrich Nietzsche's account of Ancient Greek culture, the intimacy that is created here is more Dionysian than Apollonian: that is, it reveals the structured public identity of the self and the relations that depend upon it to be contingent, and thus destabilizes them. Meanwhile it taps into a level of the subject that is seen to be deeper yet more fluid than the socially defined one. In this sense, to borrow Pierre Bourdieu's, and following him, Roy Rappaport's, notions of ritualized bodily habitus, certain elements of

Hindu interactive rituals, insofar as they engage via the gaze with a divine other, enact the 'deeper self' within the participant which is recognized by the deity. This involves the participant in an 'intimate community' of subjectivities. In this connection, Arno Bohler (2009: 120, 128) makes analogies between the 'bright, vast and open body' described in Indian Vedic and Yogic textual sources and Jean-Luc Nancy's notion of the body as a medium for 'world-wide being-with'.

## Theories of interaction: living in the trans-human community

Where the divine is able to interact as a genuinely bodied presence in time and space, interactive rituals cultivate the intimacy of space-sharing, that is, of feeling the spatially proximate presence of another body. The spontaneous, personal, real-time interaction found in the devotee's address to the deity is key to creating a relational realism that makes the divine a concrete part of the Hindu worldview. It is not only obliquely felt, but in many respects is as real as other persons and objects. Interaction with the embodied *mūrti* of a deity contributes to the creation of a 'neighbourhood' of both mortal and non-human persons. As such, embodiment here enables all sorts of beings to be bought within a spatio-temporal 'neighbourhood' defined by the routinization of regular bodily interactions within a locale. Like human persons the deity or spirit has its own private space, can be visited (though it sometimes closes its door and retreats from public view), must be cared for (through the ministrations of the priests and the gifts of neighbours) but it also helps to care for the community (through blessed food offerings of *prasāda* and protection of the home, village or land). It may possess property and engage in the commerce of food and resources on a daily basis. Its broad schedule is known, indicating its dispositions, and those who engage in *darśana* will be able to confirm that there is indeed 'someone there'.

The lives of these members of the neighbourhood are also important for constituting identities; like human neighbours whose past history, present situation and future goals all become familiar to the community, so too the narratives in which the gods and spirits are embedded define them as neighbours and cultivate important emotions of empathy and care. Bengali rituals for Goddess Parvati, for instance, create sympathy with the way in which she must take leave of her parents at the time of her wedding, and adopt a harsh new life in the mountains; this draws her within the structures of sympathy that any neighbourhood cultivates for its members. *Janmastami*, the festival celebrating the birth of Krishna, allows the community to celebrate the event of birth, empathize with the young baby and its joyful parents and cultivate emotions of affection. This affectivity is clearly an important 'glue' of communities. The '*homo duplex*' character of humankind, highlighted by Durkheim in his understanding of community as essentially bonded by instinctive emotional ties, points us to the way in which the elective community of religion often seeks to recapture the sense of a pre-industrial world of emotional ties (see on this Stjepan Mestrovic's (1997) study of the modern elision of emotion in *Postemotional Society*). Familial relations are often taken as the paradigmatic emotional relationships (not least because they feature so strongly in Western monotheistic characterizations of the divine), but Hindu worship contexts facilitate elective individual relations of affection insofar as they require genuine emotional engagement as willing servant or student, engaged friend or lover, caring parent or child. From the perspective of theories of intimacy, each offers a model for strongly affective reciprocal relations that are projected onto the gods, self-sustained within their own tropes and narratives.

But importantly, interactive practices can also directly access the agent *within* the mental, physical and social 'body'. This raw self, composed of the higher witnessing and discriminating functions of thought as we saw in Chapter 5, can be recognized and called to self-recognition by the gaze of the deity, providing a touchstone of freedom from the determining influence of our habitual identities. Such interactive practices of gaze allow practitioners to float relatively free of actual social ties, creating their own elective intimate community.

One result of the accumulation of these interactive practices is that the divine is encountered as a fully rich and complex 'person' of layers, from the core subjectivity encountered in *darśana*, to the body encountered in the *mūrti*, to the 'life-story' and disposition encountered in myth, hymn and iconography. Deities too are embodied persons in the multifaceted sense outlined in the foregoing chapters, and as such they are accessible via the materials of body and mind that make up the Hindu world. It is clear here that the idea of a community of commerce, or a symbolic nation, or even a clan or kinship identity, does not do justice to the form of intersubjective, embodied, affective intimacy found in Hindu practice. Rather the community here recalls the 'neighbourhood' of village life in which all agents are local, entwined in shared lives and mutual care. In this sense, formalized pan-Hindu rituals retain much that is common to the animist village communities of humans and spirits seen throughout Asia.

Interestingly, where Appadurai (1996) and others have suggested that media globalization is reducing the level of face-to-face interactions and intimacies, Hindu *pūjā* encounters with the divine cut through this, especially as the medium of divine embodiment is never fixed but rather infinitely expandable: new posters can be printed, online *darśan* taken and private *mūrti*s can be bought, lost, bought again and carried into new contexts, remaining a valid receptacle. The identity and authority accorded to specific temple *mūrti*s often does align with particular sectarian, regional, patronage-based and priestly claims to pre-eminence. But their influence can be disrupted by the fact that the divine is present in no one image *more* than in any other: the irreducible intimacy of the divine gaze cannot be impeded by any third party. The Hindu devotional neighbourhood is thus portable in a way that traditional animist neighbourhoods are not. And through the intimacy of the gaze, represented through the importance of the eyes in any representation, whether sculpted, drawn, imagined or physically embodied, the intimate community is infinitely renewable at its foundations, individual to individual, across and beyond the vagaries and limits of embodiment.

# 12

# Speculative practices: The reality of ideas

Practice can be mentally as well as physically embodied. From Hindu classical sources came one of the world's most prolific and conceptually sophisticated traditions of philosophical theology. It remained simultaneously philosophical *and* theological largely because the Upaniṣads had woven religious concerns about immortality and the higher possibilities for human life, with the kinds of metaphysical speculation that we have explored in foregoing chapters, resulting in a central concern with the nature of the universe and the capacities of the self that spanned both spheres. Oddly, these theological traditions of Vedānta and other systematic schools are rarely seen as 'practices' – despite the fact that they involved the participation of innumerable individuals, families, courts and whole urban centres of learning in exegetic and speculative study that constituted an all-encompassing lifestyle for most. More than a profession, the culture of reflection initiated by classical Brahmins involved skills, customs, disciplines, training and initiation, social identities and communal performances. In this sense the philosophical activities of systematic introspection, speculation and analysis were all kinds of religious 'practice' embodied in the *mental* materials of the self. The dichotomy between 'embodied' and 'intellectual' culture should thus be challenged by exploring the way in which 'philosophy as a spiritual practice', to borrow Hadot's phrase, developed over the centuries into modernity.

## Metaphysics and creative theologizing

Relatively little has been written about the fate of the Vedāntic tradition of practice after its heyday in the medieval and early modern periods. In response to the challenge of the many skeptical schools of thought, Brahminical sects of Vedāntic thought formalized their metaphysical speculation into a practice that followed standards of Mīmāṃsā exegesis, Vyākaraṇa hermeneutics, Nyāya logical analysis, commentarial conventions and formal debate. Hagiographies of the great theologian-saints such as Śaṃkara and Rāmānuja describe this form of life as a comprehensive habitus, lived out through laboriously acquired skills, within established lifestyles and communities, continuing over centuries as part of a powerful tradition that defined traditional Hindu intellectual life. Those modern scholars who have immersed themselves in the tradition have often seen this as a way of life that reaches into the present; Surendranatha Dasgupta (1922: vii), who composed the most comprehensive of all accounts of Indian philosophy and saw the Indian speculative tradition as central to any history of India, wrote of it as a living body of practice to which he had intended to make his own contribution:

> It was regarded as the goal of all the highest practical and theoretical activities ... it is not in the history of foreign invasions, in the rise of independent kingdoms at different times, in the empires of this or that great monarch that the unity of India is to be sought. It is essentially one of spiritual aspirations and obedience to the law of the spirit, which were regarded as superior to everything else, and it has outlived all the political changes through which India passed.

Yet even Dasgupta wrote of 'a passivity of centuries' (vii) during which indigenous systematic philosophy waned in India. Recent scholars have highlighted the negative effects that colonialism had on the intellectual sciences. Prior to the advent of Muslim and European intervention one sees an early modern flourishing of *navya* or 'new' styles of Nyāya logic (Ganeri 2011), Alaṃkāra poetics (Bronner 2002), grammar and its associated philosophical inquiry (Houben 2002), and also Vedānta (see Nicholson (2010) on the Bhedābheda school of thought; Gupta (2007) on Acintya Bhedābheda; McCrea (2015) on Dvaita Advaita, and others). But colonial developments, importing the 'very different, uncompromising [European] modernity that, through colonial dissemination, would eventually contest and undo the Sanskrit intellectual formation', and leading ultimately to the rise of the Western university system in India, are generally seen to have killed traditional intellectual life.

Nevertheless, there are those who have called for attention to the continuity of modern with traditional Vedānta. Brian Hatcher (2007) has argued that the intellectual tradition continued into the nineteenth- and twentieth-century 'morning after' of colonialism, and almost all of the Vedāntic sects did indeed continue their activities of reading, reflection and discussion through the seventeenth to twentieth centuries, although few within them wrote formal works of theology. What clearly diminished was the use of the traditional textual genres of philosophical theology: sūtras and bhaṣyas, dīpikas and saṃgrāhas have become increasingly rare in the cultural output of Indian culture.

But the *project* of Vedāntic metaphysics can be seen as something that went beyond formal traditions of systematic theology, spilling over into the wider contexts in which texts or thinkers expressed a holistic view of the world. The Hindu fascination with theories and images of the cosmos continued in both literary and visual imagery for the masses (often woven into iconography as in popular worship images of Śiva dancing or Viṣṇu dreaming on his serpent) and in the traditions of rational theology that thrived. Simple images, often derived from analogies in the Upaniṣads and other early Vedāntic sources, took on their own lives as ways for the populace to comprehend these worldviews and assimilate them into their own understanding. From analogical thinking in classical literature there evolved 'a long and complex history' of the use of metaphors to model the fundamental metaphysical relations that structure the universe (see, for instance, Lawrence 2005: 583; Frazier 2014: 16, 36). The Upaniṣads (and after them the Sūtras and *Sāṃkhya Kārikā* as well as philosophical discourses such as the *Bhagavad Gītā* in epic literatures, and the subsequent tradition of scholastic Vedānta theology) used *dṛṣṭānta*s liberally in their descriptions of the universe. Analogy was one of the tools used by grammarians to illustrate basic semantic concepts; Pāṇini's *Mahābhāṣya* uses them to demonstrate the basic relations of ablative derivation, instrumentality, location, possession and so on, highlighting the value of analogies for showing relationships that can otherwise be slippery philosophical concepts to explain.

This immediately semantic function of analogies underpinned their broader explanatory function in philosophical literatures, and often theological positions developed in concert with the exegesis of those images. This process can be traced in the thought of most Vedāntins, including notably Rāmānuja who mines the possibilities of the idea of an agent within a body (see Lipner (1986: 37–48) on the *śarīra-śarīrin* model), and in the subtle negotiation of early modern thinkers in the Bhedābheda school, who differentiated their ideas in terms of images of light spreading outwards (e.g. Jīva Gosvāmī; see Gupta 2007: 40–5) or sugar pervading milk (see Nicholson (2010: 47) on Vijñānabhikṣu's adding of a non-separation analogy to the standard Bhedābheda images), or objects internally differentiated like an ocean into waves, a snake into coils or any substrate and its parts or capacities (see Satyanand (1997: 297) on Nimbārka). As Hindu intellectual cultures became more complex through sectarian competition and synthesis, analysis of *dṛṣṭānta*s could even be combined in multilevelled explanations of the cosmos, structured one within another like a Russian doll (Frazier 2014: see 83–6). The openness of Vedic culture to multiple theories of everything was central to the intellectual productivity of the tradition, producing parallel paths of metaphysical thinking about the cosmos.

Ideas of emanation, as the expansion of a thing into new forms or constitutive materials, had been expressed in Upaniṣadic images of a spider emitting a web (*Bṛhad Āraṇyaka Upaniṣad* 2.1.20), a fire emitting sparks (*Muṇḍaka Upaniṣad* 2.1.1) or the sun emitting its rays (*Iṣa Upaniṣad* 1.15–16). These would in turn play an important role in the Sāmkhya-influenced cosmologies of the *Mahābhārata* and the *Purāṇa*s, various Bhedābheda Vedānta traditions and *pariṇāma-vāda* 'transformation' and *satkārya-vāda* '*in potentio*' traditions of causality. In another textual thread of ideas, the image of the universe as composed from a single bodily person (e.g. *Ṛg Veda* 10.90) was developed into theories that modelled the universe in terms of the agency of a central controller of the world (*Kaṭha Upaniṣad* 1.3–4), animating its 'limbs' (*Bṛhad Āraṇyaka Upaniṣad* 2.4.11) and serving as the force behind perception and animation (*Kena Upaniṣad*). This model underpinned the development of many theistic theories, taking the notion of embodied agency to be the most convincing way of explaining the dynamism inherent in the universe. These analogies added crucial *metaphysical* clarity to Hindu notions of theism as the expression of dynamic agency in the universe (see, for instance, Lipner (1986), Bartley (2002) and Ram-Prasad (2013: 50–5) on the philosophical conceptions of body as instrument (*prakāra*) and accessory (*śeṣa*) in Viśiṣṭādvaita thought). These traditions that affirmed embodiment and agency were challenged by Advaitic traditions that borrowed from the negative theologies found in sources such as the *Īṣa* (10–14) *and Māṇḍūkya* (7) *Upaniṣads*, sought to escape embodiment and uphold the potential purity of the consciousness that constitutes the self. Innovative new images, such as the famous Advaita descriptions of the world as being like the illusory existence of colours in a crystal, or a body imagined where there is only a tree-trunk, became popular shorthand forms of metaphysical theology for those sects, just as sparks, sunrays or a divine body served to sustain more body-positive Vedāntic theologies: together such imagistic discourse sustained earlier speculative cosmologies among communities that were unfamiliar with the original theological works.

In many ways, it was the cultures of literary and visual evocation that encouraged these ideas to take their place in the speculative imagination, transforming the self-understanding of individuals to some degree. The "Viśva Rūpa' vision that Arjuna has of Krishna in the *Bhagavad Gītā* as a being that encompasses a changing world, and the image of Śiva Naṭarāja as a divine being who dances the world into and out of existence, for example, have had a vivid afterlife in temple sculpture and popular print, recycled in tales and made viscerally comprehensible and appealing in television depictions. So too, metaphors of waves on an ocean, sparks from a fire, mirages and illusions have all entered common discourse as a kind of shorthand for ways to explain the world, and can still be found in use as explanatory techniques by both gurus and everyday Hindus. In these ways the expansion of self-understanding towards the outer limits of the world retains some currency, but the early Brahminical cultures that advocated and practised it quickly became a quieter voice, often silenced by the louder tones of logical debate.

## Scepticism, science and the shrinking of the speculative self

Upaniṣadic theories were not greatly concerned with falsity – perhaps due to their authors' awareness that no empirical a-posteriori test pertaining to the whole of being could ever be possible. Incoherence was the greatest danger in Vedic texts that were eager to argue for the way their ideas cohered with existing texts and experiences, and Vedānta extended this ideal of coherence to the textual canon, acknowledging the need to accord with the varying and sometimes self-contradictory ideas contained in the relevant textual *pramāṇa*s, the sources of each tradition. But since, as Ganeri (2008) has noted, the root texts of the tradition such as the Upaniṣads and the *Brahma Sūtras* tended to be highly dense and yet ambiguous in their meaning, it was altogether possible for assessments of validity to become creative reconstructions that created new forms of coherence where it otherwise was missing. Assessment of an idea's validity in this classical tradition was based on the idea that 'one of the most prized qualities of a philosophical work resides in its ability to enable the reader to understand patterns of inter-relatedness within a complex set of ideas' (1). Unpacking those relationships and (re-) weaving them into a coherent structure was the central theoretical practice of Vedāntic metaphysical reasoning. As sectarian competition between different traditions and their doctrines developed in the first millennium, this approach to metaphysical debate perpetuated the 'visionary' aspect of the earlier tradition, continuing to treat theorizing as a process of producing compelling and all-embracing accounts.

The Vedic ideal of coherence thus pervaded the later traditions of commentary on the assumption that the correct methods of deriving new truths from existing *pramāṇa*s would transmit the authority of that original revelatory vision because they were 'of a piece' with the original source. The Vyākaraṇa grammatical theories that developed as an interpretative science lauded this principle of coherence. These early theories sought to explain the 'semantic power' of language, and Bhartṛhari's *Vākyapadīya*, one of the oldest and most influential studies of the nature of Sanskrit, argues for a holism of meaning that fits well with the theological precedent of sources such as *Bṛhad Āraṇyaka Upaniṣad* 1.4.7 which speaks of an undivided reality that becomes divided by 'name-and-form'. Bhartṛhari argues that sentences may appear to be composites built from individual syllables and words, but in fact the meanings they convey are complete entities. A correct interpretation or extension of that meaning, by implication, partakes of the whole truth that is expressed in the original text, and a single noun (or compound of nouns together in a complex concept) could be made to say a great deal merely by the use of stems, case endings and subsidiary clauses all of which qualified that central object. The *Vākyapadīya* claimed that the coherence of the Vedas (on which the orthodox Hindu Sanskrit literatures and sciences were based) extended to the sciences based on them – sciences that of course included grammar and the *Vākyapadīya* itself (see 1.10, 1.15). Wilhelm Halbfass (1991: 38) hinted at this vision of the Vedic theoretical project in his analysis of Hindu exegetic reason:

> Both the expanded Veda itself, and the traditions of thought and exegesis which are rooted in it, are expressions of the 'principle of the word' (śabdatattva) ... Due to its inherent powers (śakti) this one and undivided principle projects itself into the world of multiplicity and separation (pṛthaktva); and the primeval 'seers' who divide the Veda into its basic 'paths' and 'branches' ... are not only speakers about, but agents and representatives of the reality of the Vedic word, and they are participants in cosmic and cosmogonic processes.

On this model, whole texts and even whole genres could be seen as sharing in a single truth that operated across the ages. Where the logical debater in the Nyāya tradition used reason for practical purposes and to assert his or her membership of the community of reasoning agents, the metaphysical speculator in the Vedic tradition used reason to access the ideas embedded in the texts, and – at least in part – to participate in 'cosmogonic' processes by assimilating them into their own thought and extending them still further.

# The modern theological imagination in Hinduism

Speculative model-making about the constitution of reality and our place within it had relatively little value in the Western university system that was exported to India. Some of the Mughal madrasas in India had incorporated Indian sources and styles of thinking into their consideration of Persian, Greek and other traditions. But the missionary platform for education that spread from the period of the earliest Jesuit missions onward generally rejected the possibility of Indian or syncretic learning. The colonial governments' attempt to 'civilize' India compounded the Westernization of Indian intellectual life: the 1854 despatch of Charles Wood, president of the Board of Control of the East India Company, to Lord Dalhousie advocated the establishment of English-speaking universities in every Indian region, all modeled on the University of London. If the formal debating cultures of classical Indian philosophy had already lost something of the Upanisadic approach through their focus on defence of existing doctrine based on exegesis, so now the modern universities of Calcutta and Delhi trained students in classical European thought and the applied sciences and would eventually give answers to cosmological questions with the language of Western physics rather than of Hindu philosophy. Frykenberg (1986) has noted that the majority of students in such institutions were orthodox Brahmins, whose traditional 'gurukula' education was replaced by this system. This was one of the ways in which conquering Europe colonized the landscape of thought as well as the geographical terrain of the subcontinent.

The nineteenth and twentieth centuries also became caught up in the West's recasting of reason as a tool of 'reform': the classical metaphysics of the Upaniṣads was put to use by Swami Vivekananda to secure equality and a sense of sociopolitical unity, and the philosophies of the *Bhagavad Gītā* and Sāṃkhya served to ground philosophies of ethical action and evolutionary transformation for Gandhi and Śri Aurobindo, respectively. But speculative cosmology and metaphysics, approached as visionary pursuits that aimed at using knowledge as a practice of personal transformation, found little place in 'modern' India where the Western tradition of natural sciences claimed to have answered so many questions. As Daya Krishna (2002: 307) remarks, by the nineteenth and twentieth centuries science 'had become the paradigmatic example of knowledge', and academic philosophy was one of the only genres of thinking which could be demarcated as a relatively autonomous realm.

Within the discipline of philosophy some scope for 'large thinking' remained, but in the Western style of universities any grand theory had to locate itself with regard to Western thinkers. Philosophers such as Hegel became useful mediators through which India could discover its own theories anew; K.C. Bhattacarya was able to give a Hegelian dialectical account of Sāṃkhya, while the great Oxford philosopher Radhakrishnan gave an idealist reading of Advaitic monism, and the Indian philosopher J.N. Mohanty saw parallels between Indian thought and the work of the father of modern Western Phenomenology, Edmund Husserl. This project of integrating Indian and European insights was, for many, unavoidable because both cultures and discourses made what seemed to be equally valid claims to truth. Some of the most creative and earnest thinkers about cosmological truth were those who attempted a conscientious synthesis, such as the young Cambridge-educated philosopher Aurobindo Ghose. Ghose, who came to be known as Sri Aurobindo once he took on the mantle of a religious teacher – and even of an original 'visionary' on his own account – sought to interpret the Upaniṣads, producing translations and commentaries on a number of them, and marrying the Hegelian ideal of the 'reconciliation and harmony of fundamental opposites' with the kind of world-emanationism found in the Sāṃkhya theory of *prakṛti*. Although he aims to follow the Indian traditional method of translation and exegesis of the primary text, and even imitates the conversational style of an Upaniṣadic discussion in some of his writings, Ghose (2003: 101) warns his Western-educated readers that the Upaniṣads will not stand up to the normal standards of Western rational critique and must be assessed as literature premised on the visions of their authors:

> The Upanishad sets forth by pronouncing as the indispensable basis of its revelations the universal nature of God. This universal nature of Brahman the Eternal is the beginning and end of the Vedanta and if it is not accepted, nothing the Vedanta says can have any value, as all its propositions either proceed from it or at least presuppose it; deprived of this central and highest truth, the Upanishads become what Mleccha scholars & philosophers think them to be — a mass of incoherent though often sublime speculations.

Aurobindo's warning about the Upaniṣads sought to defend them from the criticism of a Western-educated modern audience. But on the whole, traditional practices of learning, exegesis and imaginative speculation on the classical model dissolved in the Indian world as arranged by European colonial administrators:

> The whole world of classical knowledge and those who pursued and practised it became gradually invisible to those who came out of the new institutions modelled on the British pattern and thus produced an intellectual environment which was only aware of the western traditions in knowledge as its reference point and treated India's intellectual enterprises either as having had no value at all or as having been completely superseded by the

> developments of knowledge that had taken place in the West and were, therefore, completely irrelevant to the contemporary quest for knowledge. (Krishna 2002: 310)

One positive effect of the takeover of Western cultures of reasoning was that the sources of classical Hinduism were made more widely available beyond the non-Sanskrit-reading populace through translation and printing. With the old Brahminical community of scholars long-disrupted, a new community developed and in 1991 a *Who's Who of Sanskrit Scholars* was published to keep track of those who had sought to maintain something of the traditional practices of reflection and exegesis. Some traditional teachers and pandits have remained, often finding new popularity in the mid-to-late twentieth century and reviving the theologies of past traditions; Swami Lakshmanjoo, for instance, has continued to teach the metaphysics associated with the medieval school of Kashmiri Śaivism, while the prolific publishing output of Swami Prabhupada provided both the texts and the techniques of meditation needed for modern followers to assimilate the vision of Caitanya Vaiṣṇava Vedānta. In many cases the ability of a school to provide a compelling account of reality has remained an important part of its appeal, although in many cases the devotional aspect has long since come to be valued more highly than the metaphysical dimension. Through the intervening centuries of Hindu theology, ultimate goals such as of realization of one's true nature, devotion to a deity or meditative self-transformation of one's psychology have become more popular conceptions of liberation than the orientation of selfhood towards the world through a more global comprehension of it.

Yet traces of the earlier view remain among some of those who retained a close exegetic connection to the early literatures. Swami Vivekananda was one of Vedānta's most prolific and influential modern interpreters, sometimes criticized for an excessively informal approach to his traditional sources. But he was himself an enthusiastic close reader of classical texts such as the Upaniṣads and *Sāṃkhya Kārikā* and, distancing himself from the formal customs of India's pandit culture, he felt empowered to revisit their philosophies directly. The return to world-encompassing theory, and the importance of reidentifying the self with the universal levels of reality, rationally discovered, play an important role in his thought and are part of the style that recommended him to the broader global community in his writing and many addresses. In a talk entitled 'The Cosmos' that was delivered in New York in 1896 Vivekananda grounds his appeal to the Western audience on the way in which

> the whole mass of existence which we call nature has been acting on the human mind since time immemorial. It has been acting on the thought of man, and as its reaction has come the question: 'What are these? Whence are they?'

> As far back as the time of the oldest portion of that most ancient composition, the Vedas, we find the same question asked. (122)

The answer that he offers to questions about the nature and origin of existence provides an interesting echo of the Upaniṣads' didactic culture of rational working towards philosophical comprehension of the broadest truths. Like the figures in the Upaniṣads, he takes his audience on a reasoned journey toward a picture of the world as a whole, comprehended in terms of its underlying constitution. But where for early Brahmins rationality served to incorporate Kṣatriyas and Brahmins from other regions into a shared perspective, for Vivekananda it was his New York audience who were drawn into reflection. He takes the scientific observation of uniformity in nature to support the validity of extrapolating from specific cases (like *dṛṣṭāntas*) to the nature of the universe as a whole, and he loosely cites the *Chāndogya Upaniṣad* as a precedent for this kind of analogical reasoning:

> If it be true that the same law prevails throughout the universe, then if we take up a little plant and study its life, we shall know the universe as it is – as it has been said in the Vedas, 'knowing one lump of clay, we know the nature of all the clay in the universe'. ([1896] 1955: 124)

In this particular text, the theory of everything that he derives from his readings reflects strong influence from Sāṃkhya (he references the thought of Kapila) and builds an emanationist model of the world as a progression from subtle to gross forms of beings that 'live in the causes as fine forms'. He draws strongly on the *satkārya-vāda* view that modes pre-exist in their substrate ('there is nothing that is produced without a cause, and the cause is the effect in another form'; 127), and further associates this with the doctrine of repeated world-manifestations that were later popularized in the early medieval texts of the Purāṇas. Ultimately he builds a reasoned vision of the universe for his audience, and in the lecture that he gave to the same listeners the following week (subtitled 'the microcosm' rather than the previous week's 'the macrocosm'), he advocated that they apply this vision to the *self* as well.

Vivekananda uses other theologies than the Sāṃkhya one (particularly the later Advaitic perspective on the self) and has other agendas in mind, including the development of an ethical theory of the equality of all people out of his sources. But in his adoption of the methods of reasoned cosmology as a tool for transforming one's self-understanding, he draws on a characteristic classical approach. He was not alone in doing this, although he became perhaps the most well-known contemporary interpreter of Hindu philosophy; he represented a European-educated generation for whom the marriage of speculation on the nature of reality, with personal identity-formation, was a common spiritual practice to be combined with the modern natural sciences, rather than erased by them.

Sri Aurobindo (1998: 93–4), educated in England but conducting his own study of Indian texts, also used original classical sources as the basis for his own theology. His reading of the *Taittirīya Upaniṣad* pays careful attention to the reasoning by which it derives a conception of *brahman*, arguing for

> an Eternal behind all instabilities, a Truth of things which is implied, if it is hidden in all appearances, a Constant which supports all mutations, but is not increased, diminished, abrogated' and following closely the Upaniṣad's view of knowledge in asserting that 'to know it is to know the highest ... as it is the sum of all things, so everything else is its consequence ... so everything amounts to it and by throwing itself into it achieves the sense of its own existence.

He follows the Taittirīya's strong valuing of knowledge, holding that

> [i]t is a knowledge that is a power and a divine compulsion to change; by it his existence gains something that he does not possess in consciousness. What is this gain? It is that he is consciousness now in a lower state only of his being, but by knowledge he gains his higher being. (95)

Much influenced by Hegel, nevertheless, Aurobindo sees in the practice of knowledge recommended by the Taittirīya a means of self-transformation that relies on the idea that knowing is itself a phenomenon that can alter the very nature of the human being. In fact, the idea that the human mind is a medium of existence which can be transformed and expanded would become central to his view of self and world. Such conceptions of selfhood, then, persisted and – made accessible for the global audience at which both of these modern thinkers aimed –formed the basis of an important flourishing of cosmological speculation as a form of practice.

Brian Hatcher's (2008: 14) work on modern 'Neo-Vedāntins' brings out their practical concerns to create a philosophy that can deflect the influence of Christian missionaries while allowing them their own personal material success as spokesmen for the Hindu intellectual and spiritual community; he takes what he calls the 'informal merger of scriptural religion and the religion of reason' as an eclectic practice that is 'tinged in varying ways with the colors of Enlightenment thought ... highly reminiscent of European Deist responses to the problem of such themes as miracle and revelation in the Christian tradition'. He is surely right in identifying the influence of Western styles of natural theology on these thinkers, but this is an interpretation that also assumes a somewhat artificial divide between reason and exegesis in the practices inherited by modern Hindus. Philosophical reasoning need not be seen as a concession to Western standards; from a classical Hindu perspective it can be seen as a form of *tattva-darśana*, the expression of a vision of reality that must be *comprehended*, not merely perceived, for it to dwell fully in the mind, giving its shape to the self.

## Theory as a practice for becoming the world

The reminder from classicist and philosopher Pierre Hadot (1995) to see classical traditions of philosophical reflection as a 'way of life', and more specifically to practice it as something that 'implies a radical transformation of perspective, and contains a universalist, cosmic dimension', has been a useful corrective to the impersonal 'objectivist' tone in which philosophical and theoretical thinking about the world is routinely pursued in the modern academy. Reason can be a practice, and it can also be a form of spirituality, with all three combined into a way of life. He also criticized Michel Foucault's reading of classical practices as only concerned with the self, insisting that the specifically philosophical character of such reflection meant that they must be understood in terms not of 'interiorisation', but of 'universalisation' (211). His challenge to contemporary philosophizing addresses both traditional philosophy and that form of theory that concerns itself only with local and applied fields of knowledge, or only with scepticism, and in this he unknowingly echoes those early Indian authors of the Upaniṣads who saw philosophy as a way to acquire an 'eye of knowledge' that is also in fact the 'eye of the world'.

This understanding of the human self is as something that is continuous with the cosmos, challenging Western scientific accounts of self by highlighting the 'eidetic' fabric of being: we are made as much of *ideas* as of matter. But one implication of this self that is embodied-in-ideas is that it is also continuous with other minds insofar as theorizing tends to be depicted in the Upaniṣads as an activity of shared comprehension. Narratives about reasoning in the Upaniṣads and in related later epic, purāṇic and tantric literatures tend to underscore the process of agreement, that is, the universality of the processes of reasoning such that they enable a mental exploration shared by fathers and sons, teachers and pupils, gods and their devotees. Together characters such as Uddālaka Āruṇi and Śvetaketu, or Prajāpati and Indra, observe patterns of similarity and enact key realizations on which knowledge is based. In the *Chāndogya Upaniṣad*, for instance, we proceed through the thought exercises in the text to see (together with Uddālaka Āruṇi and his son) that entities have multiple levels of both necessary (clay) and contingent (pot) properties. The text and the audience together work through arguments and counterarguments until a position is established. These performances of public reasoning *within the text* rehearse the process in which multiple minds come into contact with each other and with the world at the level of the eidetic reality of ideas.

Numerous scholars have highlighted this public, shared quality of the self that expresses itself in certain kinds of language that prod the imagination into collective action to produce an experience 'that transcends the boundaries of inner and outer, and in which subjectivity is overwhelmed by a collective subjectivity, a shared world that is cosmic and ultimately real for those practitioners [here, "theorists"] who stand within it' (Flood 2013). Along with Flood, Jonardon Ganeri (2012b) has also noted the importance of public performances of rationality, and India's historical movement towards increasingly communal, verifiable discourses of knowledge. Our existence as part of the medium of systematic reasoning thus tends to *unite* selves within the shared embodiment of ideas.

The association of postmodernism with an assumed context relativism in which all truths are localized to a particular physical or cultural embodiment has denied the possibility of mental 'meetings' at the level of ideas. Edmund Husserl (1960: 5), the father of phenomenology, noted this isolation of minds and thoughts from each other, writing that 'philosophies lack the unity of a mental space in which they might exist for and act on one another'. In the Upaniṣads, by contrast, the didactic settings foreground just such a 'public' space: debate, realization, persuasion and agreement are all processes that empirically affirm the universality of reason as a level of reality that we all inhabit. We can thus see theory as a practice not only aimed at shared discoveries of truth, but also as a practice that regrounds the individual, if only temporarily, in a more basic, universal, shared selfhood. This 'self' is able to 'act' mentally in a way that is liberated in some degree from its situated context. Theory becomes the activity of movement along real connections (*bandhu*s, *vyāpti*s and other analogical and causal associations) that structure not only the world but also the self; it is on the level of this infinitely complex network of truths that we can meet other minds and – freed if only temporarily from our embodied identity – discover our commonality. In this respect, reason is accorded a role not dissimilar to that which it plays for Plato; it establishes thinkers in a universal polity of which they are native and equal citizens. Indeed, it is to this location that marginalized figures such as Sulabhā, the female yogi and debater of the *Mahābhārata*, sometimes revert in order to express resistance against the contingent physical bodies, social identities and narrative situations within which they are unwillingly bound. The self made of ideas supersedes physical bodies. In such cases, the self which is an 'I' becomes a 'We' or an 'All' by entering jointly into the field of thought. There it enjoys an exemplary freedom to connect with, become or assimilate other selves and to shape itself into something more comprehensive than the locally embodied, limited consciousness that it had been previously.

# 13

# Conclusion: The art of being human in the Hindu cosmos

The ideas explored in the foregoing chapters reveal a Hindu 'multiverse' – a model of the cosmos in which multiple fabrics of thought, nature, agency and social interaction are woven into a complex reality. The Hindu practitioner thus faces a tangible world that is embodied in the natural environment and in ourselves, behind which hidden possibilities lie. We have seen that many Hindu practices work to access those possibilities and bring them under human control. This special capacity lies at the heart of human creative agency in much of Hindu classical thought and the traditions to which it gives rise.

Thus knowledge facilitates control of the material embodiment that forms the wider warp and weft of reality. Hinduism has often been represented as a religious culture concerned with liberation; but the classical Hindu worldview was equally guided by the goal of artful sovereignty over these realms of embodiment. Indeed, one of the key tasks of Hindu ethics has been to discover what it means to use this agency well; that is, it asks how we should alter the world, in support of which structures of order or disorder, in cooperation with which other persons or natural forces and as which *scale* of person should we act? As the self associated with this body and identity, or as an expanded self that thinks beyond this body to identify as the community, or even the world. In many respects this is a concern that spans the 'religious' and 'secular' spheres and goes to the heart of human existence as a project of discriminating agency – or, in other terms, as an *art*.

Thus many of the fabrics or materiality and forms of embodiment offered by classical Hindu sources can be seen as a complex matrix within which the individual self negotiates its future. Of course the world presses back against the freedom of the individual, but this very struggle to shape the self and the world, through practices of reasoning and action, indicates that a fundamental realism underlies these worldviews. The causal connections that order reality may be skilfully plucked at by human agents. Matilal (1986: 357–9) focused on three rival ontologies that competed in the early centuries CE in his catalogue of Indian 'worldviews' (Buddhism's monistic phenomenalism, Nyāya's pluralism of ontological types or materials and Bhartṛhari's 'holism' which saw reality as multiple modes of a single reality). Here too we have seen a rich plurality of distinct ontologies that plot the variables of the classical self:

**a)** *material* constitution: the self is shaped by the root elements and aspects, both physical and mental, that are aggregated into its 'body';

**b)** *structural* relations: the self is shaped by the internal structure that shapes those elements into an single bodily entity;

**c)** *modal* state: the self is shaped by its cycling through different modes that determine the manifest state of the real, and the *interpersonal* interactions that relate multiple agents into a community;

**d)** *scope* of embodiment: the self is shaped by the breadth and range of its embodiment, particularly in regard to its mental material and its ability to assimilate wide-ranging and universal ideas, as well as limited local ones;

**e)** *power* of agency: the 'core' of the self is shaped by its constitution of an agent within the 'embodiment' that uses the capacities of certain mental materials to create a centre of decision-making and causal influence over its subsidiary materials.

In many respects, it is by expanding of the scope of the self's agency that the transformations considered highest can be achieved: decisions can be made from the perspective of a single time and place, or of many, or of all; of a single person, of many, or of all minds. In this respect, the broader thinking that we call 'philosophy' has a special place in elevating the self and its whole relationship with the world in which it is embodied.

## The arts of self: Hindu dualism

The body sits located within these different mental and material fabrics of reality, forming the pivot of a dualistic relationship between agency on the one hand, and its embodied expression as part of the world on the other. Crucially, this is a different dualism from the mind–body distinction of Descartes, or the 'pure awareness'–'phenomenal existence' dualism of Classical Sāṃkhya. It is a model that operates separately of the idea of a pure and passive disembodied consciousness. Rather, the distinction here is between the cluster of higher discriminating functions that form agency and the field of worldly materials which that agency shapes. For the Brahmins of many early Upaniṣads, we have seen that this agency can happen through a comprehension of the building blocks of the world and rearrangement of them through processes of physical or mental causation. This power of rearrangement, in turn, is reliant on the distinction between two different kinds of causality: *natural causality*, which automatically flows from the nature of any given element, and *discriminatory causality*, which arises as a result of the mind's ability to recognize natural causes and the situations in which they are embedded, and to create newly 'intelligent' desires, actions and causal processes. The core self consists of a special kind of intelligent causality that is actually facilitated by mental embodiment and arises through a special combination of the key materials of perception and analysis, assessment and measured motivation.

World and body share the same fundamental fabrics of reality, and so *embodiment*, that term which has become so pregnant with significance in Western theory (lauded for its capacity to capture lived, non-literate, affective, visceral aspects of life; e.g. Orsi 1997; Vasquez 2011), functions as *en-worldment* in this context. This embodied agency walks a thin line between creativity and constraint: on one hand Marcel Mauss's (2006) classic anthropological studies of 'body-techniques' and Pierre Bourdieu's (1992) account of tradition's self-perpetuation through practice, both view regularized bodily activity (*habitus*) as a restriction of the individual, and one can indeed see cultures of privatized control at work in Hindu cultures, mediating access to ritual or theological knowledge by Brahmin priests, guru initiators and *ācārya* teachers.

But on the other hand we also see how practices can be empowering means by which practitioners 'instrumentalize' their bodies as tools for transforming the environment. Ideally, human agency is more like divine agency than one would think: a sentient agent should be able to see the structures of reality through reason, and harness the powers of nature to create new realities. But first, it also has the option of rethinking and reshaping itself as an agency – becoming focused or broad in its interest, impassioned or detached, located in the body or in the broader environment as one engaged in *loka-saṃgraha*, the 'holding together' of the world. While the *Bhagavad Gītā* uses this term in the sense of a service to the structures of dharma established by the Brahminical community (as, for instance, at 3.20), we see a more literal, metaphysical and empowering model of world-grasping and world-control suggested in the earlier texts. It is disciplines of both knowledge and ritual that enable this, and the Vedas and Upaniṣads are full of stories in which even the deities themselves must make use of the same strategies of teaching and ritual as their mortal fellows. Initiation is central to much of Hindu religious culture precisely because these traditions of creative action are some of the most valuable and closely regarded resources in Hindu culture; they provide ways to chart a path of the practitioner's own making through the labyrinthine multiverse of classical Hindu reality.

Thus the struggle of human nature is to take control and direct one's own journey through the material fields of action; indeed, Jonardon Ganeri ([2007] 2012: 229–34) has argued that a theory of self holding that 'what we are is made of what we do' developed in contrast to the Ajīkika doctrine of mechanistic fatalism, and the Cārvāka belief that humans can be reduced to mere material parts. One can see here that what is important to selfhood is not the parts or the substrate that constitute it, but the coherent unifying intelligent motivation that is created by the conjunction of perception, memory, inference, reflection, taste, prediction and planning. In this context, embodiment is better understood not as any kind of materiality, but in a wholly instrumental sense as a kind of 'capacitation' of that agency, providing the necessary precondition for life as action and standing at the root of Hindu conceptions of freedom, choice and ethics.

It is also important to acknowledge that there is no such thing as death, in the sense of radical cessation, in such a worldview – there is only controlled and desirable transformation, or uncontrolled and unwilling change. Acknowledging the contingency of one's current self is *not*, then, acknowledging an end. Rather it is an acknowledgement of the imminence of new identities, stories and goals. As Haberman ([1988] 2001: 44) puts it, such views mark a distinctive Hindu 'optimism about the possibility of identity transformation'. 'Agency dualism' does not describe a self that seeks to 'put on' new identities, so much as a self that is merely an arena for possibility, constantly negotiating its own becoming.

## The world of ideas: theory as visionary practice

One of the most striking forms of self-transformation that we have seen in the foregoing chapters was that which used the generalizing capacity of thought to expand itself into something pervasive, vast and undying – a form of self which through comprehension 'becomes the world'. The discriminatory agency that defines the self in its causal relationship with the environment is itself part of a unique *eidetic* fabric of ideas that thought can access, assimilate and manipulate. We have seen that 'comprehension' – in its original linguistic derivation as a 'prehensile' grip upon something that 'comprehends' or integrates it into oneself so that we include it – is central to human engagement in the world of ideas. This too is a conception of self that lies far from contemporary Western views for which material and embodied realities are often counterposed to mental and intellectual ones. We might say there that what we comprehend is what we are, and that thought is thus a self-shaping practice that affects the very deepest levels of our ability to analyse, assess and choose.

Reason was viewed not only as an inner calculation, but as a journey into a realm of concepts that lies beneath the surface of things, conjoining what is close with what is distant via a level of shared being in which all minds partake. In this light, the activity of reasoning appears far from passive; it is a process of exploration and discovery, and analysis functions as a kind of revelation – pulling close the truths that are far. Reasoners could be like Vedic *ṛṣi*s – seers who perceive the 'real beyond the real'.

Other cultures were, like classical India, similarly inspired by the extraordinary capacity of thought to extend beyond the body and the immediate present, out into the infinite reach of the world. Here the Upaniṣads speak to the nature and purpose of philosophy – and of life understood as the journey of human consciousness through forms and expansions of understanding; in this sense the Upaniṣads address themes that Pierre Hadot has shown to be important in his study of the way in which Stoic, Epicurean and Platonic philosophy functioned as 'spiritual exercises' of self-transformation. Hadot (1995: 208) argued that for early Greek traditions of reflection, 'the feeling of belonging to a whole is an essential element . . . Seneca sums it up in four words: *Toti se inserens mundo*. "Plunging oneself into the totality of the world" . . . Such a cosmic perspective radically transforms the feeling one has of oneself'.

This 'spiritual conquest of space' (in Hadot's (1995: 243) words), which is staked out in the *Chāndogya Upaniṣad*'s exploration of principles by which what is unknown can be known seem to have become a central concern of some Vedic Brahminical traditions. But the texts hint that the goal of that self-expansion into the world was perhaps different from the goals that motivated Hadot's Greeks; where the stoics could be described as 'unconcerned by mundane affairs in their bright, eternal tranquillity . . . [spending] their time contemplating the infinity of space, time, and the multiple worlds', some of these early sources evoke a process of proactively exploring and enjoying the facets of the world itself, attaining the brightness of sun, the vitality of life-breath and wind and the sovereign control of the *ātman*. We see that the Hindu context is not necessarily aimed at detachment, although that became a major theme promoted by the *Bhagavad Gītā*. Hadot speaks of the way in which everything becomes pleasant and death becomes acceptable to the sage; this idea is also present in those sections of the Upaniṣads – particularly common in later texts shaped in dialogue with renunciant and Buddhist culture – that also prized the way in which such knowledge yielded the reward of taking one beyond death (as, for instance, the *Iṣa Upaniṣad*'s promise that correct knowledge will allow one to *mṛtyum tīrtva*, or 'pass beyond death'; verse 11).

But in some texts we also see greater enthusiasm about the power and value of embodiment, and the way in which the world in its specificity can be incorporated into the self. It is important to recognize that not all versions of *mokṣa* were as passive as classical Sāṃkhya and later Advaitic non-dualist conceptions of consciousness would have them appear. Daniel Raveh has made this point in a close reading of the eighth chapter of the *Chāndogya Upaniṣad*, in which he distinguishes the text's early idea of *turīya*, the liberated fourth state of consciousness, from later Advaitic ideas of the fourth state (which were usually grounded instead in the *Māṇḍūkya Upaniṣad*). The (probably earlier) account of *turīya* in *Chāndogya Upaniṣad* chapter eight, Raveh (2008) argues, was not devoid of ideas, consciousness and enjoyment, but actually rich in the enjoyment of 'women, chariots and relatives' about whom the liberated person realizes '*ayam aham asmīti*', or 'this is what I am!' This *ātman* is then 'the "source of will" and an enjoyer both in this world and in the Brahman-world' (331). So too Andrew Fort (1994) has explored Upaniṣadic passages that suggest an immortal life bestowed by 'knowing'; Raveh's close reading allows the specificity of this interpretation (in distinction from other texts in the Upaniṣadic corpus) to emerge. Not all texts, nor all schools of thought, saw the world as something to be abandoned: it could rather be understood, overseen and *incorporated into the understanding* to produce a vast, world-sized self. Thinking is never neutral – it is always a self-making, and one's thoughts should be treated with due care and creative attention.

In the light of these classical worldviews, one of the features most definitive of Hindu religious cultures was their grounding in an assumption that the self could be radically transformed. It was potentiality able to shift its memories, desires and personalities, its mind and body, or even its scale of selfhood into a 'new' person. The options for different types of self ranged from the limited personality rooted wholly in the immediate moment, to the integral self that aggregates multiple bodily features (or even, in possession traditions, minds) into a single person, to the world-sized self that transcends particularity altogether, playing through wind, fire and the different levels of reality. Vast possibilities lay open to any human able to take control of himself or herself, or to reach outwards with his or her native capacity of abstract thought. Thus India's fascination with the *ātman* is not merely a nostalgic movement towards recovering something pure and fixed: simplified conceptions of the *ātman* which equate it with a divine core (as later representatives of Hindu thought would come to do) do not serve the actual range of classical conceptions that generated it, nor the range of Hindu theologies into which it was subsequently developed. Embodied selves play an important role in Hindu thought. If the divine foundation of *brahman* was a concept in flux that could mean many things, so too the *ātman* and its divinity were a theme undergoing varied creative exposition.

Yet one of the distinctive themes in Hindu discussions of selfhood was its status as more than merely a finite individual; in the Upaniṣads it is celebrated as immortal, as pervasive, as capable of accessing hidden realities or encompassing distant ones, as commanding a share in the foundations of being or as possessed of extraordinary creative power over reality itself. Indeed, the divinity accorded to *brahman* can be clarified by examination of the ways in which the *ātman* exceeds itself to become more than mortal, which is to say that the nature of the self as an agent of embodiment (or 'enworldment') can serve to clarify conceptions of divinity. Hinduism is distinguished by its optimism about the possibilities offered by the self – that unique resource that we all possess; many of these foregoing texts record the awe and excitement felt by thinkers 'discovering' those possibilities of creative embodied consciousness with which we are endowed. Here we have seen it celebrated and explored as an extraordinary capacity that makes each of us Creators in our own right.

# Notes

## Introduction: Hindu worldviews and global theory

**1** Forster ([1924] 2005) did, at least, base his depictions on first-hand experience of the country, and made an interesting attempt to convey the *viraha-bhakti* tone of Kṛṣṇa devotion in the last chapters of *A Passage to India.* He recognised that India lived its own complicated life beyond the 'timeless' image imposed onto it, acknowledging in 1957 that the pre-war India he had described was much changed by the Second World War and Indian independence and partition, as well as by 'the abolition of the Native States ... the weakening of purdah and of caste ... the increase of industrialism' and 'the double impact on the peninsula of the U.S.A. and of the U.S.S.R' (307).

**2** Deleuze sets up terminology here that expresses the temporary context-specific creativity of each instance of understanding as an 'event', its character not as a constant marker of the identity of the idea, but rather as a wholly self-defined 'singularity', and the way in which truths continuously flow and alter in relation to many shared elements like a 'life'.

## Theories of self in classical Hinduism

**1** Some have challenged the idea that *puruṣa*'s purity actually indicated a 'pure translucent consciousness' – Parrott (1985: 247), for instance, argues that *kaivalya* actually signified pure 'witnessing' free from mis-identification with what it witnesses: 'Puruṣa, in his self-nature, as the indifferent witness of manifest Prakrti, complete and whole unto himself, and inactive'. On this reading the 'purity' of *puruṣa* consists in its clarity about its true nature and its freedom from false identifications with the world that it witnesses.

**2** See Beidler (1975: 16–28) for a more detailed survey of some models of the *puruṣa* from various Upaniṣads.

## Bodies made of substances and modes

**1** Translation from Mahony (1997: 27–8).

## Agency and the art of the self

1 The significance of the syllables *sat* and particularly of *tyam* is not wholly understood, but this is clearly an attempt at a Vedic style of etymology: the two syllables together make the word 'satyam', the real, but while 'sat' alone means 'what is existing', tyam has no clear meaning. In other Upaniṣads the meanings of the two syllables are reversed. This section leads to the sage Yajñavalkya's discourse on the 'honey' of all things. This presumably represents the compiled teachings of a particular lineage and includes a more developed philosophy of the true self, that is, culmination of the section of the *Bṛhad Āraṇyaka Upaniṣad* named after this speech, the *Madhukhanda*.

2 Translation: Gavin Flood and Charles Martin, *The Bhagavad Gita* (London: W. W. Norton & Company, 2015), 11–12.

3 Early forms of 'sāṃkhya' (enumeration of constituents) and 'yoga' (control and detachment) seem to be described here, in which a detached disposition of experience as the true self is based on an awareness of the material constitution of the embodied self and its agency. Yoga, here implying a kind of discriminative mental detachment, is depicted as a refuge – *yoga-sthaḥ*, a state or place – from which one can escape from natural processes and redirect one's own form of engagement and activity.

## Becoming the world through reason

1 Olivelle (1996b: 293) translates *ātman* here as body, presumably because of reference to the oral instruments for pronunciation of sound and possibly because of a caution about over-attributing statements about the *ātman* to metaphysical or spiritual discourse about the soul and its immortality. But I have tried to be more cautious here in translating *ātman* as self; it is not clear that the discussion of how the jaw and tongue create speech (1.3.4) is necessarily meant to refer to an essence of the *body* rather than of the mind, living force or other of the many meanings attributed to *ātman* in this genre.

2 This discussion of the nature of inference and its power to establish 'subtle' and unseen realities is part of a broader discussion of the means by which knowledge can be established: these usually include perception, inference and past testimony. The doctrinal point at which this definition of inference aims in this context is the establishment of an unseen source of all material existence designated in the Sāṃkhya doctrine as *prakṛti*, literally the 'pro-creative' material of things. This translation is adapted from Burley (2007).

3 Indeed, one could argue that it is precisely inductions aimed at 'phenomena as a whole' that are the strongest because they involve a 'part–whole', or mereological, relationship, rather than the chance co-terminal character of two different properties that simply happen to turn up again and again in the same phenomenon. This is a topic about which the Nyāya school

would later come to engage in debates with Buddhist thinkers, arguing that parts may effectively give us a perception of the whole of a thing (using the example of perceiving the front of a tree, by which we may safely take ourselves to perceive the tree as a whole; see Matilal (1986: 258–61)).

## Theories of everything

1 This translation is adapted from James Fitzgerald's 2003 article. I have replaced Fitzgerald's translation of *saukṣmyāt* as 'sophistication' with the more literal 'subtlety'.

2 This reading of the story of Sulabhā is given by a number of scholars including Vanita 2003, and Dhand 2009.

3 See, for instance, Jonardon Ganeri's (2012) study of 'reasoned choice', and Karin Preisendanz's (2000: 221–51) study of 'Debate and Independent Reasoning vs. Tradition'.

## Practices of materiality: Structuring and transformative rituals

1 Victor Turner, *The Ritual Process: Structure and Anti-structure* (Rutgers, NJ: Aldine, 1969): 7.

# Bibliography

## Primary texts


Agni Purāṇa: N. Gangadharan, trans., Delhi: Motilal Banarsidass, 1984.

Atharva Veda: Maurice Bloomfield, *Hymns of the Atharva-Veda*, New York: Greenwood Press Publishers, 1897.

Bhagavad Gītā: Gavin Flood and Charles Martin trans., London: W. W. Norton & Company, 2015.

Bhāgavata Purāṇa: Part I, G.V. Tagare, trans.; G.P. Bhatt and J.L. Shastri, eds., Delhi: Motilal Banarsidass Publishers, 1978.

Kātyāyana Śrauta Sūtra: H.G. Ranade, trans., Pune: Ranade Publication series, 1978.

Mahābhārata 12.308: James Fitzgerald, 'Nun Befuddles King, Shows Karmayoga Does Not Work: Sulabhā's Refutation of King Janaka at MBh 12.308,' *Journal of Indian Philosophy* 30 (2003), 641–77.

Mānava-Dharmasāstra: *Manu's Code of Law: A Critical Edition and Translation of the Mānava-Dharmasāstra*, Patrick Olivelle, trans. and ed., Oxford: Oxford University Press, 2005.

Nāṭyaśāstra: in *Aesthetic Rapture: The Rasādhyaya of the Nāṭyaśāstra*, Vol. I – Text, J.L. Masson and M.V. Patwardhan, trans., Poona: Deccan College, 1970.

The Nichomeachean Ethics of Aristotle. David Ross, trans., and Lesley Brown, ed., Oxford: Oxford University Press, 2009.

Nyāya Sūtra.

Ṛg Veda: Wendy Doniger, trans., *Hindu Myths*, London: Penguin Books, 1975.

Sāṃkhya Kārikā: in Mikel Burley, *Classical Sāṃkhya and Yoga: An Indian Metaphysics of Experience*, Abingdon: Routledge, 2007.

Śiva Purāṇa: *Śiva Purāṇa*, Part I, J.L. Shastri, ed., Delhi: Motilal Banarsidass, 1970.

Upaniṣads: in Patrick Olivelle, *The Upaniṣads*, Oxford: Oxford University Press, 1996.

Yoga Sūtras: Edwin Bryant, *The Yoga Sūtras of Patañjali*, New York: North Point Press, 2009.


## Other works


Alexander, J. (2006), *The Civil Sphere*, Oxford: Oxford University Press.

Appadurai, A. (1996), *Modernity at Large: Cultural Dimensions of Globalization*, Minneapolis: University of Minnesota Press.

Arnold, D. (2005), *Buddhists, Brahmins and Belief: Epistemology in South Asian Philosophy of Religion*, New York: Columbia University Press.

Aurobindo, S. (1998), 'Readings in the Taittirīya Upaniṣad', in Peter Heehs (ed.), *The Essential Writings of Sri Aurobindo*, New Delhi: Oxford.

Aurobindo, S. (2003) *The Complete Works of Sri Aurobindo: Volume 17*, Pondicherry: Aurobindo Sri Ashram Press.

Badiou, A. (2006), 'Lacan and the Presocratics', at lacan.com.

Bakhtin, M. (1984a), *Problems of Dostoevsky's Poetics*, ed. and trans. Caryl Emerson, Minneapolis: University of Minnesota Press.

Bakhtin, M. (1984b), *Rabelais and His World*, Bloomington: Indian University Press.

Bartley, C.J. (2002), *The Theology of Rāmānuja: Realism and Religion*, London: Routledge Curzon.

Beidler, W. (1975), *The Vision of Self in Early Vedānta*, Delhi: Motilal Banarsidass.

Bell, C. (1992), *Ritual Theory, Ritual Practice*, New York: Oxford University Press.

Benedict, R. (1961), *Patterns of Culture*, Boston: Houghton Mifflin.

Berger, P. (1967), *The Sacred Canopy: Elements of a Sociological Theory of Religion*, London: Doubleday Books.

Bhattacharya, R. (2001), 'The Frst Cause: Syncretic Bias of Haribhadra and Others', *Jain Journal*, 35 (3–4): 179–84.

Bhattacharya, R. (2012), 'Svabhāvavāda and the Carvaka/Lokāyatas: A Historical Overview', *Journal of Indian Philosophy*, 40: 593–614.

Bilimoria, P. (1993), 'Pramāṇa Epistemology: Some Recent Developments', in G. Floistad (ed.), *Contemporary Philosophy: Asian Philosophy*, 157–64, Dordrecht: Springer.

Black, B. (2007), *The Character of the Self in Ancient India: Priests, Kings and Women in the Early Upaniṣads*, Albany: State University of New York.

Bohler, A. (2009), 'Open Bodies', in Axel Michaels and Christoph Wulff (eds), *The Body in India: Ritual, Transgression, Performativity; Paragrana 18*, Berlin: Akademie Verlag.

Bourdieu, P. (1977), *Outline of a Theory of Practice*, ed. Jack Goody, trans. R. Nice, Cambridge: Cambridge University Press.

Bourdieu, P. (1992), *The Logic of Practice*, New York: Polity Press.

Brereton, J. (1999), 'Edifying Puzzlement: Ṛgveda 10.129 and the Uses of Enigma,' *Journal of the American Oriental Society*, 119 (2): 248–60.

Brockington, J.L. (1981), *The Sacred Thread: Hinduism in Its Continuity and Diversity*, Edinburgh: Edinburgh University Press.

Brodbeck, S., and Black, B. (eds) (2009), *Gender and Narrative in the Mahābhārata*, Abingdon: Routledge.

Bronkhorst, J. (1993), *The Two Traditions of Meditation in Ancient India*, Delhi: Motilal Banarsidass.

Bronkhorst, J. (2006), 'Systematic Philosophy between the Empires: Come Determining Features' in Patrick Olivelle (ed.), *Between the Empires: Society in India 300 BCE to 400 CE*, 287–313, Oxford: Oxford University Press.

Bronkhorst, J. (2007), *Greater Magadha: Studies in the Culture of Early India*, Leiden: Brill.

Bronkhorst, J. (2011), *Language and Reality: On an Episode in Indian Thought*, Leiden: Brill.

Bronner, Y. (2002), 'What Is New and What Is Navya: Sanskrit Poetics on the Eve of Colonialism', *Journal of Indian Philosophy*, 30: 441–62.
Brown, L. (2004), 'Understanding and Ontology in African Traditional Thought', in Lee Brown (ed.), *African Philosophy: New and Traditional Perspectives*, 158–78, Oxford: Oxford University Press.
Burley, M. (2007), *Classical Sāṃkhya and Yoga: An Indian Metaphysics of Experience*, Abingdon: Routledge.
Carman, J., and Marglin, F. (1985), *Purity and Auspicious in Indian Society*, Leiden: Brill.
Chakrabarti, K.K. (2007), *Classical Indian Philosophy of Induction: The Nyāya Viewpoint*, Lanham, MD: Lexington Books.
Chakravarthi, R. (2007), *Indian Philosophy and the Consequences of Knowledge: Themes in Ethics, Metaphysics and Soteriology*, Aldershot: Ashgate.
Clarke, A., and Chalmers, D. (2010), 'The Extended Mind', in Richard Menary (ed.), *The Extended Mind*, Cambridge: MIT Press.
Coakley, S. (2000), *Religion and the Body*, Cambridge: Cambridge University Press.
Connelly, P. (1997), 'The Vitalistic Antecedents of the Ātman–Brahman Concept', in Peter Connelly and Sue Hamilton (eds), *Indian Insights: Buddhism, Brahmanism and Bhakti*, London: Luzac Oriental.
Cornford, F. (1912), *From Religion to Philosophy: A Study on the Origins of Western Speculation*, London: Edward Arnold.
Dasgupta, S. N. (1922), A History of Indian Philosophy, Cambridge: Cambridge University Press.
Davis, R. (1991), *Ritual in an Oscillating Universe: Worshiping Śiva in Medieval India*, Princeton: Princeton University Press.
Davis, R. (1995), 'The Origin of Linga Worship', in Donald Lopez (ed.), *Religions of Indian in Practice*, Princeton: Princeton University Press.
Davis, R. (1997), *Lives of Indian Images*, Princeton: Princeton University Press.
Deleuze, G. (2001), *Immanence: Essays on A Life*, trans. Anne Boyman, New York: Zone Books.
Deussen, P. (1906), *The Philosophy of the Upaniṣads*, trans. A.S. Geden, London: T & T Clark.
Dhand, A. (2009), 'Paradigms of the Good in the Mahābhārata: Śuka and Sulabhā in Quagmires of Ethics', in Simon Brodbeck and Brian Black (eds), *Gender and Narrative in the Mahābhārata*, Abingdon: Routledge.
Dold, P. (2011), 'Pilgrimage to Kāmākhyā', in Hillary Rodrigues (ed.), *Studying Hinduism in Practice*, Abingdon: Routledge.
Doniger, W. (1981), *Śiva: The Erotic Ascetic*, New York: Galaxy.
Doniger, W. (1982), *Women, Androgynes and Other Mythical Beasts*, Chicago: University of Chicago Press.
Doniger, W. (1984), *Dreams, Illusions and Other Realities*, Chicago: University of Chicago Press.
Dumézil, L. (1968–73), *Mythe et Épopée*, Paris: Éditions Gallimard.
Dumont, L. ([1970] 1998), *Homo Hierarchicus: The Caste System and its Implications*, trans. Mark Sainsbury, Louis Dumont and Basia Gulati, Delhi: Oxford University Press.

Dunne, J. (2004), *Foundations of Dharmakīrti's Philosophy*, Somerville: Wisdom Publications.
Durand, G. ([1984] 1964), *L'Imagination Symbolique*, Paris: Presses Universitaires de France.
Durkheim, E. (2008), *The Elementary Forms of the Religious Life*, ed. Mark Cladis, trans. Carol Cosman, Oxford: Oxford University Press.
Durkheim, E., and Mauss, M. (2006), *Techniques, Technology and Civilisation*, Nathan Schlanger, ed., Oxford: Berghahn Books.
Eck, D. (1985), *Darśan: Seeing the Divine Image in India*, Chambersburg, PA: Anima Publications.
Edgerton, F. (1965), *The Beginnings of Indian Philosophy*, London: George Allen & Unwin Ltd.
Eliade, M. ([1958] 2009), *Yoga: Immortality and Freedom*, trans. Willard Trask, Princeton: Princeton University Press.
Erdosy, G. (1988), *Urbanisation in Early Historic India*, Oxford: British Archaeological Reports.
Erdosy, G. (1995), 'The Prelude to Urbanization: Ethnicity and the Rise of Late Vedic Chiefdoms', in F. Allchin (ed.), *The Archaeology of Early Historic South Asia: The Emergence of Cities and States*, Cambridge: Cambridge University Press.
Feyerabend, P. (1975), *Against Method: Outline of an Anarchistic Theory of Knowledge*, London: New Left Books.
Fitzgerald, J. (2001), 'Making Yudhiṣṭhira the King: The Dialectics and the Politics of Violence in the Mahābhārata', *Rocznik Orientalisyczny*, 54: 63–92.
Fitzgerald, J. (2003), 'Nun Befuddles King, Shows Karmayoga Does not Work: Sulabhā's Refutation of King Janaka at Mahābhārata 12.308', *Journal of Indian Philosophy*, 30: 641–77.
Flood, G. (1996), *An Introduction to Hinduism*, Cambridge: Cambridge University Press.
Flood, G. (2003), 'Introduction: Establishing the Boundaries', in Gavin Flood (ed.), *The Blackwell Companion to Hinduism*, Oxford: Blackwell.
Flood, G. (2004), *The Ascetic Self: Subjectivity, Memory and Tradition*, Cambridge: Cambridge University Press.
Flood, G. (2006), *The Tantric Body: The Secret Tradition of Hindu Religion*, London: I.B. Tauris.
Flood, G. (2007), *The Importance of Religion: Meaning and Action in Our Strange World*, Chichester: Wiley-Blackwell.
Flood, G. (2009), 'Śaiva Traditions', in Gavin Flood (ed.), *The Blackwell Companion to Hinduism*, Oxford: Blackwell.
Flood, G. (2012), *The Importance of Religion: Meaning and Action in our Strange World*, Oxford: Wiley-Blackwell.
Flood, G. (2013), *The Truth Within: A History of Inwardness in Christianity, Hinduism and Buddhism*, Oxford: Oxford University Press.
Flugel, Peter (2005), 'Beyond the Hindu Frontier: Jaina-Vaisnava Syncretism in the Gujarati Diaspora', *International Journal of Tantric Studies*, 7 (1): 1–43.
Forster, E.M. ([1924] 2005), *A Passage to India*, Pankaj Mishra, ed., London: Penguin Classics.
Fort, A. (1990), *The Self and Its States: A States of Consciousness Doctrine in Advaita Vedānta*, Delhi: Motilal Banarsidass.

Fort, A. (1994), 'Going or Knowing? The Development of the Idea of Living Liberation in the Upaniṣads', *Journal of Indian Philosophy*, 22 (4): 379–90.

Foucault, M. ([1969] 1972), *The Archaeology of Knowledge*, trans. A.M. Sheridan Smith, London: Routledge.

Foucault, M. (1989), *The Order of Things: An Archaeology of the Human Sciences*, Abingdon: Routledge.

Foucault, M. (1998), *The History of Sexuality: The Uses of Pleasure*, London: Penguin.

Fraser, C. (2013), 'Distinctions, Judgment and Reasoning in Classical Chinese Thought', *History and Philosophy of Logic*, 34 (1): 1–24.

Frauwallner, E. (1973), *History of Indian Philosophy, Vol. I*, Delhi: Motilal Banarsidass.

Frazier, J. (2008), *Reality, Religion and Passion: Indian and Western Approaches in Hans-Georg Gadamer and Rūpa Gosvāmī*, Lanham, MD: Lexington Books.

Frazier, J. (2013), 'Natural Theology in Eastern Religions', in Russell Re Manning (ed.), *The Oxford Handbook of Natural Theology*, Oxford: Oxford University Press.

Frazier, J. (2014), 'Vedānta: Metaphors for the Category of Existence', in *Categorisation in Indian Philosophy: Thinking Inside the Box*, London: Ashgate.

Frazier, J. (2016), 'The Overflowing Self: The Phenomenology of Possession in Biblical and Indian Mysticism', in Louise Nelstrop, Bradley Onishi (eds.), *Mysticism in the French Tradition: Eruptions from France*, London: Ashgate.

Frykenberg, R. (1986), 'Modern Education in South India, 1784–1854: Its Roots and Role as a Vehicle of Integration Under Company Raj', *American Historical Review*, 91: 37–67.

Gadamer, H. (1981), *Reason in the Age of Science*, trans. Frederick Lawrence, Cambridge, MA: MIT Press.

Gadamer, H. (1986), *The Relevance of the Beautiful and Other Essays*, trans. Robert Bernasconi, Cambridge: Cambridge University Press.

Gadamer, H. (1992), 'The Verse and the Whole', in Dieter Misgeld and Graeme Nicholson (eds), *Hans-Georg Gadamer on Education, Poetry, and History: Applied Hermeneutics*, trans. Lawrence Schmidt and Monica Reuss, Albany: State University of New York Press.

Gadamer, H. (2004), *Truth and Method*, trans. Joel Weinsheimer and Donald Marshall, Great Britain: Continuum.

Ganeri, J. (2001), *The Proper Work of Reason: Philosophy in Classical India*, Abingdon: Routledge.

Ganeri, J. (2006), *Artha: Meaning*, Delhi: Oxford University Press.

Ganeri, J. ([2007] 2012), *The Concealed Art of the Self: Theories of Self and Practices of Truth in Indian Ethics and Epistemology*, Oxford and New York: Oxford University Press.

Ganeri, J. (2008), 'Sanskrit Philosophical Commentary', *Journal of the Indian Council of Philosophical Research*, XXV (1): 107–27.

Ganeri, J. (2011), *The Lost Age of Reason: Philosophy in Early Modern India 1450–1700*, Oxford: Oxford University Press.

Ganeri, J. (2012a), *The Self: Naturalism, Consciousness, and the First Person Stance*, Oxford: Oxford University Press.

Ganeri, J. (2012b), *Identity as Reasoned Choice: A South Asian Perspective on the Reach and Resources of Public and Practical Reason in Shaping Individual Identities*, New York: Continuum.

Gaur, D.S., and Gupta, L.P. (1970), 'The Theory of Pañcamahābhūta with Special Reference to Ayurveda', *Indian Journal of the History of Science*, No.1.

Geertz, C. (1973a), 'Religion as a Cultural System', in *The Interpretation of Cultures*, New York: Basic Books.

Geertz, C. (1973b), 'Ethos, Worldview, and the Analysis of Sacred Symbols', in *The Interpretation of Cultures*, New York: Basic Books.

Giddens, A. (1992), *The Transformation of Intimacy*, Cambridge: Polity Press.

Glucklich, A. (2008), *The Strides of Vishnu: Hindu Culture in Historical Perspective*, New York: Oxford University Press.

Gonda, J. (1965), 'Bandhu in the Brāhmaṇas', *Adyar Library Bulletin*, 29: 1–29.

Gonda, J. (1969), *Eye and Gaze in the Veda*, Amsterdam: North Holland Publishing Company.

Gonda, J. (1976), *Triads in the Veda*, Royal Netherlands Academy of Arts and Sciences.

Gonda, J. (1989), *Prayer and Blessing: Ancient Indian Ritual Terminology*, Leiden: Brill.

Granoff, P. (1985), 'Scholars and Wonder-Workers: Some Remarks on the Role of the Supernatural in Philosophical Contests in Vedāntic Hagiographies', *Journal of the American Oriental Society*, 105 (3): 459–67.

Grimes, J. (2008), *Śaṅkara and Heidegger: Being, Truth, Freedom*, Varanasi: Indica Books.

Gupta, R. (2007), *The Caitanya Vaiṣṇava Vedānta of Jīva Gosvāmī: When Knowledge Meets Devotion*, Abingdon: Routledge.

Haberman, D. (1994), *Journey through the Twelve Forests: An Encounter with Krishna*, New York: Oxford University Press.

Haberman, D. ([1988] 2001),

Haberman, D. (2013), *People Trees: Worship of Trees in Northern India*, Oxford: Oxford University Press.

Hadot, P. (1995), *Philosophy as a Way of Life: Spiritual Exercises from Socrates to Foucault*, Oxford: Blackwell.

Halbfass, W. (1991), *Tradition and Reflection: Explorations in Indian Thought*, Albany: State University of New York Press.

Halbfass, W. (1993), 'On Being and What There Is', in Mervyn Sprung (ed.), *The Question of Being*, University Park: Pennsylvania University Press.

Harrison, M.H. (1932), *Hindu Monism and Pluralism: As Found in the Upanishads and in the Philosophies Dependent on Them*, Bombay: Oxford University Press.

Harvey, G. (2015), *Animism: Respecting the Living World*, New York: Columbia University Press.

Hatcher, B. (2007), 'Sanskrit and the Morning After: The Metaphorics and Theory of Social Change', *The Indian Economic and Social History Review*, 44: 333–61.

Hatcher, B. (2008), *Bourgeois Hinduism: On the Faith of the Modern Vedantists*, Oxford: Oxford University Press.

Heesterman, J. (1978), 'Veda and Dharma', in Wendy Doniger O'Flaherty and J. Duncan M. Derrett (eds), *The Concept of Duty in South Asia*, London: School of Oriental and African Studies.

Heesterman, J. (1993), *The Broken World of Sacrifice*, Chicago: University of Chicago Press.

Hegarty, J. (2012), *Religion, Narrative and Public Imagination in South Asia: Past and Place in the Sanskrit Mahābhārata*, Abingdon: Routledge.

Heidegger, M. (1978), 'Modern Science, Metaphysics, and Mathematics', in *Basic Writings*, London: Routledge.
Hiriyanna, M. (1993), *Essentials of Indian Philosophy*, Delhi: Motilal Banarsidass.
Holdrege, B. (1998), 'Body Connections: Hindu Discourses of the Body and the Study of Religions', *International Journal of Hindu Studies*, 2 (3): 341–86.
Holdrege, B. (2004), 'Dharma', in Sushil Mittal and Gene Thursby (eds), *The Hindu World*, Abingdon: Routledge.
Holdrege, B. (2015), *Bhakti and Embodiment: Fashioning Divine Bodies in Kṛṣṇa Bhakti*, Abingdon: Routledge.
Horsch, P. (2004), 'From Creation Myth to World Law: The Early History of Dharma', trans. Jarrod Whitaker, *Journal of Indian Philosophy*, 32: 423–48.
Houben, J. (2002), 'The Brahmin Intellectual: History, Ritual, and "Time out of Time" ', *Journal of Indian Philosophy*, 30: 463–79.
Hume, D. (1999), *An Enquiry Concerning Human Understanding*, Oxford: Oxford University Press.
Humphries, C., and Laidlaw, J. (1994), *The Archetypal Actions of Ritual: A Theory of Ritual Illustrated by the Jain Rite of Worship*, Oxford: Clarendon Press.
Husserl, E. (1960), *Cartesian Meditations: An Introduction to Phenomenology*, The Hague: Martinus Nijhoff.
Isayeva, N. (1993), *Shankara and Indian Philosophy*, Albany: State University of New York.
Isayeva, N. (1995), *From Early Vedanta to Kashmir Saivism: Gaudapada, Bhartrhari, and Abhinavagupta*, Albany: State University of New York.
Jackson, A.V.W. (1907), *History of India: Volume 9 – Historic Accounts of India by Foreign Travellers, Classic, Oriental and Occidental*, London: W.W. Hunter.
Jacobsen, K.A. (1999), *Prakṛti in Sāṃkhya-Yoga: Material Principle, Religious Experience, Ethical Implications*, New York: Peter Lang.
Jacobsen, K.A. (ed.), (2008), *South Asian Religions on Display: Religious Processions in South Asia and in the Diaspora*, Abingdon: Routledge.
Jacobsen, K.A (2012), 'Yoga Powers in Contemporary Sāṃkhya-Yoga Tradition', in K.A. Jacobsen (ed.), *Yoga Powers: Extraordiary Capacities Attained through Meditation and Concentration*, Leiden: Brill.
Jamieson, L. (1998), *Intimacy: Personal Relationships in Modern Societies*, Cambridge: Polity Press.
Jamieson, L. (1999), 'Intimacy Transformed? A Critical Look at the "Pure Relationship"', *Sociology*, 33: 477–94.
Jeźic, M. (2009), 'The Triṣṭubh Hymn in the Bhagavadgītā', in Petteri Koskikallo (ed.), *Parallels and Comparisons: Proceedings of the Fourth Dubrovnik International Conference on the Sanskrit Epics and Purāṇas, September 2005*, Zagreb: Croatian Academy of Sciences and Arts.
Kahrs, E. (1998), *Indian Semantic Analysis: The Nirvacana Tradition*, Cambridge: Cambridge University Press.
Kano, K. (2010), 'On the Lingas of Atman', in Johannes Bronkhorst and Karin Preisendanz (eds), *From Vasubandhu to Caitanya: Studies in Indian Philosophy and Its Textual History*, Delhi: Motilal Banarsidass.
King, R. (1995), *Early Advaita Vedaānta and Buddhism: The Mahāyāna Context of the Gaudapadīya Kārikā*, Albany: State University of New York.
Klostermaier, K. (2007), *Hinduism: A Beginner's Guide*, Oxford: Oneworld.

Krishna, D. (2002), *Developments in Indian Philosophy from Eighteenth Century Onwards: Classical and Western*, New Delhi: Centre for Studies in Civilisations.
Lakoff, G., and Johnson, M. (1980), *Metaphors We Live By*, Chicago: Chicago University Press.
Larson, G. (1969), *Classical Sāṃkhya: An Interpretation of Its History and Meaning*, Delhi: Motilal Banarsidass.
Larson, G.J. (1999), 'Classical Yoga as Neo-Sāṃkhya: A Chapter in the History of Indian Philosophy', *Asiatische Studien*, 53 (3): 723–32.
Larson, G.J. ([1987] 2014), *The Encyclopedia of Indian Philosophies, Volume Four: Sāṃkhya, A Dualist Tradition in Indian Philosophy*, G.J. Larson, R.S. Bhattacarya and K.H. Potter (eds), Princeton: Princeton University Press.
Latour, B. (2005), *Reassembling the Social: An Introduction to Actor-Network Theory*, Oxford: Oxford University Press.
Lewis, C.S. (1964), *The Discarded Image: An Introduction to Medieval and Renaissance Literature*, Cambridge: Cambridge University Press.
Lipner, J.J. (1986), *The Face of Truth: A Study of Meaning and Metaphysics in the Vedāntic Theology of Rāmānuja*, Albany: State University of New York.
Lipner, J.J. (1997), *The Fruits of Our Desiring: An Enquiry into the Ethics of the Bhagavadgītā for Our Times*, Calgary: Bayeux.
Lipner, J.J. (2010), *Hindus: Their Religious Beliefs and Practices*, Abingdon: Routledge.
Llewellyn, J.E. (2005), 'Introduction: The Problem of Defining Hinduism', in *Defining Hinduism: A Reader*, London: Equinox.
Lloyd, G.E.R. (2015), *Analogical Investigations: Historical and Cross-Cultural Perspectives on Human Reasoning*, Cambridge: Cambridge University Press.
Luchte, J. (2011), *Early Greek Thought: Before the Dawn*, London: Bloomsbury.
Lyssenko, V. (2004), 'The Human Body Composition in Statics and Dynamics: Āyurveda and the Philosophical Schools of Vaiśeṣika and Sāṃkhya', *Journal of Indian Philosophy*, No.32: 31–56.
Mahony, W. (1997), *The Artful Universe: An Introduction to the Vedic Religious Imagination*, Albany: State University of New York.
Malamoud, C. (1998), *Cooking the World: Ritual and Thought in Ancient India, trans.* David White, Delhi: Oxford University Press.
Marriott, M. (1976), *Hindu Transactions: Diversity without Dualism*, Chicago: Chicago University Press.
Matilal, B.K. (1971), *Epistemology, Logic, and Grammar in Indian Philosophical Analysis*, The Hague, Paris: Mouton.
Matilal, B.K. (1986), *Perception: An Essay on Classical Indian Theories of Knowledge*, Oxford: Clarendon Press.
Matilal, B.K. (1998), *The Character of Logic in India*, eds. Jonardon Ganeri and Heeraman Tiwari, Albany: State University of New York.
Mauss, M. (2006), 'Techniques of the Body', in Nathan Schlanger (ed.), *Techniques, Technology and Civilisation*, Oxford: Berghahn Books.
Mauss, M., and Hubert, H. (1964), *Sacrifice: Its Nature and Functions*, Chicago: University of Chicago Press.
McCrea, L. (2015), 'Over When It's Over: Vyāsatīrtha's Hermeneutic Inversion', *Journal of Hindu Studies*, 8: 97–110.

McDaniel, J. (2012), 'The Role of Yoga in Some Bengali Bhakti Traditions: Shaktism, Gaidya Vaisnavism, Baul and Sahajiya Dharma', *Journal of Hindu Studies*, 5 (1): 53–74.
McDermott, R.F. (2001), *Mother of My Heart, Daughter of My Dreams: Kālī and Umā in the Devotional Poetry of Bengal*, Oxford: Oxford University Press.
McLuhan, M. (1994), *Understanding Media: The Extensions of Man*, Cambridge, MA: MIT Press.
Mestrovic, S. (1997), *Postemotional Society*, London: Sage Publications.
Michaels, A. (2008), *Śiva in Trouble: Festivals and Rituals at the Pasupatinatha Temple of Deopatan*, Oxford: Oxford University Press.
Michaels, A. (2012), 'A Preliminary Grammar of Newar Life-Cycle Rituals', *Journal of Hindu Studies*, 5 (1): 10–29.
Michaels, A. (2016), *Homo Ritualis: Hindu Ritual and its Significance for Ritual Theory*, Oxford: Oxford University Press.
Minkowski, C. (2001), 'The Pandit as Public Intellectual: The Controversy over Virodha or Inconsistency in the Astronomical Sciences', in A. Michaels (ed.), *The Pandit: Traditional Scholarship in India*, New Delhi: Manohar Publications.
Minkowski, C., Venkatkrishnan, A. and O'Hanlon, R. (2015), 'Introduction: Social History in the Study of Indian Intellectual Cultures', *South Asian History and Culture*, 6 (1): 1–9.
Mittal, S., and Thursby, G. (eds) (2004), *The Hindu World*, Abingdon: Routledge.
Mohanty, J.N. (1991), 'Phenomenology and Indian Philosophy: The Concept of Rationality', in D.P. Chattopadhyay, Lester Embree and Jitendranath N. Mohanty (eds), *Phenomenology and Indian Philosophy*, Albany: State University of New York Press.
Mohanty, J.N. (1992), 'Phenomenology and Indian Philosophy: The Concept of Rationality', in Debi Chattopadhyaya, Lester Embree and Jitendranath Mohanty (eds), *Phenomenology and Indian Philosophy*, Albany: State University of New York.
Morgan, D. (1996), *Family Connections: An Introduction to Family Studies*, Cambridge: Polity Press.
Morgan, D. (2009), *Acquaintances: The Space between Intimates and Strangers*, Milton Keynes: Open University Press.
Müller, F. M. ([1879] 2013), *The Sacred Books of the East: The Upanishads, Part 1 of 2: Chandogya Upanishad; Talavakara (Kena) Upanishad; Aitareya Upanishad; Kausitaki Upanishad; Vajasaneyi (Isa) Upanishad*, Abingdon: Routledge.
Nakamura, H. (1973), *Religions and Philosophies of India*, Tokya: Hokuseido Press.
Narayanan, V. (2004), 'Ālaya', in Sushil Mittal and Gene Thursby (eds), *The Hindu World*, Abingdon: Routledge.
Nicholson, A. (2010), *Unifying Hinduism: Philosophy and Identity in Indian Intellectual History*, New York: Columbia University Press.
Nietzsche, F. (1993), *The Birth of Tragedy: Out of the Spirit of Music*, London: Penguin.
Nietzsche, F. (2008), *The Twilight of the Idols*, trans. Duncan Large, Oxford: Oxford University Press.
Nussbaum, M. (2001), *Upheavals of Thought: The Intelligence of Emotions*, New York: Cambridge University Press.

Ogawa, H. (2005), *Process and Language: A Study of the Mahābhāṣya Ad A1.3.1 Bhūvādayo Dhātavaḥ*, Delhi: Motilal Banarsidass.
Olivelle, P. (1993), *The Āśrama System: The History and Hermeneutics of a Religious Institution*, Oxford: Oxford University Press.
Olivelle, P. (1996a), 'Dharmaskandhāḥ and Brahmasaṃsthaḥ: A Study of Chāndogya Upaniṣad 2.3.1', *Journal of the American Oriental Society*, 116 (2): 205–19.
Olivelle, P. (1996b), *The Upaniṣads*, Oxford: Oxford University Press.
Olivelle, P. (2005), *Manu's Code of Law: A Critical Edition and Translation of the Mānava-Dharmasāstra*, Oxford: Oxford University Press.
Omoregbe, J. (1998), 'African Philosophy: Yesterday, Today and Tomorrow', in Emmanuel Chukwudi (ed.), *African Philosophy: An Anthology*, Oxford: Blackwell.
Orsi, R. (1997), 'Every Miracles: The Study of Lived Religion', in David Hall (ed.), *Lived Religion in America: Toward a History of Practice*, 3–21, Princeton: Princeton University Press.
Oruka, H.O. (1990), *Sage Philosophy, Philosophy of History and Culture*, Vol. 4, Leiden: E.J. Brill.
Padoux, A. (2011), *Tantric Mantras: Studies on Mantraśāstra*, Abingdon: Routledge.
Parrott, R. (1985), 'The Experience Called Reason in Classical Sāṃkhya', *The Journal of Indian Philosophy*, 13: 235–64.
Patil, P. (2009), *Against a Hindu God: Buddhist Philosophy of Religion in India*, New York: Columbia University Press.
Patton, L. (1996), *Myth as Argument: The Bṛhaddevatā as Canonical Commentary*, Berlin: Degruyter Mouton.
Patton, L. (2005), *Bringing the Gods to Mind: Mantra and Ritual in Early Indian Sacrifice*, Berkeley and Los Angeles: University of California Press.
Perdue, D. (2014), *The Course in Buddhist Reasoning and Debate: An Asian Approach to Analytic Thinking Drawn from Tibetan Sources*, Boston: Shambala Publications.
Perrett, R.W. (1998), 'Truth, Relativism and Western Conceptions of Indian Philosophy', *Asian Philosophy*, 8 (1): 19–29.
Phillips, S.H., and Tatacharya, N.S.R. (2004), *Epistemology of Perception* (including text and translation of the perception chapter of Gangeśa's *Tattva-cintāmāṇi*)', New York: Columbia University Press.
Pintchman, T. (ed.) (2007), *Women's Lives, Rituals in the Hindu Tradition*, Oxford: Oxford University Press.
Pollock, S. (1985), 'The Theory of Practice and the Practice of Theory in Indian Intellectual History', *Journal of the American Oriental Society*, 105 (3): 499–519.
Pollock, S. (2001), 'New Intellectuals in Seventeenth Century India', *The Indian Economic and Social History Review*, 38: 3–31.
Pollock, S. (2006), *The Language of the Gods in the World of Men: Sanskrit, Culture and Power in Premodern India*, Chicago: Chicago University Press.
Pollock, S. (2008), 'Is There an Indian Intellectual History? Introduction to "Theory and Method in Indian Intellectual History"', *Journal of Indian Philosophy*, 36: 533–42.
Potter, K. ([1963] 1991), *Presuppositions of India's Philosophies*, Delhi: Motilal Banarsidass.

Preisendanz, K. (2000), 'Debate and Independent Reasoning vs. Tradition: On the Precarious Position of Early Nyāya', in Ryutaro Tsuchida and Albrecht Wezler (eds), *Festschrift Minoru Hara*, 221–51, Reinbek: Dr. Inge Wezler Verlag.

Preisendanz, T. (2010), 'Reasoning as a Science: Its Role in Early Dharma Literature, and the Emergence of the Term Nyāya', in Brendan S. Gillon (ed.), *Logic in Earliest Classical India*, Delhi: Motilal Banarsidass (Papers of the 12th World Sanskrit Conference).

Prentiss, K.P. (1999), *The Embodiment of Bhakti*, New York: Oxford University Press.

Preston, J. (1985), 'Creation of the Sacred Image: Apotheosis and Destruction in Hinduism', in Joanne Punzo Waghorne and Norman Cutler (eds), *Gods of Flesh, Gods of Stone: The Embodiment of Divinity in India*, Chambersburg, PA: Anima Publications.

Radhakrishnan, S. (1957), *A Sourcebook in Indian Philosophy*, Princeton: Princeton University Press.

Raheja, G. (1988), *The Poison in the Gift*, Chicago: Chicago University Press.

Ram-Prasad, C. (2007), *Indian Philosophy and the Consequences of Knowledge: Themes in Metaphysics, Ethics and Soteriology*, Aldershot: Ashgate.

Ram-Prasad, C. (2013), *Divine Self, Human Self: The Philosophy of Being in Two Gītā Commentaries*, London: Bloomsbury.

Raveh, D. (2008), 'Ayah aham asmīti: Self-Consciousness and Identity in the Eighth Chapter of the Chāndogya Upaniṣad vs. Śankara's Bhāṣya', *Journal of Indian Philosophy*, 36: 319–33.

Reynolds, P. (1991), *Stealing Fire: The Atomic Bomb as Symbolic Body*, Palo Alto: Iconic Anthropology Press.

Roberts, M.V. (2014), *Tastes of the Divine: Hindu and Christian Theologies of Emotion*, New York: Fordham University Press.

Rodrigues, H. (ed.) (2011), *Studying Hinduism in Practice*, Abingdon: Routledge.

Sachau, E. ([1887] 1971), *Alberuni's India*, London: Trubner and Co.

Samuels, G. (2005), *Tantric Revisionings*, London: Ashgate.

Samuels, G. (2008), *The Origins of Yoga and Tantra*, Cambridge: Cambridge University Press.

Satyanand, J. (1997), *Nimbārka: A Pre-Śaṃkara Vedāntin and his Philosophy*, New Delhi: Munshiram Manoharlal.

Sax, W. (2009a), 'Performing God's Body', in Axel Michaels and Christoph Wulf (eds), *Paragrana 18.1: The Body in India: Ritual, Transgression, Performance*, Akademie Verlag.

Sax, W. (2009b), *Ritual Healing and Social Justice in the Central Himalayas*, Oxford: Oxford University Press.

Schopenhauer, A. ([1969] 1818), *The World as Will and Representation*, trans. E.F.J. Payne, Mineola: Dover Publications.

Sen, A. (1997), 'Indian Traditions and the Western Imagination', *Daedulus*, 129: 1–26.

Sen, A. (2006), *The Argumentative Indian: Writings on Indian History Culture and Identity*, New York: Picador.

Sengupta, S. (2010), 'Saṣṭhi: Between the Forest and the Lying-in-Chamber: The Formation of a Goddess', *Journal of Hindu Studies*, 3: 216–37.

Sharma, A. (2000), *Classical Hindu Thought: An Introduction*, Oxford: Oxford University Press.

Shulman, D. (2012), *More than Real: A History of the Imagination in South India*, Cambridge, MA: Harvard University Press.

Smith, B. (1988), *Reflections on Resemblance, Ritual and Religion*, Delhi: Motilal Banarsidass.

Smith, B. (1994), *Classifying the Universe*, Oxford: Oxford University Press.

Smith, F. (2006), *The Self-Possessed: Deity and Spirit Possession in South Asian in South Asian Literature and Civilisation*, New York: Columbia University Press.

Smith, J. (1991), *The Epic of Pabuji*, Cambridge: Cambridge University Press.

Spivak, G. (1997), 'A Memoir', in *Relativism, Suffering and Beyond: Essays in Memory of Bimal K. Matilal*, New Delhi: Oxford.

Staal, F. (1995), 'The Sanskrit of Science', *Journal of Indian Philosophy*, 23: 73–127.

Staal, F. (1996), *Rituals and Mantras: Rules without Meaning*, New York: Peter Lang.

Staal, F. (2008), *Discovering the Vedas: Origins, Mantras, Rituals, Insights*, New Delhi: Penguin Books.

Taylor, C. (1989), *Sources of the Self: The Making of the Modern Identity*, Cambridge, MA: Harvard University Press.

Thoreau, H.D. (1962), *The Journals of Henry David Thoreau*, Vol. 8, eds. B. Torrey and F. Allen, New York: Dover Books.

Tillich, P. (1951), *Systematic Theology*, Chicago: University of Chicago.

Timalsina, S. (2009a), 'The Brahman and the Word Principle (Śabda): The Influence of the Philosophy of Bhartṛhari on Maṇḍana's *Brahmasiddhi*', *Journal of Indian Philosophy*, 37: 189–206.

Timalsina, S. (2009b), *Consciousness in Indian Philosophy: The Advaita Doctrine of 'Awareness Only'*, Abingdon: Routledge.

Timalsina, S. (2012), 'Body Self and Healing in Tantric Ritual Paradigm', *Journal of Hindu Studies*, 5: 30–52.

Timalsina, S. (2013), 'Gauḍapāda on Imagination', *Journal of Indian Philosophy*, 41: 591–602.

Turner, V. (1969), *The Ritual Process: Structure and Anti-Structure*, Rutgers, NJ: Aldine.

Turner, V. (1974), *Dramas, Fields and Metaphors: Symbolic Action in Human Society*, Ithaca, NY: Cornell University Press.

Urban, H. (2010), *The Power of Tantra: Religion, Sexuality and the Politics of South Asian Studies*, London: I.B. Tauris.

van Gennep, A. (1960), *The Rites of Passage*, eds. Monica Vizedom and Gabrielle Coffee, Chicago: University of Chicago Press.

Vanita, R. (2003), 'The Self Is Not Gendered: Sulabhā's Debate with King Janaka', *NWSA Journal*, 15 (2): 76–93.

Vasquez, M. (2011), *More Than Belief: A Materialist Theory of Religion*, Oxford: Oxford University Press.

Vivekananda, S. ([1896] 1955), *Jnana-Yoga*, New York: Ramakrishna-Vivekananda Center.

Vivekananda, S. (1999), 'The Real Nature of Man', in *The Complete Works of Swami Vivekananda*, Vol. 2, 70–87, Calcutta: Advaita Ashrama.

Waghorne, J., and Cutler, N. (eds) (1985), *Gods of Flesh, Gods of Stone: The Embodiment of Divinity in India*, New York: Columbia University Press.

Watson, A. (2014), 'The Self as a Dynamic Constant: Rāmakaṇṭha's Middle Ground between a Naiyāyika Eternal Self-Substance and a Buddhist Stream of Consciousness-Moments', *Journal of Indian Philosophy*, 42: 173–93.

Werner, K. (1978), 'The Vedic Concept of Human Personality and Its Destiny', *Journal of Indian Philosophy*, 5: 275–89.

White, D.G. (1998), *The Alchemical Body: Siddha Traditions in Medieval India*, Chicago: Chicago University Press.

White, D.G. (2009a), *Sinister Yogis*, Chicago and London: University of Chicago Press.

White, D.G. (2009b), 'Yogic Rays: The Self-Externalisation of the Yogi in Ritual, Narrative and Philosophy', in A. Michaels and C. Wulff (eds), *The Body in India: Ritual, Transgression, Performativity*, Berlin: Akademie Verlag.

White, L. (1967), 'The Historical Root of Our Ecological Crisis', *Science*, 155 (3767): 1205–206.

Witzel, M. (1979), *On Magical Thought in the Veda*, Leiden: University of Leiden.

Witzel, M. (1987), 'On the Localisation of Vedic Texts and Schools', in *India and the Ancient World: History Trade and Culture before A.D. 650*, 174–213, Leuven: Department Orientalistiek.

Witzel, M. (1996), 'How to Enter the Vedic Mind? Strategies in Translating a Brahmana Text', *Translating, Translations, Translators From India to the West*. Harvard Oriental Series, Opera Minora 1, Cambridge: Harvard Oriental Series.

Witzel, M. (1997), '*The Development of the Vedic Canon and Its Schools: The Social and Political Milieu*', in Michael Witzel (ed.), *Inside the Texts, Beyond the Texts*, 255–345. Columbia, MO: South Asian Books.

Wright Mills, C. ([1959] 2000), *The Sociological Imagination*, New York: Oxford University Press.

Wujastyk, D. (2009), 'Interpreting the Image of the Human Body in Pre-modern India', *International Journal of Hindu Studies*, 13 (2): 189–228.

Wulf, C. (2013), *Anthropology: A Continental Perspective*, Chicago: University of Chicago Press.

Wulff, D.M. (1984) *Drama as a Mode of Religious Realisation: The Vidagdhamādhva of Rūpa Gosvāmī*, Chico, CA: Scholars Press.

Wynne, A. (2007), *The Origin of Buddhist Meditation*, Abingdon: Routledge, Abingdon.

Zaehner, R.C. (1962), *Hinduism*, Oxford: Oxford University Press.

Zimmerman, F. (2011), *Jungle and the Aroma of Meats: An Ecological Theme in Hindu Medicine*, Delhi: Motilal Banarsidass.

# Index